THE NIBELUNGENLIED: A LITERARY ANALYSIS

the nibelungenlied:
a literary analysis

hugo bekker

university of toronto press

© University of Toronto Press 1971
Printed in Canada by
University of Toronto Press
Toronto and Buffalo
ISBN 0-8020-5235-5

FOR ELIZABETH

ACKNOWLEDGMENTS

BY KIND PERMISSION of the editors of the *Germanic Review*, "Kingship in the 'Nibelungenlied,'" *GR*, XLI (1966), 251–63, and "The *Eigenmann*-Motif in the 'Nibelungenlied,'" *GR*, XLII (1967), 5–15, are incorporated into this volume in the studies on Brunhild. Endeavors have been made to hone the pertinent arguments presented in those articles, and to add desirable notes on literary criticism of the Brunhild figure.

The manuscript of this book was finished when Mowatt and Sacker's *The Nibelungenlied: An Interpretative Commentary* appeared. Because it seemed desirable to relate their work to this, various notes have been inserted to present interpretations advanced by the *Commentary*'s authors. Whereas the present work might benefit from taking portions of Mowatt and Sacker's introduction as its own, there are differences – some basic – between the *Commentary* proper and the suggestions presented in the following pages. Hence most of the citations have been allowed to stand by themselves to give the reader the opportunity to draw his own conclusions about divergent views.

I wish to express my debt of gratitude to the late W. Robert Jones for going over the manuscript and cleansing it of stylistic impurities.

This volume was published with the aid of the Publications Fund of the University of Toronto Press.

CONTENTS

INTRODUCTION

THE FOLLOWING STUDIES are based on the view that the *Nibelung-enlied* is a literary monument worthy to be read for its own sake. This is not to deny the validity and importance of the scrutiny of the epic's known or assumed sources. After all, the *Nibelungenlied* was not written in a vacuum; its antecedents are multiple and complex, and the manner in which the poet dealt with them is very much a matter of relevant investigation.

Unfortunately, endeavors to reconcile the two basic and sometimes mutually antagonistic approaches to the epic have so far been unsuccessful. Over against the imposing number of critics who are persuaded that the historico-genetic approach is the best, there is an equally impressive number who want to read the epic in the manner in which we read *Tristan*, whose author whatever he may have brought in the form of a message – if bringing a message was his purpose at all – is generally credited with improving on his source.[1] Whereas Lachmann[2] may be seen as the spearhead of the movement dedicated to the scrutiny of sources – in his wake we encounter the activities of such critics as A. Holtzmann, E. Kettner, R. C. Boer, A. Heusler, D. von Kralik, G. Nordmeyer, J. Bumke – early representatives of the literary-critical approach are such critics as J. Körner, E. Tonnelat (too much neglected), F. Neumann, and M. Thorp. These, and many with them, like to take the sources for granted, to read the *Nibelungenlied* as a

1 This fact does not affect the basic cleavage separating the various approaches to Gottfried's poem.
2 K. Lachmann, *Ueber die ursprüngliche Gestalt des Gedichts von der Nibelungen Noth* (Berlin, 1816). For the works of the following critics mentioned, see the Bibliography.

poetic unit, and to discuss it from whatever basis seems relevant.

Many bases have turned out to be valid, and together they bear testimony to the complexity of the poet's artistic ability. This is what Batts has to say:

> Man darf sagen, dass der Dichter ein äusserst selbstsicherer Mann
> gewesen sein muss, um sich so gegen die herrschende Dichtung zu
> stellen, und man muss auch folgern, dass das Nl. und besonders
> die Personen des Liedes vollkommen unabhängig von der Tradi-
> tion und ohne Beachtung der Quellen zu betrachten sind, wenn
> man die Absichten des Dichters kennenlernen will; denn ein
> Dichter, der bereit ist, den zeitgenössischen Geschmack derart
> zu affrontieren, muss auch fähig sein, die Personen der alten
> Quellen nach eigenem Gutdünken umzuformen und zu gestalten.[3]

Less drastic, Singer speaks of the poet of the *Nibelungenlied* as bringing a "new design upon the Nibelungen tradition."[4] The following
chapters concern themselves with facets of this "new design."

It is well to establish emphatically at the outset that this new
design does not aim at psychological character delineation.[5] While this

---

3 M.S. Batts, "Die Tragik des Nibelungenliedes," *DB*, xxvi (1960), 43. See also
M. Ittenbach, *Das Nibelungenlied: Dichtung und Schicksalsgestaltung* (Brüssel,
1944), pp. 45 f.

4 C.S. Singer, "The Hunting Contest: An Interpretation of the Sixteenth *Aventiure*
of the *Nibelungenlied*," *GR*, xlii (1967), 179. To indicate this new design is also
the purpose of studies seeking to point out the structural devices in the epic. Cf.,
e.g., F. Knorr, "Der künstlerische Aufbau des Nibelungenliedes," *ZfD*, lii (1938),
73–87; F. Maurer, "Die Einheit des *Nibelungenliedes* nach Idee und Form," *DU*, v
(1953), 27–42; idem, "Ueber den Bau der Aventiuren des Nibelungenliedes," in:
Festschrift für Dietrich Kralik (Horn, 1954), pp. 93-98; J. Fourquet, "Zum Aufbau
des *Nibelungenliedes* und des *Kudrunlieds*," *ZfdA*, lxxxv (1954/55), 137-49;
W. Richter, "Beiträge zur Deutung des Mittelteils des *Nibelungenliedes*," *ZfdA*,
lxxii (1956), 9-47; H. Eggers, *Symmetrie und Proportion epischen Erzählens*
(Stuttgart, 1956); idem, "Vom Formenbau mittelhochdeutscher Epen," *DU*, xi
(1935), 81 ff.; B. Wachinger, *Studien zum Nibelungenlied: Vorausdeutungen,
Aufbau, Motivierung* (Tübingen, 1960); M.S. Batts, *Die Form der Aventiuren im
Nibelungenlied* (Giessen, 1961); B. Nagel, *Das Nibelungenlied: Stoff, Form, Ethos*
(Frankfurt, 1965), pp. 53 ff.

5 This has already been suggested by Mary Thorp in "The Unity of the *Nibelun-*

view goes counter to several recent evaluations of the *Nibelungenlied*, it does not contradict the remarks made by those whose procedures leave room for the claim that the characters they depict are types rather than individuals, representative rather than unique in the modern sense of the word. Such a claim cannot only be made for Siegfried,[6] but also for Brunhild as she emerges from the pages of the fourth and fifth chapters in the present work. And regarding Hagen we can say that he resembles Iago: Iago, too, is a character who, according to Spivack,[7] is "representationally" rather than "individualistically" developed. It is because of these considerations that the chapters headed by the names of the various prominent characters deliberately refrain from seeking to establish all-round evaluations that might tend to pass them off as characters whose "individuality" the poet meant to draw.

From this point of view Weber, however persuasive in the main, seems too intent on discovering complex psychological entities – the term "modern" comes to mind. In this sense also I understand Kuhn's critique of Weber's book:[8] Kuhn is not so much against careful reading as against a type of psychological dissecting which constitutes a criterion too rich to be applicable to the manner of portrayal followed in the *Nibelungenlied*. Indeed, though there are many important hints scattered throughout the epic that give us insights into the various characters, it can be said that they are, one and all, "hollow" men and women (cf. chapter IX, p. 154).

The relevance of the approach here used recently received unexpected support. After these studies had acquired their essential form,

genlied," *JEGP*, XXXVI (1937), 479 f.: "The poet would seem to be little interested in characters as such; there is very little individualization in any part of the work." Whether, as Miss Thorp suggests, the alternative is an epic in which we must look for plot, is a different matter. H. de Boor, *Geschichte der deutschen Literatur*, II (München, 1964), p. 158, observes: "Jüngste Forschung droht ... durch gewaltsame Deutungsversuche eine planvolle Einheitlichkeit zu erzwingen. Unvoreingenommene Betrachtung wird es unterlassen, in der Kriemhild des ersten und des zweiten Teils eine folgerichtige psychologische Entwicklung zu suchen."
6 See Singer, "The Hunting Contest."
7 B. Spivack, *Shakespeare and the Allegory of Evil: The History of a Metaphor in Relation to His Major Villains* (New York, 1958).
8 Hugo Kuhn, review of G. Weber, *Das Nibelungenlied: Problem und Idee* (Stuttgart, 1963), in: *ZfdA*, XCIV (1965), Anzeiger, 1 ff.

Stout's book,[9] which is thoroughly historico-genetic in its approach, turned out to present a view strikingly similar to my suggestions about Hagen. Stout shows that the relevance of one type of evaluation can be vindicated by that of another. Additionally, his book again and again lends support to the suggestion implied in the statement that Hagen and Iago are brothers under the skin: Hagen, too, might lend his name to a book dealing with "the history of a metaphor."

Further, it is an implication of these remarks that the *Nibelungenlied* is not a work telling us how the wicked are punished by the good, or how the good destroy the evil. At least in *this* sense the epic has no moral to tell, and the following chapters have again and again reason to suggest that the question of guilt or innocence is irrelevant in an epic in which the poet goes out of his way to stifle any such question.[10]

With characterization ruled out as a device contributing to unity, it may not be an easy matter to cut a swath through the maze of critical materials on the *Nibelungenlied* and still arrive at positive suggestions pointing to the literary coherence, depth, integrity, and meaning of the epic. It must be left to the reader to decide whether this work has been successful in avoiding the various pitfalls along the way and in presenting a unifying view.

The attempt to present such a view made it advisable to provide a number of cross references in the text. If adequate to their intended purpose, they should help the reader to stay abreast of the implications flowing from the particular argument of the moment.

In this connection, the approach used in these studies – consultation of the text, and little digression from the text, so as to understand the *Nibelungenlied* as the poet wanted it understood – has affected the nature of the footnotes. Many of them deal with the conflicting views of other critics. By indicating the sources of interpretations and contentions, they play an important role in an analysis which by its very method must be frugal in its references or comparisons to other epics

9 J. Stout, *Und ouch Hagene* (Groningen, 1963).
10 Cf., for contrast, K. Bollinger, *Das Tragische im höfischen Epos* (Bonn, 1938); H. Flügel, "Die Schuld der Nibelungen," in: idem, *Geschichte und Geschicke: Zwölf Essays* (München-Kempten, 1946), pp. 191-219; W. Fechter, *Siegfrieds Schuld und das Weltbild des Nibelungenliedes* (Hamburg, 1948); W. Hempel, " 'Superbia' als Schuldmotiv im *Nibelungenlied*," *Seminar*, II (1966), 1-12.

of the period and must forgo broad cultural or sociological excursions on a comprehensive historical basis.

The often indirect approach used in these studies calls for a word of explanation in so far as it may seem a cumbersome way of presenting the various arguments. In the Hagen chapters, for instance, the salient points do not begin to emerge until later in the discussion. This method of delivery is due to the poet's way of presenting his materials. He often does it indirectly and thus compels the reader to scrutinize a number of minor details in order to induce the main arguments from them. Besides, much of what we learn about Hagen is learned in retrospect; for example, his position with regard to the hoard. Elsewhere, too, the poet's diffuse portrayal calls for an indirect approach by the reader, as in the second chapter when the discussion of the various requests for a free exit entails remarks about the valor of the Huns.

From the above it follows that the approach applied in the following chapters has a "naive" rather than an "intellectual" bias, and must therefore do without abstracting statements. There may be a disadvantage to this inability to be persuasive without constant reliance on the primary material, but there is also a benefit: the conclusions arrived at can only be refuted by an equally close scrutiny of the text. Whatever the outcome of such a confrontation, the *Nibelungenlied* will benefit from it.

Finally, in so far as some of the interpretations presented here deviate drastically from established criticism on the *Nibelungenlied* – and as such may not be acceptable to all readers – it is hoped that they will be received as attempts to shed new light on old problems.

THE NIBELUNGENLIED: A LITERARY ANALYSIS

i

GEMS, CLOTHES,
FESTIVITIES

THE TITLE OF THIS CHAPTER derives from the conviction that clothes, gems, and festivities are of consequence in the *Nibelungenlied* in so far as they are representative of a noble way of life. Together with other devices, which will also be mentioned, they emphasize parallel or contrasting situations and suggest additional dimensions of meaning. The larger part of the discussion that follows seeks to glean insights from several passages dealing with manifestations of this representative function.

The first verse of the *Nibelungenlied* – "Uns ist in alten maeren wunders vil geseit ..."[1] – brings to mind tales of a gray and shadowy past, tales with a once-upon-a-time opening. In such tales, what at first glance seem to be digressions are in effect desirable and indispensable data enhancing the self-consistency and verisimilitude of the realm from which such stories issue. In this realm, the likely and the impossible, the down-to-earth and the magic, stand side by side, without the narrator's feeling self-conscious about a procedure in which motivation meanders from the plausible to the implausible and back again.[2]

1 Quotations are taken from the edition by H. de Boor in *Deutsche Klassiker des Mittelalters*, 17th ed. (Wiesbaden, 1963). In instances when details in the text are used as bases for arguments, various versions and translations will be cited to present differing opinions on debated questions.
2 Disregard of this matter-of-fact procedure leads to such emphases on contrasts as W. J. Schröder detects between "Zeit" and "Vorzeit" in *Das Nibelungenlied: Versuch einer Deutung* (Halle/Saale, 1954), passim. But many evaluations of the *Nibelungenlied* to the contrary, the epic was not written by a poet who played Hebbel some seven hundred years too early by juxtaposing representatives of

In this realm also, what seem to be omissions are not omissions but superfluous matters which, if incorporated into the flow of the material, would fail to add to the integrity of the story. And if lack of explicit detail seems to deprive us of a full understanding of the motivational forces at work, the fault may be ours rather than the narrator's, since we may not be reading the story as he intends us to read it.

Whereas the view of the *Nibelungenlied* as a story grants the fact that there are inconsistencies to be found in the epic, and that its development of plot and its delineation of characters may be flawed, it will be one of the tasks of these studies to suggest perfectly logical answers for at least some of the alleged discrepancies. In this connection, one of the implications of the argument conducted so far has it that the editor responsible for the c* version, while stylistically smoother and more factual in his approach than his predecessor, had little eye for the subtle technique employed by the author of the B* text – and even less eye for the subtle implications involved. Again and again the "smoothing" procedure and the tendency to divide the cast into "good" and "bad" characters serves as an interesting contrast to the complex concepts detectable in the B* text.[3]

different cultures. B. Nagel, "*Das Nibelungenlied,*" *ZfdP* LXXVI (1957), 278 f., supports the poet's interest in presenting a unified story with these words: "Es gehört zu den Haupttendenzen des *Nibelungenliedes,* dass es die aus Sage und und Märchen überkommenen magischen und mythischen Elemente bewusst zurückdrängt, ja recht eigentlich ausgeschaltet hat. ... Alles erscheint hier im hellen Licht der 'normalen' Tageswelt." On this "normal" level, the magic and the mythical are to be accepted as integral parts of the events occurring in this world, and are to be taken at face value. In this connection, it is good to remember that the poet of the *Nibelungenlied* is a contemporary of Gottfried von Strassburg, who expects us to view the love potion in his *Tristan* as a motif which he borrows from his sources, but which he uses to convey in a limited number of lines the love that comes to prevail between Tristan and Isolde. Of course, as K.C. King has reminded us in "The Message of the *Nibelungenlied:* A Reply," *MLR,* LVII (1962), 541, "The 'heroic' is *ipso facto* concerned with persons who stand in some way outside the usual conventions."

3 D.G. Mowatt and Hugh Sacker, *The Nibelungenlied: An Interpretative Commentary* (University of Toronto Press, 1967), p. 26, make a related point: "That the *Nibelungenlied* was little understood at the time is suggested by its continuation, known as *Die Klage,* which follows it in virtually all manuscripts. This senti-

The introductory strophe to the *Nibelungenlied* does not draw our attention to old tales in general, but to tales of a special kind:

1 Uns ist in alten maeren   wunders vil geseit
  von helden lobebaeren,   von grozer arebeit,
  von fröuden, hochgeziten,   von weinen und von klagen,
  von küener recken striten ...

We are told in ancient tales of marvels unending, of laudable
heroes, of heavy toil, of joys, festivities, of weeping and of
wailing, of bold warriors' battles ...

and of these tales we shall hear one that deals with a well-born maid, "ein vil edel magedin" (2). Much later we are told that the story is at an end – "hie hat daz maere ein ende" – and that it is called the fate of the Nibelungs, "der Nibelunge not" (2379). There is therefore a connection between the "vil edel magedin" and the "not" of the Burgundians. By means of this connection the poet informs us of the manner in which he wishes us to read his story: the relation between Kriemhild and the fall of the Burgundians is the relation between cause and effect.

The narrator's apparent intention, then, is to tell us a story, one story, not two or more sewn together more or less successfully with perhaps a careless and disturbing seam showing through here and there or a thread hanging loose.[4] That the poet is interested in having

mentalizing banality, which most modern scholars reject as worthless, appears to have been accepted by the medieval audience as an essential continuation of the *Nibelungenlied.*" Also de Boor, *Geschichte*, p. 167, has a view on the matter: "Schon die nächsten Nachfahren haben die Grösse des Nibelungenliedes in der gleich-wägenden Behandlung von Spiel und Gegenspiel nicht begriffen, weil sie den tie-feren Hintergrund, das germanisch-heroische Schicksalsdenken nicht rein nachzu-leben vermochten." The latter statement holds true particularly when we identify "den tieferen Hintergrund" with poetic artistry and ingenuity, as well as with the implications flowing from the structural devices employed in the epic (cf., e.g., Introduction, note 4).

4 To repeat a view implicit in the Introduction, this way of reading the epic is not intended to disparage the many endeavors that have been made to heighten our understanding of the epic by tracing its materials back to various sources. The historico-genetic approach has yielded too much valuable information to be

his epic understood as a homogeneous unit is also suggested by the way in which the introductory strophe telescopes the data elaborated in the epic proper. Strophe 1, so to speak, comprises all the *Nibelungenlied*. In the quickest way possible it directs our attention to the tremendous panorama about to unfold. Similarly, the last verse – "hie hat daz maere ein ende" – traverses decades and vast spaces with a backward glance, directing our attention in one sweep to what we have seen.

The narrator's intention to present a unified story is also suggested by the manner in which, in the first *Aventiure* and elsewhere, predictory elements are used. When we meet Kriemhild in the second strophe we are informed immediately that many men will lose their lives because of her. We gleaned this information also from the relation between this first mention of Kriemhild and the mention of the Burgundians' "not" in the final line. Whereas the latter relation is an example of self-revealing and self-referential patterns[5] in the *Nibelungenlied*, the information we receive about the Burgundians in the second strophe comes to us in the form of a prediction pointing to that same "not" of the closing verse. There is therefore a double link – one self-referential, the other predictory – between strophes 2 and 2379, and therefore a double indication that the *Nibelungenlied* begs to be read as a continuous story.[6]

A few strophes later in the first *Aventiure* we learn more about the fate of the Burgundians. They will travel to the land of Etzel (5) and will die as a result of the quarrel between two women (6). The death of Siegfried is predicted only later – through Kriemhild's falcon dream and the following conversation with her mother (13 ff.), and by the

slighted. To put it briefly, the present chapter – and those following – is concerned with the unifying elements in the *Niberlungenlied* as the в* text presents it, and with the way in which these elements affect our reading of the epic.

5 The designations "self-revealing" and "self-referential" do not cover identical aspects, though they often apply simultaneously. Nor is the one of a higher, because more illuminating, order than the other. In the following pages these two terms will be used repeatedly, either together or individually. In the latter case, the term used is either thought to be the more important applicable or, as also happens, the only one.

6 The argument conducted so far does not preclude the possibility that the classification of the *Niblungenlied* as a story may turn out to be inadequate (cf. chapter IX, p. 161).

poet directly (19). Thus the death of Siegfried enters as an element of the plot only after the basic outline of the epic has been drawn. The author makes use of predictory elements in such a fashion as to establish Siegfried's death as but an event, however important, within the *Nibelungenlied*, and he makes efforts to prevent this major incident from breaking the epic into two parts.

In this connection Wachinger's suggestion comes to mind regarding a consciously applied structural device working by means of predictions in the *Nibelungenlied*, but against this is another statement made by Wachinger: "Jeder Teil drängt auf seine Katastrophe zu."[7] With this claim Wachinger comes close to discarding the most important implication of the insights gleaned from his scrutiny of predictory elements. For that matter, Wachinger is not the only one to speak of "part I" and "part II" of the *Nibelungenlied* and thus perpetuate the notion of a narrative with a broken back. Indeed, the habit has become so ingrained that it is difficult now to speak of the epic without making references to "part I" and "part II." One study proclaims: "Wenn wir Anhaltspunkte für ein Handlungsgerüst im Nibelungenlied suchen, dann müssen wir von der allgemein angenommenen Zweiteilung des Gesamthauses des Werkes ausgehen."[8] Nagel takes this position: "Zu berücksichtigen ist ... die Grossgliederung des Epos in *zwei Hauptteile* sowie die tektonische Funktion der als Zäsur wirkenden *Zwischenpartie*. Das setzt freilich voraus, dass das Gedicht als ein Gesamtentwurf erfasst ist und seine Unterteilung im Blick auf dieses Ganze durchgeführt wird."[9] Mergell, however, speaks of the *necessity* of viewing the *Nibelungenlied* as "ein einheitliches Kunstgebilde."[10]

It may well be that this habit of speaking of "part I" and "part II" has affected our evaluation of both events and characters. We have learned to view Hagen, for instance, as a figure who comes into his own in "part II"; a presumably broken-backed narrative has led us to conceive of the earlier Hagen as "such and such" – often enigmatic, and certainly so in scenes occurring before the decision that Siegfried

7 Wachinger, *Studien*, pp. 27, 17.

8 J. Szöverffy, "*Das Nibelungenlied*: Strukturelle Beobachtungen und Zeitgeschichte," *WW*, xv (1965), 134.

9 Nagel, *Das Nibelungenlied*, p. 101.

10 Bodo Mergell, "*Nibelungenlied* und höfischer Roman," "*Euphorion*, xLV (1950), 327.

must die – but as never quite the man he is in later days when, in addition to all the epithets found applicable to him before, he is thought to be demonic. This demonic quality is usually seen as emerging in Hagen's encounter with the *merwip* in the twenty-fifth *Aventiure* and in the immediately following episode of the Danube crossing. Regarding Hagen and other prominent characters with lives spanning all of the epic, we have looked for – and found – more or less drastic changes because the structure of the *Nibelungenlied* is thought to warrant them. It will become evident, however, that Hagen as well as Kriemhild display essential traits or dispositions that are part of them from the beginning until the very end of the epic, and that make perfectly logical, if not inevitable, the Hagen and the Kriemhild we encounter in the later *Aventiure*. By that token, it may be more felicitous to speak of developments in these figures rather than of drastic changes – though not developments in the psychological sense.

Now, if the poet of the *Nibelungenlied* makes it evident that he wishes to relate one continuous story, we might profit by taking his suggestions and observing what other means he employs to cast his materials into the desired mold. For aside from the predictory elements liberally sprinkled throughout the poem, the nature and portent of which have been investigated elsewhere,[11] there is another unifying device at work. It is one of the purposes of this chapter and those following to scrutinize some examples of this device, and to delineate whatever implications we may encounter.

It may be loosely designated as parallelism.[12] The *Nibelungenlied* displays it in abundance. There is verbal parallelism; there is parallelism of motifs; and there is parallelism of symbolic values. The latter type becomes manifest when a particular scene or episode is compared

11 A. Gerz, *Rolle und Funktion der epischen Vorausdeutung im mittelhochdeutschen Epos* (Berlin, 1930); A. Bonjour, "Anticipations et prophéties dans le *Nibelungenlied*," *EG*, VII (1952), 241-251; S. Beyschlag, "Die Funktion der epischen Vorausdeutung im Aufbau des Nibelungenliedes," *Beiträge*, LXXVI (1954), 38–53); H. Linke, "Ueber den Erzähler im *Nibelungenlied* und seine künstlerische Funktion," *GRM*, x (1960), 370–85; Wachinger, *Studien*, chapter I.

12 Whereas Nagel, *Das Nibelungenlied*, pp. 118 f., in his section on "Parallelen" delineates examples in order to highlight the architectural devices used in the epic, the present discussion seeks not so much applications of this device as those implications flowing from them that cast light on situations, events, or characters.

with another and thus provides insights that are not readily available by other means. These three types are not always easily distinguishable; each partakes in some measure of the nature of the other two. The discussion of examples belonging to the first group in particular is bound to spill over into the realm of the other two. Hence no attempts are made to keep the three separated.

Verbal parallelism involves word repetition. The opening paragraphs of this chapter gave an example of it when "maere," as it occurs in the first as well as the last verse of the epic, was mentioned as a unifying device and as displaying an example of self-referential patterns in the structure of the *Nibelungenlied*. The significance of such unifying functions is not pre-empted just because certain events are depicted repeatedly and therefore make some repetitions unavoidable. And again, meaningful self-referential or self-revealing patterns do not automatically issue from mere repetition, but depend on the way the poet makes a virtue of necessity and thus turns repetition into an advantageous and informative device. Indeed, there are instances in which the study of the parallelistic device not only provides the possibility of gaining fresh insights, but is the best means by which to arrive at a satisfactory solution to some vexing problem. The discussion of some cases of parallelism will show how they occur and what can be gleaned from them if we take as our object of study not the poet's assumed intentions but his actual achievements.

360 "Ir sult vil rehte merken   waz ich iu, frouwe, sage:
    daz ich selbe vierde   ze vier tagen trage
    ie drier hande kleider   und also guot gewant,
    daz wir ane scande   rumen Prünhilde lant."

"Now mark what I tell you, my lady: the four of us for four days
are to wear three sets of clothes each, and of such quality that we
can leave Brunhild's land without disgrace."

From this strophe we learn that Gunther asks Kriemhild to prepare clothes for each of the four travelers to Islant. In each set there is a white suit (362), worn by Siegfried and Gunther when they arrive at Isenstein (399). One suit in each set is black (365); Hagen and Dankwart wear one during that same arrival (402). In each set is also a suit green "alsam der kle" (362). Aside from the visual and suggestive contrast between the white of the kings and the black of their followers we hear also that Siegfried and Gunther are two of a kind:

399 Reht' in einer maze   den helden vil gemeit
von sneblanker varwe   ir ros unt ouch ir kleit
waren vil geliche.

Completely identical were the dashing heroes; their horses and clothes were of the same snow-white color.

The white clothes convey their wearers' equality of rank and so belie the tenor of the landing scene immediately preceding (396 ff.) in which Siegfried pleases Gunther by pretending to be subservient to him. The clothes motif applied in strophe 399 gives an example of self-revealing patterns in the *Nibelungenlied*.

Closely linked to the strophes quoted is the gem motif. This occurs first in the second *Aventiure* which tells of gems that have been forced out of shields on the occasion of a joust in Santen, and lie strewn about in the grass:

36 man sach ouch da zebrochen   vil manege buckel starc,
vil der edelen steine   gevellet uf daz gras
ab liehten schildes spangen,   von hurten daz gescehen was.

You could also see many stout bosses broken, and many precious stones forced from shining shield-plates and strewn about in the grass by lance-thrusts.

A similar motif occurs in Siegfried's death scene:

985 Swie wunt er was zem tode,   so krefteclich er sluoc,
daz uz dem schilde   draete genuoc
des edelen gesteines.

However deadly his wound, he flailed so violently that many precious stones were forced off the shield.

Later, in the thirty-third *Aventiure*, we read:

2212 Wie rehte grimmecliche   vil swerte darinne erklanc!
vil der schiltspangen   uz den slegen spranc;
des reis ir schiltgesteine   verhouwen in daz bluot.

*How savagely rang the din of swords in there! many shield clasps
flew from their mountings; smashed gems splattered into the
blood.*

In the first of these instances we deal with a festive occasion, and the
gem motif helps to convey by means of visual imagery the mood of
gay abandon and joy prevailing at the court of Santen – not, however, without making us realize that the gems lie there forgotten,
their sparkle obscured in the downtrodden grass. This instance
parallels, yet also contrasts with, the second, in which the splendor
of stones whirling to the ground is like the soon ruined final glory of
the hunter Siegfried. This time the gems are reminiscent of
meteorites; we see them move and catch fire for only a moment, in
order then to see them lose their luster in the bloody grass. Our attention is now directed to destruction and waste, and we see a similarity between Siegfried's manner of dying and the way the gems are
lost. Aside from being strewn first in downtrodden and then in
blood-reddened grass, at a later moment gems are said to be broken
and to splatter into the blood flowing in streams in Gran's banquet
hall. This third instance of the gem motif closes a trio of related allusions which parallel the ever bloodier course of events in the epic.

The gem motif also lends significance to the strophe in which
Kriemhild cuts the cloths for the suits to be used on the trip to Islant:

362 Die arabischen siden   wiz also der sne
        unt von Zazamanc der guoten   grüen' alsam der kle,
        dar in si leiten steine; des wurden guotiu kleit.
        selbe sneit si Kriemhilt,   diu vil herliche meit.

*The Arabian silks, white as the snow, and silks of Zazamanc, green
as clover, in which they laid precious stones; these were fine clothes.
Noble Kriemhild herself cut the cloth.*

Is it sheer accident that the mention of gems sewn on comes immediately after the mention, not of the white or the black cloth, but
of the green?[13] I suggest that it is not and that, owing to these lines,

13 The thrust of the argument here presented would be enhanced if we could read
strophe 360 as a request for twelve rather than forty-eight suits. So far, commen-

the final verse of the strophe acquires ominous overtones, since the green of the cloth and the gems sewn on forewarn us of the role which Kriemhild will play in the preparations leading to the death of Sieg-fried in flower-dotted grass. It is as if the poet by adjectival repetition had underscored his intention to link Kriemhild's role in the tailor scene to the role she plays in bringing about Siegfried's death: it is she, "diu vil herliche," who cuts the cloth and sews on the stones, and it is Siegfried, "der vil herliche" (985), who knocks gems off the shield with which he flails away at Hagen. The reversal in this paral-lelism – Kriemhild's sewing the gems on versus Siegfried's knocking them off – is intriguing: in the fabric of the noble life to which Kriem-hild and Siegfried are committed, gems are of consequence and be-come symbolic for the richness and *fröude* to which this life is dedi-cated.[14] In the moment of death, however, when the essence of life is laid bare just before it is extinguished, such symbolism is destroyed.

tators and translators have thought in terms of the latter number, except perhaps D.G. Mowatt, *The Nibelungenlied: Translated* (New York, 1962), who renders the strophe thus: "The four of us, for four days, will need three changes of clothing each." Mowatt leaves open the question whether "ie" of the third verse could be read as a reference to "ich selbe vierde" rather than "vier tagen." Admittedly, there is mention in the following strophes of furs being used, but we read that they serve to line silk materials. In the reading here suggested, the geographical designations in the strophes 362/365 – Zazamanc, Morocco, Lybia – refer to the green, white, and black silks. "Die arabischen siden" (362) is therefore not a strictly geographi-cal reference but designates a type of silk coming from Morocco, the silk from Lybia being black; or, vice versa, the white Arabian silk comes from Lybia, and the silk from Morocco is black – the silk from Zazamanc being green in either case. This reading is not far fetched. For one thing, K. Bartsch, *Der Nibelunge Not: Mit den Abweichungen von der Nibelunge liet*, i. Bd. (Leipzig, 1870), p. 57, gives for "die arabischen siden" of strophe 362 as a possible alternative "aller hande siden." For another, the poet indicates that strophes 364 and 365 are in part a repetition of what we have been told in strophes 362 and 363; the closing verse of 363 – "nu hoeret michel wunder   von der liehten waete sagen"/"*Now hear astounding things about their dazzling clothes*" – is the sign of the redundance to come. Arabian silk, then, comes from Lybia or Morocco for the same reason that Panama hats come from Ecuador. Read in this manner, it is perfectly possible that strophe 360 constitutes a request for four times three rather than four times twelve suits.
14 The point hardly needs elaboration and is readily verified in the many passages

The detection of ominous overtones seems also warranted since – in contrast to the black and white suits – green suits are nowhere said to be worn by anyone at any time. They function only to relay the relationship between the tailor scene and the way in which Siegfried's death is prepared. Moreover, the scene relating the preparations of the suits for the Islant trip as well as that ending in Siegfried's death show Hagen to be responsible for engaging Kriemhild's help (cf. 346 and 895 ff.).[15]

Because of this suggested parallelism, a twofold meaning applies to Gunther's remark to his sister that her help is essential – "ane dine helfe kundez niht gesin" (354). The obvious reference is to Kriemhild's making the suits and merely shows how Gunther – who in this particular case has no choice but to ask someone – is in the habit of relying on help. The oblique reference is an allusion to the information given by Kriemhild regarding Siegfried's vulnerable spot between the shoulder blades when, instead of glittering jewels, she sews a cross on Siegfried's suit.

The far-flung strophes quoted, then, are closely related and together form an example of the self-revealing and self-referential patterns with which the poet works. In this pattern of allusions found in these references to cloth, grass, and gems there is also room for Siegfried's lying down prior to the race that ends in his death (974), and for Hagen's advice to the Burgundians that they lie down prior to his rowing them across the Danube (1570). In each instance the act of lying down in the grass acquires symbolic overtones – and reflects

describing the splendor of the court. The following strophe, for instance, is but one of the many relaying the significance of precious stones.

712 Do so in ir hohen eren   sazen und heten genuoc.
     waz goltvarwer geren   ir ingesinde truoc,
     perlen unt edel gesteine   verwieret wol dar in!

So they sat in great honor and surrounded by abundance. Pearls and precious stones sewn into the golden sleeves of their festive clothes ...

15 See F. Panzer, *Das Nibelungenlied: Entstehung und Gestalt* (Stuttgart, 1955), p. 328, for the view that the poet attached great importance to the tailor scene – Lachmann's opinion about it as "unecht" notwithstanding.

on Hagen. The Burgundians, too, are "about to die," and Hagen is like a Charon, rowing across in his little boat those destined to meet their end on the other side of the river.

If we are willing to lend credence to the suggestion implicit in the above remarks, to the effect that these references to cloth and gems serve a purpose beyond that of embellishing the narrative, we may say that there is a "philosophy" of clothes to be gleaned from the *Nibelungenlied*.[16] But whereas in the landing scene at Isenstein and in the tailor scene clothes tell us something specific, the implications in general are less explicit, less self-revealing or self-referential. Clothes are mentioned often; they play a role on every court occasion. They are usually donned to reflect the honor of their wearers (65 ff., 362 ff.), or to confer honor upon their beholders (564 ff.). Elsewhere, however, clothes are used to taunt: Etzel's minstrels, who come to invite the Burgundians to Gran, haughtily offer their splendid attire to anyone who wants it, since they themselves have no further use for it (1434).

On a different plane, clothes add color to the numerous court occasions. The poet delights in speaking of clothes, usually as worn by the ladies, or of armor as worn by the men. Here, too, he applies parallelism in the repetitive system of the clothes motif. Several times, for instance, he speaks of swords being so long as to reach down to their wearers' spurs (73, 401, 591). In each instance Siegfried is involved, either alone or with one or more companions.

We can say that the poet has a pictorial eye in these dress descriptions, however generally worded they tend to be. Particularly the women's clothes should be looked at.[17] Except for the women named, the majority of them are passive and fail to participate in the events taking place. The men, however – again with some notable exceptions – are shown in action. Each sex is attentive to the qualities of the other: the men look at and admire passivity; the women look at and admire action. The world depicted in the *Nibelungenlied*, if action is to be regarded as more desirable than inaction, is in ideal a male

16 See chapter III for further remarks on the importance of clothes.

17 Panzer, *Das Nibelungenlied*, p. 193, comments: "Die Beschreibungen, die unser Dichter von seinen Frauen gibt, vermögen ... keinerlei Anschauung im einzelnen zu vermitteln. Denn diese Frauengestalten sind aus eitel Licht gebildet, sind aufgelöst in ein Strahlen und Schimmern, in dem ihre helle Haut, das Gold und die Edelsteine ihrer Gewänder ineinander fliessend sie umwittern."

world,[18] even though the activity of the *buhurt* serves to bring *fröude* to the ladies (cf. 599 and 795).

With our attention thus turned to chivalry, we can see that parallel to the clothes motif runs another repetitive motif, that of festivals: "fröuden, hochgeziten" the poet calls them in the first strophe. These festivities fulfil a structural and unifying function in that they occur in all the far-flung locales of the narrative, in Worms as well as in Santen, at Etzel's court as well as at Isenstein and Bechlaren. The *pièce de résistance* on these occasions is the *buhurt* with its contests of skill and strength. Those participating are like actors displaying their talents before the admiring onlookers. Theirs is like a command performance; there always comes an order to stop the jousting, and this order is always given by or in the name of the highest authority present (cf. 36, 598, 657, 1355). In a way, the duty of these jousting knights is to bring "fröude" by imitating it, i.e. by their play (cf. 599 and 795).

For that matter, joy is not merely desirable but a dire necessity, both on and off the field of combat. Witness, for instance, Siegfried's statement to his mother that he wishes to be unconcerned before the heroes, "ane sorge vor allen wiganden" (61).[19] Joy is to be acted, and fear and anguish must remain covered, at least by those who find themselves in leading positions. That is the reason why Gunther at one point hides his worries (148) and refuses to speak of them except to an intimate and trusted friend (155). And later he seeks isolation; he is troubled but realizes that he must not violate the rule that "fröude" is to remain unspoiled (647). In the *Nibelungenlied*, in which fear is thus to be subdued and hidden by "played joy," "fröude" may become desperate, a mask with a frozen smile.[20]

18 See, in this connection, remarks on the position of women in the epic – chapter III, pp. 64 ff. and chapter VII, pp. 114 ff.

19 To my knowledge, this line is interpreted by all commentators as an indication of Siegfried's cocksure confidence in the face of enemies. Here, however, "wiganden" is read as "heroes" and thought to refer to Siegfried's men, so that the line comes to convey his determination to appear untroubled before his retainers.

20 Nelly Dürrenmatt, *Das Nibelungenlied im Kreis der höfischen Dichtung* (Bern, 1945), pp. 129 and 173, speaks of the *solemnity* of the festivities in the epic. In their notes on 31 and 127, Mowatt and Sacker, *The Nibelungenlied*, speak of the dreary ceremonial which obtains at Gunther's court and of "the tediousness inherent in such recurrent rituals."

As we have seen, the jousters are also expected to adhere to a certain pattern of behavior. And this is the disturbing element on the occasion of the joust in Gran: the possibility exists that Volker is blatantly refusing to adhere to the pattern expected, and that he is defying authority in public – as he does later when he gives his definition of what a true hero must sometimes do despite the wishes of those in authority:

2268 Do sprach der videlaere: "der vorhte ist gar ze vil,
swaz man im verbiutet,   derz allez lazen wil.
daz kan ich niht geheizen   rehten heldes muot."

Then the fiddler spoke, "There is too much fear when a man abstains from whatever he is forbidden to do. I cannot call that the courage of a true hero."

It is small wonder that Etzel decides that the death of the Hun by Volker's hand was an accident. If it were not, Etzel would be faced with the choice whether or not to countenance Volker's public defiance of authority. At Gran's joust reality has broken to the surface. When that happens, "fröude" may turn forever into its opposite,[21] and Etzel therefore attempts to put the lid on the box from which anarchy may issue, the alternative to played joy and harmony. The attempt to deny this reality, to keep on "playing," is only partly successful, and leaves the onlookers with a sense of doubt as to why the play was marred: did the Hun's horse really stumble, as Etzel claims (1896), or did it not? At any rate, it is ironic that of all the blood to flow in Gran the first is shed on a festive occasion. Etzel cannot deny, try as he may, that it is the musician Volker, that able performer, that bringer of "fröude" *par excellence,* who strikes the first dissonant note carrying death in its wake, and ends the peaceful play. The games in the *Nibelungenlied* are over now and we hear no more of the implicitly or explicitly lauded positive values of harmony and joy; reality has intruded and is here to stay. With Etzel perhaps seeing what he wants to see, with the Burgundians making no claims of ac-

---

21 Cf. Wachinger, *Studien,* pp. 25 f., and F. Maurer's essay on *Leid* in *Studien zur Bedeutungs- und Problemgeschichte, besonders in den grossen Epen der Staufischen Zeit* (Bern/München, 1951), pp. 33–38.

cidents but grimly surrounding the scene, weaponed to the teeth (1890 f.), the play has ended on an angry note, ominous and full of portent.

This is not the first time that *leid* ensues from a highpoint of *fröude* – as exemplified in the *buhurt*. The phenomenon occurs frequently. To mention only a few instances: Brunhild weeps during her bridal banquet (618); the quarrel between the queens occurs during court festivities (815); the attack on Dankwart's men takes place during a banquet (1921); so does the attack on the other Burgundians (1951); Rüdeger's sorrow results from his newly established friendship with the Burgundians during festive occasions. All these examples indicate "wie liebe mit leide ze jungest lonen kan," the emergence of suffering from happiness (17), and together they support the tenor of the closing strophes:

2378 mit leide was verendet   des küniges hohgezit
      als ie diu liebe   z'aller jungeste git.

> *The king's feast had ended in sorrow, as all joy in the end becomes sorrow.*

In this connection it bears pointing out that as the epic progresses not only is there less and less mention of festive clothes – that follows naturally from the development of the events relayed – but increasing mention is made of armor donned for grimmer business. The turning point for the change comes at the moment when hostilities have not *quite* broken into the open: Kriemhild's Huns, when she goes "under krone" to speak to Hagen and Volker, wear armor under their festive garb. This is the last instance of a reference to clothes accompanied by an allusion to their rich and festive appearance – "ich waen' si under siden   die liehten brünne tragen" (1775). From now on clothes are no longer mentioned as lending color to events. In fact, there is no additional mention of clothes other than those of the Hun who, precisely because of the beauty of his attire, meets his end in the joust with Volker. It is significant of the poet's method of delivery that at Gran's banquet – an occasion where formerly he would not fail to draw attention to rich apparel – there is not the slightest mention of clothes. Here, as elsewhere, what the poet does not say it just as important as what he says.

At the moment of the Hun's death complete disintegration is averted only because Etzel comes down from his window and imposes his authority on the players. (After all, he is still the king of the game, who cannot condone rude treatment of the guest performers.) The window motif, used some fifteen times, is of some consequence, and it is misleading to claim that these window scenes are borrowed from the literature of the period and are often misused.[22] Actually, we may gain from looking at some of these scenes to see how and to what effect the poet employs them. At Bechlaren, for instance, we encounter open windows twice. When Kriemhild passes through on her way to Etzel, the double mention of opened windows looking down on the scenery of Rüdeger's domains, before which the company sits talking — "diu venster an den muren   sah man offen stan" (1318), "si sazen gegen dem lufte   unde heten kurzewile groz" (1320) — enhances the element of hospitality with which the poet has endowed the episodes at Bechlaren. Later, those who stay behind open the windows when the Burgundians and Rüdeger with his men ride off to Etzel's court and their doom. The poet uses the occasion to say that there is anguish on the part of those left behind:

1711 Do wurden allenthalben   diu venster uf getan,
      der wirt mit sinen mannen   zen rossen wolde gan.
      ich waen' ir herze in sagete   diu krefteclichen leit.
      da weinte manic vrouwe   und manic waetlichiu meit.

*Everywhere the windows were opened wide. The host and his
retainers were about to mount their horses. I believe their hearts
told them of terrible things to happen. Many a lady and many a
fair maiden wept.*

Such — usually vague — premonitions and feelings of anguish themselves form a repetitive pattern, emerging again and again throughout the narrative and indicating that in the world of the *Nibelungenlied* foreign places and persons are to be dreaded and, if possible, avoided. Siegmund and Sieglind warn their son against

---

22 Hugo Kuhn, "Ueber nordische und deutsche Szenenregie in der Nibelungendichtung," in: *Edda, Skalden, Saga; Festschrift für Felix Genzmer* (Heidelberg, 1952), p. 282.

Worms and its inhabitants (51 ff.); they *know* Hagen and *Gunther*.[23] Kriemhild dreads her brother's going to Islant and suggests that he find himself a queen closer by (371). No one is free of this fear, except Siegfried,[24] who is afraid only once – and that with good reason (cf. chapter IV, p. 76) – when he sees Brunhild performing in the games (451). The Bavarian ferryman, fearful of enemies entering the country, refuses to transport Hagen across the Danube (1558). There is a vivid awareness of ever threatening enmity and danger from abroad when Rüdeger sees Eckewart approach Bechlaren and assumes that enemies cannot be far off (1641 ff.). There is usually fear at leavetaking, and in general there is the awareness of possible enemies (cf., e.g., 67 f., 477, 1018, 1205, 1511, 1542). An occasional assumption that someone approaches as a friend turns out to be naive (cf. 2171 ff.). The ever present awareness of peril is also indicated by those strophes that indicate whether travelers reach their destination unmolested (1302) or are confronted by enemies (cf. the twenty-sixth *Aventiure*). In short, Islant, Worms, Etzel's land, Santen, Bavaria, all appear dangerous, because alien.[25] Fear thus being man's condition, Siegfried's trust in everything and everyone is as naive, if not thoughtless, as Giselher's optimism when Rüdeger approaches the banquet hall (2171 ff.).

So, too, there is fear in those remaining in Bechlaren. This anguish is made manifest by the women opening the windows to wave goodbye to their men. Now that conversation has become impossible, these women wish to continue visual communication. Windows, if closed, cut one off from present or – through the premonitions of disaster that accompany the opening of windows – future events; opened, these windows afford a look at life down below where the action goes on, while the spectators are condemned to remain exactly what they are, spectators, forming as it were a chorus commenting with pantomime on the goings-on.

---

23 Wachinger, *Studien*, pp. 35 f., has his own view of the fear expressed by Siegfried's parents.

24 Indeed, Siegfried's "constant blindness to danger" is conspicuous. Cf. Singer, "The Hunting Contest," p. 180.

25 Related to this, though presented in a rather different framework of evaluation, Mowatt and Sacker speak in *The Nibelungenlied*, note on 1999, of guests as the bringers of disorder and destruction.

This passivity at windows applies also to the central characters. Kriemhild, standing at the casement as though looking for the arrival of friends (1716), remains stationary until she goes to confront Hagen and Volker. She leaves her theater box as it were and begins to act, entering the stage and affecting the course of events.[26] Men depicted at windows are also inactive. The first instance occurs when Hagen is looking down at Siegfried, who has just arrived in Worms. Hagen does not begin to act until he has advised Gunther to be polite to the foreign visitor (101). Another window scene involves Etzel. Told that he is looking at Hagen (1752), Etzel begins to reminisce. In a second instance, he follows a pattern of behavior similar to Kriemhild's: he comes down from his window to act, and subdues the disorder that threatens to erupt when Volker kills the Hun in the joust (1893 f.). There is also inactivity when Dietrich von Bern sits down in a casement and perhaps attempts to recognize the situation for what it is. When Hildebrand's message finally forces him to see what is happening, he also leaves the window and goes into action against Hagen and Gunther (2324 ff.).

This enumeration reveals traits in the characters who first occupy a window and then leave it to act. Hagen leaves the window after speaking of Siegfried's past, and he maintains a cautious attitude towards the visitor (cf. chapter VII, pp. 120 f.); whatever the ultimate reason for his demeanor, he wants peace and harmony.[27] When Volker kills the Hun at the joust, Etzel begins to act in an effort to maintain order and at least a semblance of peace. Dietrich's action upon leaving the window is derived from his awareness that neutrality is no longer possible, since it has become appallingly evident that the neutral are also drawn into the maelstrom of events, and that Hagen and Gunther may run amuck if they are not subdued. This

26 Reference is made to the essay by J. Bumke, "Die Quellen der Brunhildfabel im Nibelungenlied," Euphorion, LIV (1960), 4–28, in which the "important" scenes are said to have theatrical qualities, strongly evoking spatial dimensions. Hugo Kuhn, "Die Klassik des Rittertums in der Stauferzeit, 1170–1220," Annalen der deutschen Literatur (ed. H. O. Bürger, Stuttgart, 1952), p. 156, speaks of "eine Kunst ausgesprochen künstlerischer Szenenregie."

27 J.K. Bostock, "Realism and Convention in the Nibelungenlied," MLR, LVI (1961), 231, denies this view of Hagen as one who wishes for harmony. But see chapter VII, p. 120.

series of attempts at keeping harmony (Hagen), at re-establishing at least a semblance of order (Etzel), or at preventing worse things from happening (Dietrich), like other motifs, mirrors the course of events. It also casts into relief the role which Kriemhild adopts when she leaves the window to destroy. Though she is not immediately successful in her attempt, harmony is the last thing she has in mind.

Etzel is not the only one who endeavors to keep peace and order. On a considerable number of occasions one or more of the other kings impose their authority to prevent disorder. Such attempts are practiced by Gunther (127, 872, 1967), Gernot (119 ff.),[28] Giselher (866), Dietrich,[29] Siegfried,[30] and even Kriemhild, who counsels peace to the Nibelungs who are ready to avenge Siegfried's death (1031 ff.). To be sure, in Kriemhild's case there is no interest in harmony for its own sake, but an awareness that the opponents are too numerous.

Related to this perpetual concern that harmony be retained[31] are two incidents in which a character suddenly gives in to the arguments of the person with whom he is conversing. Siegmund, at one moment of his conversation with Siegfried regarding the latter's intended trip to Worms, notices that his advice goes unheeded. He then suddenly shifts course and is now eager to help Siegfried as much as he can:

53"Unt wil du niht erwinden," sprach der künec do,
  "so bin ich dines willen   waerlichen vro
  und wil dirz helfen enden   so ich aller beste kan."

  "If you do not want to change your mind," said the king, "I am truly happy for your sake, and I shall help you to succeed as well as I can."

28 Panzer, *Das Nibelungenlied*, p. 222, speaks of Gernot as the mediator.
29 Cf. B. Nagel, "Das Dietrichbild des *Nibelungenliedes*, I. Teil," *Zfdp* LXXIX (1960), 226 f. Nagel's suggestion that Dietrich endeavors to retain "geselligen Einklang" is from the present point of view an understatement, for "Einklang" is now not merely desirable but highly necessary; harmony is this society's oxygen.
30 Bostock, "Realism," p. 222.
31 While pursuing a rather different line of thought, Mowatt and Sacker speak in *The Nibelungenlied*, note 2060, of heroism as less a positive value than a last desperate reaction to imminent and unavoidable danger: "Everyone ... fights reluctantly."

Siegmund's acquiescence does not suggest fond indulgence of father to son but results from his awareness that the conversation with Siegfried may end negatively, words having a tendency to go their own stubborn way. Gunther's sudden acquiescence in Brunhild's request regarding the visit of Siegfried and Kriemhild to Worms is similar:

731 Si gertes also lange   unz daz der künic sprach:
"nu wizzet daz ich geste   so gerne nie gesach.
ir muget mich sampfte vlegen.   ich wil die boten min
nach in beiden senden,   daz si uns komen an den Rin."

*She kept pressing until at last the king said: "Believe me, I never
liked to see guests as much as them; you need not to persuade me.
I shall send messengers to the two of them to invite them here to
the Rhine."*

Does Gunther suddenly collapse because he, too, is willing to do anything to retain harmony? As the reader knows, Gunther cannot be much interested in seeing Siegfried again; Siegfried was a key figure in an affair which Gunther has little pleasure remembering. Even so, he gives in to Brunhild. It is ironic that his attempt to retain harmony with his queen becomes the cause of disharmony on a gigantic scale.

Other parallels can be found in the recognition scenes. Those involving Siegfried are remarkable in that on several occasions he is recognized without the beholder's having met him before. This is true with Hagen (84), with the kings of the Nibelungs of whom Hagen speaks (90), and also with the messenger who brings Brunhild tidings of the arrival in Islant of Gunther and his companions (411), as well as with the queen of Islant herself when she meets the four visitors.[32]

32 The suggestion implicit in the remarks by Weber, *Das Nibelungenlied*, pp. 26 and 36, that Brunhild and Siegfried know each other is doubtful; Siegfried knows *of* Brunhild in the way she – and others, for instance her messenger and Hagen – knows *of* him. See chapter IV, p. 87, and for contrast, cf. Mowatt and Sacker *The Nibelungenlied*, note 378, who speak of the "homecoming" symbol, "which draws its strength from the emotions connected with childhood, or even earlier, recollections. Evidently, the yearning is basic enough to dispense with plot mechanics or history (cf. Mr. Polly and his pub, or the Jews and their promised land)."

There is undoubtedly something striking about the physical appearance of the Santen youth to mark him so easily, though of course such recognitions are a common epic device. But more remarkable are the three passages that mention Hagen's ability to recognize strangers: Siegfried upon his first arrival in Worms (86), Rüdeger (1180), and the minstrels who come to invite the Burgundians to Gran (1432). This ability is remarkable because there seems to run through the later *Aventiure* a series of suggestions that Hagen does not see well. When he and Volker are sitting on a bench, it is Volker who sees Kriemhild and her Huns coming, and who notices the suggestive broadness of the shoulders under the flowing silk of their garb (1772 ff). Later it is again Volker who detects the sheen of a helmet in the dark (1837), and still later he points out to Hagen the approach of Iring and his men (2032). Hagen's three recognitions, compared to the three occasions when Volker serves as his eye, on the one hand highlight Hagen's peculiar mnemonic ability and, on the other, perhaps recall Hagen's loss of an eye earlier in his career.[33] It is thus inevitable that Rüdeger's daughter, seeing Hagen for the first time, is afraid of him and must be urged by her father to kiss the Burgundian (1666 ff.).

Some examples of parallelism mentioned in this chapter have led to suggestions that tend to modify or sharpen our understanding of certain details in the *Nibelungenlied*. More important, some of these suggestions are not readily available by means of other interpretative methods. Whereas the cases of parallelism dealt with in these pages arise in the main from the "courtly" orientation that permeates the epic, the following chapter will investigate instances of parallelism that derive from qualities equally important in establishing the general tenor of the epic, those related to battle activities.

33 This suggestion relies on "outside" material, i.e., *Waltharius Poesis*. An attempt to find support for this inference would have to rely on the "inside" claim that Etzel's speech on Hagen as he knew him in the past alludes to the Latin poem, and on the consideration that A. Renoir, "*Nibelungenlied* and *Waltharii Poesis*: A Note on Tragic Irony," *PQ* (1964), 14–19, detects allusions to Hagen's role in the *Waltharius* when Rüdeger's death is depicted.

ii

HUNS AND
BURGUNDIANS

IN THE THIRTY-SECOND *Aventiure*, after the nine thousand Burgundians under Dankwart have been slain, Hagen's brother has one of his awe-inspiring moments in this strophe:

1939 "So we mir dirre leide,"   sprach Aldrianes kint.
    "nu wichet, Hiunen recken,   ir lat mich an den wint,
    daz der luft erküele   mich sturmmüeden man."
    do sah man den recken   vil harte herliche gan.

    "Alas for this grief," Aldriane's son said, "stand back, you Hunnish
    knights, and let me out into the open, so that the breezes may
    cool me, a battle-weary man." And he proceeded with magnificent
    stride.

It is not certain whether the Huns let Dankwart through because they cannot help but admire his prowess, or because they fear him; whether they make a path free and perhaps even line it as a sort of honor guard, or whether upon his approach they scatter. The following strophe, involving Huns other than those in the building in which the fight began, does not solve the ambiguity:

1940 Also der strites müede   uz dem huse spranc,
    waz iteniuwer swerte   uf sinem helm erklanc!
    die niht gesehen heten,   waz wunders tet sin hant,
    die sprungen hin engegene   dem von Burgonden lant.

Thus the strife-worn man jumped out of the building. What fresh swords clanged on his helmet! Those who had not seen his miraculous feats now sprang forward to meet the Burgundian.[1]

But the attitude of the Huns in this matter seems to be of little consequence, the poet's attention being focused on Dankwart; this is *his* hour of glory. If we stop to wonder at all, we are inclined to assume that fear rather than admiration on the part of the Huns dictates the manner of Dankwart's exit, since a few strophes later we are told that frightened Huns attempt to avoid Dankwart by retreating to higher steps on the stairway leading into the banquet hall:

1950 Swelher durch sin ellen   im für die stiege spranc,
       der sluoc er eteslichen   so swaeren swertes swanc,
       daz si durch die vorhte   uf hoher muosen stan.
       ez het sin starkez ellen   vil michel wunder getan.

1 In his edition of 1870, Bartsch offers as alternate for 1939 f.:
1939 "Owe mir dirre leide,"   sprach Aldrianes kint,
       "nu wichet, Hiunen recken,   ir lat mich an den wint,
       daz der luft erküele   mich sturmmüeden man."
       do begunder an ir willen   in strite gegen der türe gan.

       Der helt in grozem zorne   zuo dem huse spranc.
       waz iteniuwer swerte   uf sinem helme erklanc!
       die niht gesehen heten,   waz wunders tet sin hant,
       die muosen da beliben   von dem von Burgonden lant.

"Alas for this grief," Aldriane's son said,
"stand back, you Hunnish knights, and let me out into the open
so that the breezes may cool me, battle-weary man."
Then, despite their efforts, he began fighting his way toward the door.

In great wrath the hero leaped toward the house.
What fresh swords clanged on his helmet!
Those who had not seen his miraculous feats
had to die by the hand of the Burgundian.

The ambiguity is gone; instead there is a hiatus between Dankwart's leaving one building and going to another. In addition, the scene becomes repetitive when read in conjunction with the following strophe, and the "improvement" is far from convincing.

Those who through their valor ran from the stairs to meet him,
he struck such heavy sword blows that they had to retreat again
in fear. His powerful valor worked great wonders.

But here, too, the question regarding the Huns' valor remains unanswered, since in this strophe Dankwart is not dealing with fully
armed warriors but with Huns carrying drink and food (cf. 1948),
who, moreover, are crowded on the staircase and therefore have
little freedom of movement when fighting. Even so, though some of
them have courage enough to seek to stop Dankwart, we seem to
have little reason to think highly of the Huns. The poet calls those
attacking Dankwart and his nine thousand "ungetriuwe" (1935), and
Panzer seems quite correct in observing the implication "dass die Hunnen auf der Wertskala unserer Dichtung allgemein einige Grade
tiefer stehen."[2] It is to be remembered, however, that the poet uses
"ungetriuwe" also with respect to Gunther (893, 876 f.) and Hagen
(915), while elsewhere his word on Hagen is equally unfavorable (cf.,
e.g., 906, 971, 981).

The only Huns of whom we have heard in any detail at all by
the time Dankwart makes his exit are those who are with Kriemhild
when she has her exchange with Hagen and Volker, the Hun killed by
Volker at the joust, Bloedelin, and the Hun who warned Dankwart
about Bloedelin's intentions (1928). Those in Kriemhild's following we
know to be afraid of Volker and Hagen, though at least part of their
reaction to Kriemhild's request to kill the two Burgundians stems from
the *admiration* her men have for Hagen's feats of war — by now historical and already somewhat legendary — when he served Etzel in
twenty-two battles (cf. 1796 ff.). As for the Hun killed by Volker,
the only thing we know about him is the dashing quality of his
appearance:

1885 Do sahens' einen riten   so weigerlichen hie,
     daz ez al der Hiunen   getet deheiner nie.
     ja moht' er in den ziten   wol haben herzen trut.
     er fuor so wol gekleidet   sam eines edeln ritters brut.

Then they saw a man riding with such bravado as none of the
Huns had displayed. He may very well have had a sweetheart at
this time, and he was decked out like a young wife of the nobility.

2 Panzer, *Das Nibelungenlied*, p. 135.

This appearance strikes Volker as disagreeable and so becomes the cause of the Hun's death. By that token, the little scene is just as informative about Volker as about the Hun himself, if not more so, and it tells us nothing about the dead man's valor or lack of it. Bloedelin of course is treacherous, though not to the same degree as the person spurring him on with promises of gold, domains, and Nudung's beautiful widow for a wife (1906 f.). Even if we imagine that Kriemhild has mentioned to Bloedelin the possibility that he would be Etzel's heir if the little Ortlieb were out of the way – an insinuation for which there is not the slightest warrant anywhere in the epic – Bloedelin's treachery would still be outdone by the boy's mother. It seems malicious that Bloedelin holds not only Hagen's brother, but also the nine thousand Burgundians under him, responsible for the death of Siegfried (1923 ff.), but this notion that guilt is to be shared by associates parallels Hagen's determination that Rüdeger's men must pay for the death of their master (2222), and is indeed a common attitude in medieval epic and romance. As for the Hun who warns Dankwart, the poet has nothing unfavorable to say about him.

If, then, the Huns are to be thought of unfavorably, the poet so far has given little or no tangible and irrefutable evidence or even hints of it. His own unfavorable judgments are evenly distributed between the Burgundians – mainly in relation to the murder of Siegfried – and the Huns. On our part it is at best a matter of feeling rather than of objective knowledge that the Huns are cowards and incapable of any magnanimity. That feeling may come from the confrontation scene in which Kriemhild is pitted against Hagen and Volker, as well as from a previous occasion: the Nibelungs had retired to Santen without having revenged Siegfried's death at the hands of the Burgundians. It is true that the Nibelungs are prepared to fight despite the great odds against them, and, like Hagen on a later occasion (1937), tighten their helmets to begin their business (1032); but they are restrained by Kriemhild, who tells them to wait for a better day since the numbers of the Burgundians are overwhelming. It is quite possible to read these two scenes – with their parallel motifs of helmets being tightened and of one side wanting action while the other decides to be prudent – as indications of Kriemhild's erstwhile prudence in contrast to her later determination to take revenge, rather than as indications of the valor of the Nibelungs and the cowardice of the Huns.

A second request to leave a building comes from Dietrich von Bern:

1992   ... "mir ist niht getan.
    lat mich uz dem huse   mit iuwerm vride gan
    von disem herten strite   mit dem gesinde min:
    diz wil ich sicherlichen   immer dienende sin."

   "I have not been wronged. Under your safe-conduct let me go out
   of this building, with my retainers away from this fierce encounter.
   I pledge that I shall be in your debt forever."

In the scene in which Dietrich's request occurs, the Burgundians with Gunther as their spokesman strike our attention, and we sense a certain degree of grandeur in Gunther's bearing. This is one of *his* moments. But aside from the political motivation discernible in the granting of Dietrich's request,[3] part of the grandeur evoked is a reflection of Dietrich's imposing demeanor, and part of it derives from the poet's preoccupation with the scene as he sees it. By way of contrast, not ever the briefest mention is made of the reaction of the Huns to Dankwart's request.

A third request comes from Gernot:

2096 "So sol iu got gebieten,   daz ir friuntlichen tuot.
    slahet uns ellenden,   und lat uns zuo z'iu gan
    hin nider an die wite: daz ist iu ere getan.

   "Swaz uns geschehen künne,   daz lat kurz ergan.
    ir habt so vil gesunder,   und turrens' uns bestan,
    daz si uns sturmmüede   lazent niht genesen.
    wie lange suln wir recken   in disen arbeiten wesen?"

   "In God's name, do us the kindness, let us wretches come out into
   the open, and make an end of us. That would do you honor.

   "Whatever may happen to us, let it be brief. You have so many able
   bodied men who, if they dared confront us, could kill us, battle
   worn as we are. How long shall we continue in this torment?"

3 Bostock, "Realism," p. 232.

Gernot's request appeals to his opponents' sense of honor and is about to be granted by the Huns – and by Etzel – when Kriemhild intervenes. This readiness to let Gernot and his companions out of the banquet hall after seven thousand Huns have been slain under questionable circumstances (see below) raises again the doubt that also arose when Dankwart wanted to leave the scene of slaughter in the preceding *Aventiure*. Are the Huns really less capable than the Burgundians of displaying a magnanimous attitude towards enemies in dire straits? Gernot's request indicates that he at least thinks it worthwhile to appeal to the Huns' sense of honor. Correctly so, for it is this sense of honor that causes the Huns to fear Volker more than Hagen: the former is most formidable in insulting his enemies (cf. 1820 f., 1846, 2015, 2027).[4] All in all, if we had an opportunity to hear of the Huns' behavior in somewhat greater detail, we might not take it to be a matter of course that their code of conduct, compared to that of the Burgundians, is far less noble. The dearth of information about the Huns makes it not at all certain that the epic shows the tendency "die Hunnen als Menschen und Kämpfer minderen Ranges von den Burgunden abzuheben."[5]

The requests of Dankwart, Dietrich, and Gernot present a development that more or less parallels the course of events in Gran in so far as the reactions to these requests increasingly indicate threatening doom, either for the Huns or for the Burgundians. In Dankwart's case it is possible that the Huns grant the demand, but his nine thousand are all dead. In Dietrich's case, the granting of the demand seems politically motivated and involves a man to refuse whom would be tantamount to turning a neutral observer into an enemy; in this case the Burgundians stipulate that the Huns in the hall are not to be included in the free exit – one of them attempts to sneak out with the Amelungs, but is killed by Volker (1999). In Gernot's case, the Huns are ready to grant the request, but the answer is a flat refusal by Gernot's own sister. Kriemhild has already reached the stage where she remains unmoved by the misfortunes of others, in contrast to the Huns, who seem more capable of exercising mercy – even if only to kill the remaining enemies out in the open – than the Burgundians. She is unmoved by pity, and maintains a rigid seclusion within herself. She has lost her humanity

---

4 See chapter IX, p. 154, on the fear of insults as blemishes of one's honor.
5 Nagel, "*Das Nibelungenlied*," p. 297. See also Wachinger, *Studien*, p. 130.

before she violates the dignity of kingship by kneeling before Rüdeger for the sake of revenge (see chapter III, p. 52).

Another motif connected with the battle activities is what for lack of a better term we may call the Job tiding. In the campaign against the Saxons, after Siegfried has taken Liudegast prisoner, he is confronted by thirty of the Dane's men. Killing twenty-nine of them, Siegfried allows the thirtieth to escape, apparently with the deliberate purpose of having him report the calamity to Saxon headquarters:

191 Die drizec er ze tode   vil werliche sluoc.
　　er liez ir leben einen.   balde er reit genuoc
　　und sagte hin diu maere,   waz hie waz gescehen.
　　ouch mohte mans die warheit   an sime rotem helme sehen.

　　Very bravely he slew these thirty dead. He let one of them live,
　　who rode off speedily and reported what had happened. The truth
　　could be told by his red helmet.

The second tiding of this nature is brought to the banquet hall by Dankwart, the sole survivor of the massacre depicted in the thirty-second *Aventiure*:

1951 Also der küene Dancwart   under di tür getrat,
　　daz Etzeln gesinde   er hoher wichen bat,
　　mit bluote was berunnen   allez sin gewant;
　　ein vil starkez wafen   daz truog er bloz an siner hant.

　　Vil lute rief do Dancwart   zuo dem degene:
　　"ir sitzet al ze lange,   bruoder Hagene.
　　iu unde got von himele   klag' ich unser not:
　　ritter unde knehte   sint in den herbergen tot."

　　When brave Dankwart stood in the threshold he asked Etzel's
　　men to stand back. His armor was streaming with blood, and he
　　carried a strong weapon naked in his hand.

　　Dankwart shouted loudly to the warrior, "you have been sitting all
　　too long, brother Hagen, to you and to God in heaven I cry out our
　　calamity: the knights and squires lie dead in their lodgings."

A similar message is brought to Dietrich by Hildebrand, to the effect that not only Rüdeger and his men, but also all the Amelungs are dead:

2318 Do sprach meister Hildebrant: "Wer sol zuo iu gen?
      swaz ir habt der lebenden,   die seht ir bi iu sten.
      daz bin ich alterseine: die andern die sint tot."

Then master Hildebrand spoke: "Who should come to you? What-
ever men you have alive, you see standing beside you: and that
is I alone; the others are dead."

Again a movement is discernible that parallels the course of events. Siegried – playful as ever – leaves one Dane to get away unwounded, though his helmet is splattered with blood. Dankwart's manner of exit from the scene of the massacre is left vague and we are uncertain whether he is allowed to get away because the Huns respect or because they fear him; though unwounded himself, he is drenched with the blood of the slain (cf. 1956). Hildebrand escapes Hagen's furious efforts to kill him only by running away after he has been wounded (2306).

A third motif accompanying the battle activities is that of battle wrath. It is first mentioned when Siegfried arrives in the land of the Nibelungs and knocks at the castle door:

488 Er sprach:"Ich bin ein recke   nu entsliuz uf daz tor.
     ich erzürne ir eteslichen   noch hiute da vor,
     der gerne sampfte laege   unt hete sin gemach."

He said, "I am a knight. Now open the door. Before the day is
done I shall raise the wrath of some who prefer to lie comfortably
in their beds."

On this occasion we already have reason to wonder about the intrinsic nature of this anger.[6] It is alluded to again and again in the later *Aventiure,* as when Dietrich answers Kriemhild's plea for help:

6 Singer, "The Hunting Contest," has given an explanation why Siegfried acts this way towards his own men.

1984 "Wie sol ich iu gehelfen,"   sprach her Dietrich,
   "edeliu küneginne?   nu sorge ich umbe mich.
   ez sint so sere erzürnet   die Guntheres man,
   daz ich an disen ziten   gefriden niemen enkan."

"How should I help you, noble queen?" Dietrich said. "I have
worries enough for myself. Gunther's men are in such wrath that
right now I cannot assure anyone's safety."

Battle anger is also displayed by Hagen when he deals with Iring (2061), and later, after Rüdeger has had his verbal exchanges with the kings and Hagen and Volker, he begins the only thing left to do in this fashion:

2206   ... den schilt huop Rüedeger,
   des muotes er ertobete,   done beit er da niht mer.[7]

   ... Rüdeger raised the shield; His battle fury rose and he hesitated
   no longer.

Hagen also experiences battle wrath when he sees Rüdeger and Gernot dead (2221).[8] So do Hagen and Hildebrand when they face each other

7 Nagel, *"Das Nibelungenlied,"* p. 278, detects a difference between Rüdeger's *Kampfzorn* and that of other battlers.
8 The following strophe is spoken by Hagen:

2222   ... "ez ist uns übel komen.
   wir haben an in beiden   so grozen schaden genomen,
   den nimmer überwindent   ir liute und ouch ir lant,
   die Rüedegeres helde   sint unser ellenden pfant."

   ... "Things have taken a bad turn. We have lost so much in these two
   that their people and their lands will never recover. Rüdeger's warriors
   stand forfeit to us, outcasts."

Hagen, like Bloedelin (cf. 1925), exercises a type of logic by which relatives or followers of one killed are responsible for that death, and must pay the consequences. This adherence to the notion of guilt shared by associates thus provides the impetus for further disaster.

(2275), and a few strophes later Hildebrand is again said to be in battle fury: "Do vaht alsam er wuote der alte Hildebrant"/"*Old Hildebrand fought like a man possessed*" (2282). Dietrich, after he has conquered his own anger (2325 ff.), notices that Hagen is of murderous mind, "vil grimmes muotes" (2349), and when Dietrich meets Gunther, the king of the Burgundians is also enraged and maddened, "sere erzürnet und ertobt" (2358). The interesting thing in all these instances of *Kampfwut*[9] is the implication that the mind of the person possessed by it becomes unhinged and can no longer exercise discipline over the hand. The hand thus becomes independently active, and the fury alluded to is a blind fury, incapable of cool reasoning or objective calculation.[10]

The image of the hand as an independent "actor" thus becomes of consequence in the *Nibelungenlied*. What with the events portrayed, it is small wonder that hands are mentioned some two hundred and fifty times, and that the distribution of these references favors the *Aventiure* dealing with warfare.[11] By way of a few examples, the hand is not mentioned in the first two *Aventiure*, but occurs twenty-one times in the fourth, which deals with the Saxon campaign. The *Aventiure* relating Rüdeger's death mentions the hand eleven times; that dealing

9 Several critics have dealt with this *Kampfzorn*. Wachinger, *Studien*, p. 134, finds that "in der Welt des *Nibelungenliedes* der Kampf an sich schon etwas Grosses und Erstrebenswertes sein kann. Das zeigt sich besonders in den Reizreden, die den Kampfgeist immer wieder bewusst aufpeitschen." Nagel, "Das Dietrichbild, 1. Teil," p. 272, gives his elucidation a metaphysical twist when he contrasts Dietrich's self-discipline and the battle wrath of Hagen and Gunther in the last *Aventiure*. And in the second part of his Dietrich study, *Zfdp*, LXXIX (1960), 48, he states: "Es ist kein Zufall, dass überall, wo im *Nibelungenlied* solche Besessenheit waltet, der Name des Teufels begegnet und so z.B. Hagen (2311) und Volker (2001) – als die von der wildesten Kampfwut besessenen Burgunden – jeweils Teufel genannt werden."

10 Cf. Mowatt and Sacker, *The Nibelungenlied*, note 1781: "In these contests bravery means something close to blindness." Incidentally, whereas in the previous chapter instances of acquiescence were interpreted at attempts to retain harmony, it is now possible to argue that this motif of giving in is related to that of *Kampfzorn* in so far as here, too, the mind seems incapable of sustaining its function.

11 The instances when the poet speaks of white hands will be discussed in chapter IX.

with the battle between the Burgundians and the Amelungs has nine-teen mentions of the hand. It is quite natural, then, that most often the hand is said to carry a sword, to pick up or raise a shield, or to perform some other act related to battle. And it is obvious, in relation to the *Kampfwut* motif, that there is nothing "reflective" about such hands. On the contrary, they are active without the restraining influence and guidance of reason. Siegfried's words addressed to the Nibelungs in strophe 488 are intended to rouse battle anger for precisely this pur-pose: to render more easily vulnerable to their opponent those in whom it is aroused. The Bavarian ferryman seeks to rouse Hagen's anger for the same reason (cf. 1561), and Dietrich's overcoming his own anger aids him in subduing Hagen and Gunther (cf. 2349). When the individual skirmishes with Hagen and Gunther are over, Dietrich's "thoughtful" hands bind those of Hagen and Gunther.[12] Whereas Panzer interprets the cases of *Kampfwut* in the epic as so many in-stances of Germanic *Heldentum*,[13] from the present point of view we can only say that the hand references resulting from this *Kampfwut* relate to the poet's penchant for working with visual imagery (cf. chap-ter IX, pp. 150 ff.).

Another example of parallel motifs involves two clusters of words related to murder. Such a cluster begins to emerge on the occasion of the plot laid against Siegfried. The first to refer to murder is Gunther, who advises against murderous wrath, "Lat beliben den mortlichen zorn" (872), when Hagen and Ortwin press for Siegfried's death. After Hagen has thrown the killing spear and has boasted that now all the Burgundians' worries are over,

994"Ir muget iuch lihte rüemen,"   sprach do Sifrit,
    "het ich an iu erkennet   den mortlichen sit,
    ich hete wol behalten   vor iu minen lip.
    mich riuwet niht so sere   so vrou Kriemhilt min wip.

    "Nu müeze got erbarmen   daz ich ie gewan den sun,
    dem man daz itewizen   sol nah den ziten tuon,
    daz sine mage iemen   mortliche han erslagen.
    möht' ich," so sprach Sifrit,   "daz sold' ich billiche klagen."

12 Cf. Mowatt and Sacker *The Nibelungenlied*, on strophe 2349: "This is the only hint in the *Nibelungenlied* that a knight could use his intelligence while fighting."
13 Panzer, *Das Nibelungenlied*, p. 187.

"You can easily boast," Siegfried said, "if I had recognized your murderous intent, I should have saved my life. Nothing worries me more than my wife Kriemhild.

"God have mercy that I ever sired a son, to whom people in future will act according to custom because his kinsmen have murderously slain someone. If I could," said Siegfried, "I should have good reason to lament it."

Kriemhild, finding Siegfried's body before her door, laments:

1012 "Owe mich mines leides!   nu ist dir din schilt
       mit swerten niht verhouwen;   du list ermorderot."

"Alas, my woe! But your shield is not ruined by swords; you have been murdered!"

Incidentally, it seems unwarranted to find fault with this last strophe in relation to strophe 985, in which Siegfried is said to ruin his shield by beating Hagen with it. The explanation for the alleged contradiction is very simple: whereas in strophe 999 we are told that Siegfried is laid upon *a* shield, Kriemhild cannot possibly be expected to know that it does not belong to Siegfried who, being rich, was the owner of many shields. There is ample evidence elsewhere in the epic that shields become useless and need replacement after short service. Strophe 2059, for instance, shows that Iring's shield, having become worthles after his fight in the banquet hall, must be replaced. The fact that Siegfried's shield is ruined after he has beaten Hagen with it shows that shields in the *Nibelungenlied* are not too solidly constructed.

A little after Kriemhilds' lament that Siegfried has been murdered, Siegmund says to her:

1023 ..."Owe der reise   her in ditze lant,
       wer hat mich mines kindes   und iuch des iwern man
       bi also guoten friunden   sus mortlich ane getan?"

... "Alas for the journey to this land; who among such good friends has so murderously done away with my child and your husband?"

And the poet on the occasion of the renewed bleeding of Siegfried's wounds states:

1044 Daz ist ein michel wunder; vil dicke ez noch geschiht;
     swa man den mortmeilen bi dem toten siht,
     so bluotent im die wunden, als ouch da geschach.

That is a great miracle; it still happens very often. Whenever one sees the murderer with the slain, the dead man's wounds bleed.

Despite a number of what could be considered unprovoked and unnecessary killings, there is only one other cluster of occasions when terms for murder are used. In the thirty-third *Aventiure*, in which we read of the death of seven thousand Huns in Gran's banquet hall, a great and savage slaughter is announced: "do huop sich under degenen ein mort vil grimmec unde groz" (1961). A little earlier we have been told that Ortlieb died because of Hagen's murderous hatred, his "mortlichen haz" (1913), and in the thirty-seventh *Aventiure* we are reminded that the massacre began at midsummer, "z'einen sunewenden der groze mort geschach" (2086).

Hagen, confronting Iring with murder on his mind, is "der mortgrimmige man" (2060). Murder lust, which in strophe 1913 begins with Hagen and stays with him, comes to infest all the Burgundians, at least in Kriemhild's estimation when she refers to the Burgundians as murderous men, "die mortraechen" (2099). Even the cordial relationship between Rüdeger and the Burgundian kings is quickly eroded by "mortraeche":

2207 Die zwene stuonden hoher, Volker und Hagene
     wand' ez im e gelobten die küenen degene.
     noch vant er also küenen bi den türn stan,
     daz Rüedeger des strites mit grozen sorgen began.

     Durch mortraechen willen so liezen in dar in
     Gunther unde Gernot, si heten helde sin.

The two, Hagen and Volker, stood aside, for the bold warriors had promised him this. He found others equally brave standing at the door, so that he began the fight fearing greatly.

Gunther and Gernot, with murderous intent, let him enter, like true heroes.

As I understand it, the last phrase constitutes a condemnation of the kings.[14]

To speak of significant verbal parallelism on the basis of the two clusters related to murder would seem on the surface to be preposterous; surely there can be no question of a consciously intended link between Siegfried's death and the bloodbath at Etzel's court. After all, Siegfried's death is cold-blooded murder, whereas in Gran we are dealing with battling in which, gruesome though it is, all participants take their chances fairly. Or do they?

We have been reminded by a critic of the custom of appearing without weapons on festive court occasions.[15] This custom prevails in Islant (cf. 406 f.) as well as in Gran (1861 ff.) and Worms (cf. 75, 128, 1864). To assume, as Panzer does,[16] that the poet forgets this item of practical and prudent court etiquette when dealing with the episode in the banquet hall is hardly a solution to the questions which the thirty-third *Aventiure* raises regarding the circumstances in which the killing of the seven thousand Huns takes place. Actually, if it is true that forgetfulness and careless oversight are the poorest and – to the poet – least complimentary explanations to be used,[17] then we should wonder

14 In relation to this enumeration of murder references it is difficult to see the thrust of the statement made by Wachinger, *Studien*, p. 67, note 1: "In der berühmten Strophe 2086, mit der die Ereignisse dieser kurzen Sommernacht wuchtig eingeleitet werden, wird das einzige Mal im *Nibelungenlied* für die Not der Burgunden das Wort 'mort' gebraucht: z'einen sunewenden der groze mort geschach." Does Wachinger mean that in strophe 2086 we deal with the only reference to the murder of the Burgundians under Dankwart, in contrast to the other references in which the Huns are the victims? In his footnote to this same strophe, de Boor, edition cited, is equally partial to the Burgundians: "Die Bezeichnung *mort*, nur hier für den Burgundenkampf verwendet, enthält ein Urteil des Dichters."

15 Panzer, *Das Nibelungenlied*, p. 412.

16 *Ibid.*, pp. 411 f.

17 See in this connection Nagel, "Das Dietrichbild, 1. Teil," p. 29: "Bei Kunstwerken hohen Ranges sollte man überhaupt zögern, begegnende Widersprüche eilfertig als geistige Fehlleistungen des Verfassers zu deuten, als ob es schlechthin nicht in Frage käme, einem Dichter etwas Tiefsinniges und Ungewöhnliches zuzutrauen. Es ist schon der Mühe wert, um eine Erklärung zu ringen, die die Ehre des Dichters nicht schmäht und das scheinbar Unsinnige seiner Darstellung als sinnvoll erkennen lässt. Jedenfalls wird positive Unterstellung dem Geiste der Kunst grundsätzlich eher gerecht als ... Makelei."

what exactly happens in the hall, how and when things happen, and why they happen. To be sure, the Huns wear helmets (1970, 1974, 1981, 2003, 2906) and armor (1868, 2006), but nowhere in the episode do we read of their using weapons until the moment when Huns from the outside attempt to enter the hall in the thirty-fourth *Aventiure*.

Of course, the Huns' innocence was suspected earlier when it seemed to Volker that those in the retinue of Kriemhild "under krone" wore armor under their clothes (1775). On that occasion the Huns did wear weapons, and Hagen assumed (correctly) that they were meant against him. Superficially, however, the treacherous intentions of Kriemhild's party were not "legally" ascertainable. Going "under krone" as she did, protocol might well have been the ostensible reason why the Huns wore their fighting gear. Besides, though everyone except Etzel knew soon enough of Kriemhild's plans for Hagen, these plans did not yet imply treachery against all the Burgundians, at least not as far as Volker knew. He remained uncertain of her intentions until the moment when she appealed to the Huns in her following to dispatch Hagen and himself (cf. 1792). And even then Kriemhild's decision to kill Volker together with Hagen could be seen as a matter of necessity; it still did not prove her readiness to kill all the Burgundians. That did not become evident until she persuaded Bloedelin to kill the nine thousand men under Dankwart. On that occasion, too, it was odd that at best only some of these Burgundians were able to get hold of proper weapons (1931), and a little arithmetic indicates the conditions under which Dankwart's men met death: three thousand armed Huns killed nine thousand partly armed Burgundians at the cost of only some five hundred lives on the side of the attackers (cf. 1932). In addition, the activities of the nine thousand in that episode were indicated to consist in the endeavor to *defend* themselves:

1930 Vil lute rief do Dancwart   daz gesinde allez an:
     "ir seht wol, edeln knehte,   wie ez wil umbe gan.
     nu wert iuch ellenden,   deiswar des gat uns not,
     swie uns diu edele Kriemhilt   so rehte güetlich enbot."

Loudly Dankwart called to his followers, "You see for yourselves, noble squires, how things will go. Now defend yourselves in this alien land; need compels us, no matter how kindly the noble Kriemhild invited us."

1932 Wie grimme sich do werten   diu ellenden kint!
si triben uz dem huse   die gewafenten sint,[18]
doch beleip ir tot dar inne   fünf hundert oder baz.
do was daz ingesinde   von bluote rot unde naz.

How fiercely the forlorn squires defended themselves! They drove the armed men out of the building. But five hundred of them were left dead inside, and the retainers were red and wet with blood.

1935 Diu ungetriuwen brahten   für daz hus ein michel her.
die ellenden knehte   die stuonden wol ze wer.
was half ir baldez ellen?   si muosen ligen tot.
dar nach in kurzen stunden   huop sich ein vreislichiu not.

The traitors amassed a huge army before the building. The foreign retainers defended themselves well. What did their bravery help them? They had to die. Soon after that, a terrible tragedy occurred.

It is these considerations that give the only "in character" explanation for Dankwart's claim that he was only a child at the time of Siegfried's death and cannot be held responsible for Hagen's deed:

1924"Neina, herre Bloedelin,"   so sprach do Dancwart,
"so möhte uns balde riuwen   disiu hovevart.
ich was ein wenic kindel   do Sifrit vlos den lip.
ine weiz niht waz mir wizet   des künec Etzelen wip."

"But no, Lord Bloedelin," answered Dankwart, "otherwise we should dearly regret our visit here. I was a little child when Siegfried died. I do not know what king Etzel's wife has against me."

Dankwart, no coward, was responsible for his men, and it was the awareness of this responsibility – shared at some time or other by each of the leading Burgundians, as well as by Liudegast during the Saxon campaign (cf. 1839), and the immediate cause of the deaths of Gernot

18 This verse seems to say that only the Huns are armed.

and Giselher[19] – that led Dankwart to lie in an attempt to stave off the danger looming for the defenseless men under his care.[20]

All this constitutes no proof that the Burgundians murder seven thousand Huns in the banquet hall. But then, only one line is devoted in this episode to the desperate activity of the Huns: "Ouch werten sich vil sere   die Etzelen man" (1972). The verse contains the same verb as that used to describe the activities of Dankwart's men in the preceding *Aventiure*. By the sound of it the Huns in the banquet hall are defending themselves as best they can, either perhaps, like some of Dankwart's men (1931), with benches, or with weapons gathered from fallen enemies. Even Dietrich von Bern – whose position, to be sure, is one of attempted neutrality, and who does not want to aggravate anyone – upon Kriemhild's plea for help can in this *Aventiure* speak only in terms of defending himself (1984).

And then there is Etzel, first deeply insulted in his fatherly pride (1918), and later witnessing the decapitation of his son at the hand of the same Hagen (1961). Nevertheless, there is not the slightest hint anywhere in the thirty-third *Aventiure* that Etzel becomes active with weapons, whereas the Burgundian kings do (1967). There is, indeed, a difference between the attempts of the Burgundian kings to retain or re-establish peace, and the attempts made by Etzel. At the joust in Gran the Burgundians warn their retainers but fail to persuade them. Etzel exercises greater authority over his men than do his royal colleagues over theirs (1893 f.). If we also consider that Etzel does not react to Hagen's insulting remark about Ortlieb's sickly look (1918), it seems that the kingly – and courtly – business of keeping harmony and peace stands a better chance with Etzel than with the Burgundian kings.[21]

19 See strophes 2216 f. and 2292 f., in which Gernot and Giselher leap to arms, no longer willing to see their men killed.

20 See Mowatt and Sacker, *The Nibelungenlied*, on strophe 1924, and for contrast, cf. Panzer, *Das Nibelungenlied*, p. 242: "Die stark betonte Jugend mag den auffallendsten Widerspruch veranlasst haben, der im Liede begegnet, indem der Dichter Dancwart dem Blödel versichern lässt, er sei 'ein wenig kindel' gewesen, als Sifrit emordet wurde."

21 In this connection, Dürrenmatt, *Das Nibelungenlied*, p. 290, delivers a puzzling statement: "Der Nibelungendichter [vergisst] doch nicht, dass Etzel auf der

As a matter of fact Etzel does not react until the new hurt done to him by Hagen in the thirty-fourth *Aventiure* (2020) causes him to leap for his shield. The provocation now is hardly of a higher order than that received from Hagen in the banquet hall unless, ironically, Etzel were to be seen as a hero of the old Germanic tradition who *must* seek revenge at Hagen's latest affront. But if this were so, Etzel the Hun rather than Gunther the Burgundian – who stayed home during the Saxon campaign (see 174 f.) – would be the true hero-king. Of course, as some of the considerations in this chapter imply, Germanic *Heldentum* is far from all of a piece in the *Nibelungenlied*, and the hero-king concept is not a rewarding criterion with which to evaluate the crown-bearers in the epic. (See also chapter VIII, p. 143). Etzel, we must surmise, does not leap to arms in the hall simply because there are no weapons for him to get hold of (cf. also 1861 ff.).

Furthermore, it is only after Hagen has assured himself that armed Huns are unlikely to force their way into the hall – Volker having joined Dankwart to block the entrance and exit of the building – that he truly becomes active:

1980 Do von Tronege Hagene   die tür sah so behuot,
    den schilt warf du ze rucke   der maere degen guot.
    alrerst begond' er rechen   daz im da was getan.
    do heten sine viende   ze lebene deheiner slahte wan.

Gegenseite der Burgunden, der eigentlichen Helden, steht, und stellt ihn deshalb nicht als den in jeder Hinsicht vollkommenen höfischen Richter dar." Weber, *Das Nibelungenlied*, p. 80, speaks of Etzel as "in seinen schon etwas greisenhaft wirkenden Friedenstugenden merklich eingerostet." This remark is also less than convincing in view of the concern of everyone in the epic to retain peace. Nagel, *Das Nibelungenlied*, p. 180, is more persuasive: "Ueberraschen muss, dass von den Königen der Hunnenherrscher Etzel den Geist der Kurtoisie am stärksten in sich aufgenommen zu haben scheint" – though there is little surprising about this if we allow ourselves to think that for a king the adherence to "Kurtoisie" depends primarily on the enhancement of *fröide* and harmony. While exercised under different circumstances, Etzel's concept of kingship shows similarities with Brunhild's (see chapter IV, passim). Mowatt and Sacker find in *The Nibelungenlied*, note 1968, that "Etzel is more consistent as a king-figure than Gunther, in that he never shows any heroism at all." Cf. also their note on strophe 2012.

When Hagen of Tronje saw the door so well guarded, the splendid
fighting man threw his shield on his back. Now he began in earnest
to revenge what had been done to him, so that his enemies gave
up all hope of living.

In this strophe Hagen appears as the scything angel of death in person.
On this occasion, though he does not have Siegfried's horn-like skin,
his "hurnin hut" (100), he, too, seems invulnerable, but the reason for
this may be quite different from that constituting Siegfried's erstwhile
confidence in battle.

It is true that, if the Burgundians are the only ones armed in the
banquet hall, Wolfhart's assumption that he can work through to the
door to gain the open is preposterous, but Wolfhart *is* a Hotspur who
tends to speak before he thinks, and Dietrich, knowing his man, tells
him to stop his foolish talk (1933). Rüdeger may later pick up the shield
of someone fallen before he rushes into battle (2206), but Dietrich is
unwilling to become involved and will not allow his men to serve
themselves with the equipment of some dead Burgundians, thus preventing them not only from working their way out of the hall, but
also from engaging in the battle – perhaps to help the (defenseless)
Huns.[22]

The question touched upon in these paragraphs remains unanswered, and all we gain is doubt. But that very doubt is of consequence in that it seems to be a consciously applied device by means of
which the poet brings our minds into an ambivalence which it will be
difficult to resolve. For one thing, this doubt detracts from the valor
of the Burgundians in the thirty-third *Aventiure*, and we carry this
doubt with us as we read on, so that it continues to color our conception of the Burgundians' prowess and bravery. The statement, for instance, that Giselher is the best of the Burgundians in storming the
enemy (1971) now turns out to be an accolade of doubtful value. And
the strophe in which, according to Weber,[23] the best is evoked in
Gunther – "er was ein helt zen handen,   daz tet er groezlichen schin"/
"He gave abundant evidence that he was an excellent warrior" (1968)

22 Bostock, "Realism," p. 232, concerning himself with an entirely different
question, takes it for granted that Dietrich and presumably therefore also Wolfhart
and the other Amelungs in the hall are without weapons.
23 Weber, *Das Nibelungenlied*, p. 73.

– acquires the possibility of being heavy with irony. Also doubtful is Weber's claim that "eben diese Saalschlacht für Volker zur Bewährungsstunde wird,"[24] since Volker stands inside the door, while Dankwart on the outside withstands the armed Huns who try to come through to aid their comrades inside the building.

The doubt emerging here is in the first place the poet's doubt. He presents a slice of bloody life and draws no conclusions, at least no overt ones. Instead he seems to be saying: "Here it is, now try it for yourselves."[25] By refusing to become engaged, he engages us. But with all his discipline and seeming aloofness he does leave indications of the directions we should look for answers to nagging questions, and it would seem that the pointers in the thirty-third *Aventiure* consist of the repetitious use of terms related to murder.

This suggestion implies that the poet's doubt is not to be understood as a personal doubt. That would be nonsensical and would constitute the accusation that he is patching things together without much thought. The scrupulous care with which, for instance, he has woven into his materials the strands of gem, grass, and cloth references (chapter 1, pp. 10 ff.) is sure evidence of his integrity as a poet. His doubt, then, is a technical device by which he enables us to decide things for ourselves. It also follows that Nagel is correct in noticing "eine zwiespältige Haltung des Dichters versus dem bindungslosen Heroismus der Nibelungenmäre"[26] – though correct in a manner rather different from that intended by Nagel himself. Elsewhere he says:

> Unangemessen ist es, wenn das Nibelungenlied als das Epos der unzulänglichen Helden (W.J. Schröder, "Deutungsversuch", 64) gekennzeichnet wird, was durch die verwundbare Stelle auf Sifrits Rücken "trefflich" charakterisiert sei. *Es geht nicht an, solchen modernen Tiefsinn in dem mhd. Epos unterzubringen*, zumal der Dichter selbst nicht müde wird, immer zu betonen, dass es die besten und herrlichsten Helden sind, deren Tatenruhm in seinem

---

24 *Ibid.*, p. 62. That Volker's stature as a fighter comes through convincingly elsewhere is a different matter.

25 Perhaps Wachinger, *Studien*, p. 103, is referring to this doubt when he finds that "Dürftigkeit, Brüchigkeit und Mehrsträndigkeit als stilbildend und strukturbestimmend zu begreifen sind."

26 Nagel, "Das Dietrichbild, 1. Teil," p. 260.

Epos verkündet wird. Der Superlativ des Heldentums wird
nicht nur auf Sifrit, sondern sehr nachdrücklich auch auf Hagen ...
und die Burgunden überhaupt angewandt, deren kämpfer-
ische Ueberlegenheit gegenüber allen anderen Völker-
gruppen für den zweiten Teil des Liedes geradezu thematische
Bedeutung besitzt.[27]

The approach adopted in this paragraph contradicts the outlook pre-
vaeling in Nagel's Dietrich studies, of which the citation given (see
above, note 17) strikes an entirely different chord. Besides the ironic
use of superlatives disproves Nagel's view that the poet's words must
be taken literally at all times.[28]

One more remark may be made regarding the conditions under
which the seven thousand Huns are killed: some thousand Burgundian
knights (cf. 1573) dispatch all these Huns at the cost of much less than
four hundred lives on the Burgundian side.[29] Do not these numbers
bear testimony to an unsavory aspect of the heroism in the banquet
hall?

It has been suggested that in the *Nibelungenlied*, in contrast to,
say, the *Gudrun*, numbers are used consistently and "realistically,"[30]

27 B. Nagel, "Probleme der Nibelungenlieddichtung," *Zfdp*, LXXV (1956), 68,
italics added.
28 Cf. H. Sacker, "On Irony and Symbolism in the *Nibelungenlied*: Two Prelimi-
nary Notes," GLL, XIV (1960/61), 271 ff. The implications of the Miltonic device
(see below) and the chapters on Hagen help to support Sacker's findings.
29 Reference is made to strophe 2124:

Der wirt wolde waenen,   die geste waeren tot
von ir arbeite   und von des fiwers not.
do lebte ir noch dar inne   sehs hundret küener man.

The host assumed the visitors had died from the toil of battle and the
terror of the flames. But inside six hundred bold men were still living.

These six hundred are still alive after they have killed Etzel's seven thousand Huns
and done battle as well against armed groups under Irnfrit and Hawart, the latter
with a thousand men under his command (cf. 2083). Incidentally, strophe 2031
states that the Danes and Thuringians must first arm themselves before they rush
into battle. They, at any rate, have abided by the rule to go without weapons on
court occasions.
30 Panzer, *Das Nibelungenlied*, p. 164.

thus making it possible to attach some value to their distribution.[31] In addition to being consistently used, numbers appear to have a more general importance in the epic. True as it is that medieval literature takes delight in the glitter of baubles, it does not follow that their mention in the *Nibelungenlied* serves only to embellish the narrative. The gem motif as discussed in chapter 1 (pp. 10 ff.) in itself refutes such a claim. But, more pertinently, the series of occasions on which, for instance, the giving of armbands is mentioned constitutes more than a unifying element resulting from the mere repetition of the motif; the number of armbands given is indicative of the relation between donor and receiver. Kriemhild gives twenty-four to Siegfried (558) and twelve to Rüdeger's daughter (1322); Hagen gives six to Eckewart (1634), and Volker receives twice that number from Gotelind (1706). The number six or its double also occurs in relation to the kisses bestowed here and there. Upon her arrival in Etzel's land, Kriemhild kisses twelve Huns (1352) carefully chosen by Rüdeger who knows the hierarchical values prevailing at Etzel's court. Gotelind kisses six Burgundians passing through Bechlaren (1652); her daughter kisses the same six (1665 f.). The occurrence of the number six or its multiples in the armband and kiss motifs warrants the conclusion that there is some interest in numbers in the *Nibelungenlied*. It will become evident in later chapters that the poet relies on numbers to provide insights into key events which without those numbers are obscure and liable to result in contradictory evaluations.

The Burgundians singled out to be kissed by Gotelind and her daughter comprise, aside from the three kings, Hagen, Volker, and Dankwart. The honor done to them in this manner sets them apart from and above the other Burgundians. This bestowal of distinction is also evident in other motifs, for example in that of the *widerkere* (cf. below, p. 46); it is a device encountered again and again in the epic. Lacking a better term, we may speak of the Miltonic treatment given at some time or other to each of the socially prominent figures. Just as

---

31 See B.Q. Morgan, "On the Use of Numbers in the *Nibelungenlied*," *JEGP*, XXXVI (1937), 10–20. On medieval interest in numerology in general, see M. Ittenbach, *Deutsche Dichtungen der salischen Kaiserzeit* (1937); J.A. Huisman, "Exkurs über die symmetrische Zahlenkomposition im Mittelalter," in: *Neue Wege zur dichterischen und musikalischen Technik Walthers von der Vogelweide* (Utrecht, 1950); E.R. Curtius, *Europäische Literatur und Lateinisches Mittelalter* (Bern/München, 1961), pp. 491 ff.

Milton's Satan in *Paradise Lost* is depicted with all the grandeur with which the imagery of kingship can endow him, and just as the same imagery in *Paradise Regained* is applied to Christ, Hell's opponent, so in the *Nibelungenlied* each figure sooner or later becomes the focus of attention and receives aggrandizing accolades and adjectives.[32]

This treatment is applied to Siegfried first. As long as he lives, no one can vie with him in prowess. Of course, Siegfried has the cloak that makes him invisible and his hardened skin, a "hurnin hut," and that helps. But even aside from that he is clearly superior to those around him, no matter whether the action of the moment deals with knightly games (130), war (fourth *Aventiure*), hunting (sixteenth *Aventiure*), or love (48). Only of him is it said that he mows a path through the ranks of the enemy, not once but three times (206). Ambiguously enough, in the strophes spoken by the messenger bearing tidings to Kriemhild about the outcome of the campaign against the Saxons (226 ff.), many of the superlatives are applied to Kriemhild's brothers (cf. 231 ff.), though nothing is said in detail of their fighting. Besides, however admirable, their warring is but a "wint" (228) – nothing at all compared to Siegfried's. It seems that Gernot and Giselher receive accolades couched in superlatives because of their rank.[33]

While the central position of Hagen in the epic after Siegfried's death never allows our attention to stray long or far from him, he relinquishes our attention every so often to make room for someone else. The most obvious example concerns Volker, who, owing partly to Kriemhild's evaluation of him (1768), partly to the persistently recurring violin motif, and partly to the dread which his acid tongue arouses in the Huns, puts Hagen in the shade.

Dankwart, too, receives the Miltonic treatment (cf. above). It is these three, Hagen, Volker, and Dankwart, who in their prowess with

32 When Panzer, in *Das Nibelungenlied*, pp. 150 f., speaks of "Aufschwellung" he deals with a specific form of what in this chapter is called the Miltonic device.
33 Sacker, "Irony and Symbolism," pp. 271 ff., finds that the liberality of the Burgundian kings as mentioned in the first *Aventiure* is relayed in the Miltonic manner. There are also cases in which the device is used without much of an attempt to disguise it. For instance, the festivities in Worms upon Brunhild's arrival are depicted in superlatives and are said to be the grandest ever (711). Soon after, however, they are found to be inferior to the festivities in Santen when Kriemhild arrives there (787).

weapons are more outstanding than either of the Burgundian kings.[34] Examples of the device are found in some gleanings from the events occurring in Gran. While detailed descriptions of Dankwart and then of Hagen and Volker are presented as they fight, there is no such abundance of information about their kings' deftness with weapons. As in the war against the Saxons we are told that the kings fight marvelously (cf. e.g., 2279) but the statements are general and brief in comparison to those relating the feats of other battlers. Only when it is their time to die do the kings receive a more personalized aggrandizement. The first to receive this treatment is Gernot, who kills Rüdeger and is killed by him; he is belatedly raised to a high level of eminence in battle and honored by meeting death at the hand of so able an adversary as Rüdeger, who before confronting Gernot practices the battle maneuver known as the *widerkere*: that is, he mows a path through the Burgundians and returns to his rank (2213).

A similar treatment is accorded Giselher, who is destined to kill and be killed by Wolfhart. It has been pointed out (cf. above, note 19) that the immediate cause of Gernot's and Giselher's deaths is their concern for the welfare of their Burgundians. This care is laudable – though it shows itself too late to be very effective, and it is a *conditio sine qua non* with kings and leaders in general: Siegfried goes scouting during the Saxon war (179 f.); Liudegast stands guard for his Danes (182 f.); Dankwart lies in an attempt to save his nine thousand from being butchered; Dietrich and Rüdeger, concerned with the welfare of their retainers, forbid them to participate in Gran's *buhurt* (1873 ff.); Hagen as a matter of course stands guard at the door of the banquet hall (1828), and Volker joins him.[35]

Wolfhart, we gather, is one of the ablest warriors confronting the

34 This remark dovetails with the suggestion that the epic centers around the court nobility. Cf. S. Beyschlag, "Ueberlieferung und Neuschöpfung: Erörtert an der Nibelungenlied-Dichtung," *WW*, VIII (1957), 211 f. Regarding Hagen, cf. chapters VII and VIII.

35 Incidentally, during their second watch Hagen and Volker engage in deliberate speech, "rede vil spaehe" (2009). The verse has been said to have a courtly ring, but in the environment in which it occurs, it is more likely that the phrase conveys the ponderous exchanges between two tired and death-threatened men who attempt to find a way out of the desperate situation in which they and the other Burgundians find themselves.

Burgundians. At any rate, he fights through the ranks of his opponents three times (2292), a feat equalled only by Siegfried (206). Whereas Rüdeger and Wolfhart are the only adversaries of the Burgundians to whom the *winderkere* motif is applied, of Gunther's men Dankwart (1946), Volker (1976) and Hagen (2290) merit this honor-lending motif. Gernot and Giselher receive it only indirectly, by dying at the hands of Rüdeger and Wolfhart respectively, and by being the causes of their deaths.

The eldest of the Burgundian kings also achieves eminence as a warrior only towards the end of his life. The manner of endowing him with glory is more forced than with Gernot and Giselher. In strophes 2357 ff., his physical bravery and ability with the sword are lauded, and we hear of his exhaustion (2360), which makes his defeat by Dietrich plausible. We are told also about Hagen's fatigue (2351). With Hagen we have little doubt that there is good reason for this weariness — witness his muscular activity as depicted in strophe 1980, no matter whether the Huns are thought to wear arms or not — but with Gunther we tend to pass the weariness off as a device to render him tardy homage.[36]

This and the previous chapter have endeavored to show that the parallelistic devices in the *Nibelungenlied* are of consequence, and that the intra-comparative approach — so far applied mainly to cases of verbal parallelism or parallelisms involving motifs — is valid and rewarding. The number of parallels is so large that the mere enumeration of them would be an endless task. More examples will be discussed in the following chapters, which center on specific characters, since in those instances the implications to be derived from them contribute to our understanding of the individuals.

It has also become evident that on occasion the parallels serve to create and reinforce a more imaginative unity than mere repetition

36 Cf., for contrast, Nagel's evaluation of Gunther's end in *"Das Nibelungenlied,"* p. 281: "Wenn ihm aber dann im letzten Augenblick eine Aristie zuteil wird, indem er nämlich im Endkampf noch 'ein ellen lobelich' (2357), 'einen herlichen muot' (2359) bewährt, so muss das doch wohl als menschliche Entlastung dieses unglücklichen Charakters angesehen werden, der sich wenigstens angesichts des Todes — und ganz auf sich selbst gestellt — aus Zwiespältigkeit und Schwäche freikämpft in die Entschiedenheit und Stärke eindeutigen Heldentums. ... Er weiss als der zu sterben, als der er hätte leben sollen."

could provide. By using them the poet engages our interest, prompts our perpetual activity, urges us to intervene and to be vigilant, and to use the checks and balances built into the structure of his narrative as so many opportunities to verify or modulate our appreciation of situations and events. By that token, scrutiny of the parallels may provide a key to some crucial episodes in which the poet has exercised to a higher degree than usual his penchant for making statements so terse as to raise questions.

iii

KRIEMHILD

THE INVESTIGATION of the window motif in chapter I showed that Kriemhild is the only person in the *Nibelungenlied* who leaves a window in order to destroy. She is also the one who does not want harmony for its own sake (chapter I, p. 21), and who – in contrast to the Huns – is unwilling to exercise any form of mercy. There are several other occasions on which Kriemhild (obliquely) reveals or even indicts herself. Each of these instances is of consequence, for the epic provides but a few hints about her development in the course of time. For instance, in this strophe Kriemhild kneels only rhetorically:

1765 "Daz wold' ich immer dienen, swer raeche miniu leit.
　　alles des er gerte, des waer' ich im bereit.
　　ich biute mich iu ze füezen," sprach des küniges wip:
　　"rechet mich an Hagene, daz er vliese den lip."

　　"*I should be forever grateful to him who avenged my grief. All that
　　he would demand, I should be prepared to give to him. I beg at
　　your feet,*" *said Etzel's queen:* "*Avenge me on Hagen that he may
　　lose his life.*"

Hence her words are of no consequence, and there is no effort on the part of those addressed to meet her request; the Huns realize that they are no match for Hagen and Volker, and therefore they cannot be concerned (cf. 1794 ff.). Besides, rhetoric will not suffice; it must be acted out, and Kriemhild is as yet unprepared to abandon her royal prerogatives. On the contrary, she relies on them, and presently goes "under krone" (1770) when confronting Hagen and Volker.[1] And though she

1 This interpretation in no way invalidates Schröder's claim that Hagen's offense,

deems it advisable to support her request for help against the two
Burgundians with promises of rich reward, her plea sounds almost like
a command – she is still mindful of the demeanor of kingship. In that
connection it is perhaps an ironic touch of the poet's that in strophe
1765, on one of the comparatively few occasions when Kriemhild is
designated by a reference to her position, "des küniges wip," the appellation draws attention to the discrepancy between her words and her
bearing.

Later, *vis-à-vis* Rüdeger, things have changed, but by then the
queen of the Huns has twice had to ask Dietrich von Bern to come to
her aid (1899, 1983 ff.), even after he had punctured the sham of her
superiority with the epithet *valandinne*, "she-devil" (1748); at that
time Dietrich had already been her moral superior.[2]

1899 ..."fürste von Berne,   ich suoches dinen rat,
     helfe und genade: min dinc mir angestlichen stat."

     ... "*Prince of Verona, I seek your advice, help and mercy; I am
     in dire straits.*

When Kriemhild thus asked Dietrich's help for the first time it was not
he of Bern, but his retainer Hildebrand who saw fit to put the queen
into her place, even if in public. And when she sought Dietrich's help
a second time, all pretence was gone.

1983"nu hilf mir, ritter edele,   mit dem libe dan
     durch aller fürsten tugende   uz Amelunge lant!
     wand' erreichet mich Hagene,   ich han den tot an der hant."

     "*Help me to get away, noble knight, By the honor of all the princes
     of Amelungland. It will be my death if I fall into Hagen's hand.*"

because of Kriemhild's crown, comes to carry political-diplomatic overtones. See
W. Schröder, "Die Tragödie Kriemhilts im Nibelungenlied," *ZfdA*, xc (1960/61),
134. On a different plane, the scene provides one of the evidences that Hagen –
here in contrast to Volker (cf. 1780) – disregards not only the power of symbols but
the symbols themselves. Cf. in this connection chapter viii, pp. 145 ff.
2 Cf. Nagel, "Dietrichbild, ii. Teil," p. 28 ff.

1985"Neina, herre Dietrich,   vil edel ritter guot,
　　laza hiute schinen   dinen tugentlichen muot
　　daz du mir helfest hinnen,   oder ich belibe tot."

"No, no! lord Dietrich, worthy noble knight, show your generous
spirit today by helping me to get away from here, or it will be my
death."

Cornered now, Kriemhild readily recognized the superiority of Dietrich, whether it lay in his person or in his regal rank. When facing
Rüdeger, Kriemhild acts out her submission, not to a king, but to her
own vassal, and kneels at his feet (2152).

Panzer detects "eine immanente Paradoxie"[3] in this action, and
true enough, it *is* paradoxical when we consider the difference in rank
between Kriemhild and Rüdeger. But more paradoxical is the fact that
Kriemhild, while now actually kneeling, uses her regal position to force
Rüdeger to do her bidding. When in danger of her life, her submission
to Dietrich, though real enough – particularly in the second request to
him – remained a verbal one. Before Rüdeger she is not in immediate
peril, and it is blind lust for revenge that here brings her to her knees.
Moreover, a comparison of the words to the Huns in strophe 1765
with the action before the lord of Bechlaren shows that by means of
the repetitive use of this motif – the two requests to Dietrich reveal-
ingly intervening[4] – the poet conveys the "gradual fall" of Kriemhild
as a moral being, not so much because she, the queen, kneels before her
own vassal, as because she does it for the sake of revenge. Only for
revenge is kingly dignity abandoned.[5]

---

3 Panzer, *Das Nibelungenlied*, p. 178.
4 Before Kriemhild actually kneels, her subservience to Bloedelin is as rhetorical
as it was to the Huns, but it serves a wider purpose, since now she wants the death
of nine thousand Burgundians (cf. 1904).
5 See W. Schröder, "Die epische Konzeption des Nibelungenlied-Dichters," *WW*,
XL (1961), 201: "Nicht Kriemhild hat die Rache, die Rache hat sie." Cf., in this
connection, W. Betz, "Der Gestaltwandlung des Burgundenunterganges von Prosper Aquitanus bis Meister Konrad," in: *Gestaltprobleme der Dichtung: Festschrift*
für Günther Müller (Bonn, 1957), p. 6.

Kriemhild's forgetting the demeanor of kingship is all the more striking when we remember that on the occasion of the queens' quarrel she bedecks herself and her retinue with splendor:

831"Nu kleidet iuch, mine meide," sprach Sifrides wip.
   "ez muoz ane schande beliben hie min lip.
   ir sult wol lazen schouwen, und habt ir riche wat.
   si mac sin gerne lougen, des Prünhilt verjehen hat."

   Man moht' in lihte raten, si suochten richiu kleit.
   da wart vil wol gezieret manic vrouwe unde meit.
   do gie mit ir gesinde des edelen küniges wip
   (do wart ouch wol gezieret der schoenen Kriemhilden lip).

   Mit drin und vierzec meiden, di brahte si an den Rin,
   di truogen liehte pfelle geworht in Arabin.
   sus komen zuo dem münster die meide wol getan.
   ir warten vor dem huse alle Sifrides man.

   Diu liute nam des wunder, wa von daz geschach,
   daz man die küneginne also gescheiden sach,
   daz si bi ein ander niht giengen alsam e,
   da von wart manigem degene sit vil sorclichen we.

   Hie stuont vor dem münster daz Guntheres wip.
   do hete kurzewile vil maniges ritters lip
   mit den schoenen vrouwen, der si da namen war.
   do kom diu vrouwe Kriemhilt mit maniger herlichen schar.

   Swaz kleider ie getruogen edeler ritter kint,
   wider ir gesinde daz was gar ein wint.
   si was so rich des guotes, daz drizec künige wip
   es möhten niht erziugen, daz tete Kriemhilde lip.

   Ob iemen wünschen solde, der kunde niht gesagen
   daz man so richiu kleider gesaehe ie mer getragen
   also da ze stunden truogen ir meide wol getan.
   wan ze leide Prünhilde, ez hete Kriemhilt verlan.

"Now dress yourselves, my maidens," said Siegfried's wife, "for I cannot be disgraced here. Make it obvious what beautiful clothes you have; Brunhild will then gladly take back what she has said."

They needed no persuading, but took out their splendid robes. Many a lady and her maiden was gorgeously adorned. There went with her retinue the noble king's wife (the beautiful Kriemhild was also magnificently attired).

With forty-three maidens whom she had brought to the Rhine; they wore shining gowns wrought in Arabia. So they came to the minster, these fair maidens. All Siegfried's men were waiting in front of the building.

The people wondered why it happened that the queens were thus separated and no longer went together as they did before. Many warriors had to suffer for that in the end.

Gunther's wife was already standing before the minster; and many knights diverted themselves with the beautiful ladies they saw there, when lady Kriemhild arrived with a great and glorious company.

Whatever fine clothes had ever adorned the daughters of noble knights, it was as nothing compared to those of her following. She was so rich in possessions that thirty queens could not amass what she had.

No one, however he tried, could say that such rich clothes as were worn by her fair maidens had ever before been seen. If it were not to affront Brunhild, Kriemhild would not have done it.

From these strophes it becomes evident that Brunhild does not return to her apartments to change. Bumke has it that both queens prepare for the confrontation.[6] Whereas the ambiguous strophe 832 on which he seems to base this opinion is quite freely translated by de Boor in

6 Bumke, "Quellen," p. 12.

his bilingual edition,[7] the same author, in a note in his edition after Bartsch, interprets "des edelen küniges wip" of the third verse to refer to Kriemhild.[8] Bartsch himself took this appellation as applying to Brunhild,[9] and in his edition of 1870 gives as alternate for "des edelen küniges wip" the phrase "des edeln wirtes wip."[10] Neither of these readings solves anything, since both leave undecided the question whether "des edelen küniges wip" goes to change her dress or proceeds directly to the minster. In the presence of such equivocal interpretations, reliance on the "inner probability" of the quoted passage yields the view that Brunhild does *not* change her dress: the passage deals exclusively with the dressing of Kriemhild and her retinue; not a word is said about Brunhild's attire. Moreover, it would be a matter of course for a poet with a penchant for the Miltonic device (cf. chapter II, pp. 45 ff.) – *if* he meant to convey the notion that Brunhild dresses up also – to give descriptions of such dressing activities twice: first that of Brunhild's party and then, in grander superlatives, that of Kriemhild's. Besides, the first verse of strophe 836 – "Swaz kleider ie getruogen   edeler ritter kint" – does not compare the splendor of Kriemhild's group with that of Brunhild's – a natural contrast to be mentioned if Brunhild had dressed up also – but is a general statement simply indicating the riches which Kriemhild is capable of displaying. Finally, the last verse in strophe 837 – "wan ze leide Prünhilde,   est hete Kriemhilt verlan" – suggests that Brunhild does *not* dress up for the confrontation.

And so, despite Weber's view that Brunhild "immer am Aeusseren, Grob-Sichtbaren hängt,"[11] Kriemhild attaches more importance

7 H. de Boor, *Das Nibelungenlied: Zweisprachige Ausgabe*, Sammlung Dietrich, vol. 250, strophe 832:

> Sie liessen gern sich mahnen   Mit ihrem schönsten Kleid
> schmückten sich die Frauen   und machten sich bereit.
> Auch Kriemhilt liess sich kleiden   mit königlicher Pracht.
> Dreiundvierzig Jungfraun,   die sie zum Rheine mitgebracht, ...

8 De Boor, in *Deutsche Klassiker*, note to 832.

9 K. Bartsch, *Das Nibelungenlied* (Leipzig, 1923), note to 832.

10 Bartsch, *Der Nibelunge Not*, strophe 832.

11 Weber, *Das Nibelungenlied*, p. 40. See also Mowatt and Sacker, *The Nibelungenlied*, note 118: "It is noticeable that Sifrid (here) and Brünnhilde (especially

to pomp and circumstance than does the queen of the Burgundians. Siegfried's wife is of the view that clothes make the queen, and that her dress will play a vital part in the decision to come. Kriemhild's clothes must help to make the truth come out, the truth as Kriemhild sees it or claims to see it. Of course, as far as the reader is concerned, Kriemhild in this episode is dressing up the truth. Brunhild, however, waits in front of the minster, full of confidence because she knows and feels herself to be all queen.[12]

In this manner, the clothes philosophy brought to bear on the quarrel between the queens is of consequence; it teaches or verifies impressions gained elsewhere about Brunhild and Kriemhild. That Brunhild has this self-assurance follows also from her nonchalant and insulting command given over the shoulder that Hagen and Dankwart must receive their weapons back:

447 Wol hort' diu maget edele   waz der degen sprach
     mit smielendem munde   si über ahsel sach:
     "nu er dunke sich so küene,   so traget in ir gewant,
     ir vil scharpfen wafen   gebet den recken an die hant."

   The noble maiden heard what the warrior said, and looking over
   her shoulder said with a smile: "Since he considers himself so
   brave, bring them their armor, and put the knights' sharp swords
   into their hands."

Brunhild *knows* that she is invincible and need not fear a mere quartet of visiting Burgundians.[13] As regards Kriemhild, we have already dealt with an incident suggesting that for her the outward mark of kingship constitutes kingship itself; in the twenty-fifth *Aventiure*, many years after the quarrel, Kriemhild has retained her tendency to identify innate qualities with outward show. Her reason for going

in stanza 821) are more conscious of rank than is anyone else in the *Nibelungen-lied."*

12 Lida Kirchberger, "The Crown in the *Nibelungenlied*," *Monatshefte*, XLVIII (1956), 267, speaks in a similar vein of Siegfried when she refers to his "inner attributes of royalty" which make it unnecessary for him to wear the symbols of kingship.

13 Brunhild's self-assurance will be discussed in greater detail in chapter IV.

"under krone" when she confronts Hagen and Volker is of the same nature as her decision to dress up before meeting Brunhild.

Lida Kirchberger[14] detects in Gunther a similar tendency to rely on the outward marks of kingship. During the landing scene at Isenstein he is pleased because Siegfried leads his horse and helps him mount it (396). There thus seems possible a grouping which puts Brunhild and Siegfried – both innately kingly and not feeling the need for outward display – over against Gunther and Kriemhild. The implications are of consequence, as will be shown in the following chapter. For the moment it suffices to say that this grouping is an example of the *Sein-Schein* contrast found to be embedded in the epic by several critics.[15] This contrast, however, is different from that detected by D. G. Mowatt.[16]

We learn, or at least may surmise, something else from the quoted dressing-up passage and the scenes following it. Before the quarrel Kriemhild and Brunhild have been in the company of each other for ten days. The question of why Brunhild has never noticed the ring on Kriemhild's hand or the belt she wears until Kriemhild draws her attention to them at the height of the insults (847 ff.) is disconcerting[17] until we realize that the ring as well as the belt are put on by Kriemhild when she dresses for the confrontation scene. Part of her proof of alleged superiority over the queen of the Burgundians relies on Kriemhild's using her opponent's erstwhile possessions. What rightfully belonged to Brunhild is here used to prove Kriemhild "right"[18] – cf. "Ez muoz ane schande   beliben hie min lip" (831). The symbolic value of ring and belt thus becomes more complicated and is made to carry more implications than would appear at first glance. This new value reveals, I think, a type of truth, in the language of symbol, that is of consequence in the framework of the *Nibelungenlied* as a whole (cf. chapters iv and v, passim). Though this symbolic significance calls for

14 Kirchberger, "The Crown," p. 268.

15 Wachinger, *Studien*, pp. 25 ff.; Linke, "Ueber den Erzähler," p. 374, and others.

16 D. G. Mowatt, "Studies towards an Interpretation of the *Nibelungenlied*," *GLL*, xiv (1960/61), 263 f.

17 See Kuhn, "Szenenregie," p. 285, note 9: "Warum sieht und erkennt Brünhilt den Gürtel erst jetzt?"

18 Compare this statement made by Sacker, "Irony and Symbolism," p. 277: "That Kriemhild wears the belt and ring is as significant as that Siegfried took them."

close scrutiny, for the moment we can infer from Kriemhild's "arming" herself with ring and belt that she goes to the minster fully intending to devastate Brunhild with her "knowledge" of what happened ten years ago in her enemy's bridal chamber. Kriemhild, as it were, by wearing the belt wears Brunhild's despoiled honor as a trophy.[19]

In this connection, whereas it has been suggested that Kriemhild at one time feels guilty – when she warns Siegfried not to go to war against the Saxons – there is no indication that she is guilty by any objective standard. For like all the characters in the *Nibelungenlied*, Kriemhild is a believer in the testimonial power of symbols.[20] She therefore knew from the very moment Siegfried gave her the belt and ring that he had vanquished Brunhild[21] (without Siegfried having to *say* anything), and she logically assumed that such vanquishment was equatable with possessing. Hence Kriemhild does not lie knowingly when she sardonically accuses Brunhild of having been the *Kebse* of an *Eigenmann*, and it is ironic that this accusation provides Brunhild with the basis from which to mete out Siegfried's punishment. For Kriemhild herself indicts Siegfried. Her insult, if the double untruth in it is removed, turns into the statement that Siegfried as *king* did *not* make Brunhild his *Kebse*, and that, as we shall see in the following chapter, becomes the reason why Siegfried must die.

Kriemhild, then, comes to know as much as anyone else from the quarrel and oath scenes – that is, everything except how Brunhild defines Siegfried's guilt or lack of it. And she still does not know Hagen, and assumes that he, too, was informed by the testimonial power of belt and oath, and that he would think and act accordingly:[22] she therefore tells him readily about Siegfried's vulnerable spot.[23]

19 This holds true even though I think that Brunhild's honor was despoiled for a different reason than is generally assumed (see chapters IV and V, passim).

20 See in this connection chapter VI, p. 113.

21 See chapter IV, passim.

22 See chapters II, p. 51, n. 1, and VIII, pp. 145 ff., for the true state of affairs regarding Hagen's bearing towards symbols.

23 Because it will be argued later – see chapter VII, p. 128 – that there is no bond of loyalty between Brunhild and Hagen, it may in the present context be suggested that Kriemhild expects the help of Hagen – a relative – as a matter of course. This expectation has nothing to do with her unconscious desire to harm Siegfried. The latter view is advanced in *The Nibelunglied* by Mowatt and Sacker, who see fit

Kriemhild, of course, has long since fallen into the habit of "co-operating" with the forces that ultimately bring about Siegfried's demise, and she is prone to revealing herself as well in her actions, her words, and her thoughts. In addition to her self-revelations when dressing up for the confrontation with Brunhild, when being active in the tailor scene (with its parallel in her later action of sewing a cross on Siegfried's suit), when becoming involved in events after standing passively at a window, or when kneeling before Rüdeger, there is her decision to marry Etzel. During her deliberations she has two main thoughts on the matter: "If I marry Etzel the world will blame me" (1248); and "Marriage to Etzel will bring me the opportunity to take revenge" (1259). Taken together these thoughts amount to the acknowledgment that the world will blame her for her revenge. This inadvertent self-accusation, emerging when the two strophes are read in relation to each other, *seems* to be contradicted by her thought at a later moment:

1395 Ez lag ir an dem herzen   spat' unde vruo,
      wie man si ane schulde   braehte dar zuo
      daz si muose minnen   einen heidenischen man.
      die not die het ir Hagene   unde Gunther getan.

> *From dawn to dusk she pondered how she, all innocent, had been caused to love a pagan man. This sorrow Hagen and Gunther had inflicted upon her.*

At the time, the decision to marry Etzel had been her own; her brothers only *advised* her to accept Etzel's offer. Hagen in fact opposed the marriage (1203 f.), and Gunther exerted himself much less than Giselher, her dearest brother (1243 f.). The conclusion is clear: Kriemhild's decision was free in so far as it followed the well intended advice of her brothers and her mother, but it was not free in so far as Hagen's and Gunther's involvement in Siegfried's death "compelled" her to marry Etzel for the sake of revenge.

to say that Hagen is irresistible to any woman but Brunhild (note on 447), that there is a touch of possible satisfaction in Kriemhild's first reaction to Siegfried's death – "du list emorderot" (note on 1012) – and that to her Hagen comes to figure as a sort of substitute for Siegfried (note on 1572).

In such rather covert ways the poet delineates a Kriemhild whose language and actions reveal her inadequate ability to cope with her position as Siegfried's wife or widow. For the poet depicts Kriemhild's life as centered on Siegfried, and he sees her love for Siegfried as inevitable,[24] as is indicated by the moon similes.

283 Sam der liehte mane   vor den sternen stat,
      des scin so luterliche   ab den wolken gat,
      dem stuont si nu geliche   vor maneger frouwen guot.
      des wart da wol gehoehet   den zieren helden der muot.

As the bright moon stands out from the stars and shines so clearly through the clouds, just so she stood in front of many fine ladies, raising the hearts of the gallant warriors.

Enlightening though Fechter's remarks[25] are on this strophe, the moon simile is in the present context particularly significant because it establishes a link between Kriemhild and Siegfried, the latter in much the same manner being compared with the moon:

817   ... "nu sihestu wie er stat,
      wie rehte herliche   er vor den recken gat,
      alsam der liehte mane   vor den sternen tuot?
      dez muoz ich von schulden tragen   vroelichen muot."

... "But look how he stands there! How splendidly he outshines the other knights, as the bright moon outshines the stars! For this my heart has every right to swell with joy."

The link is meaningful because the simile applied to Siegfried is spoken by Kriemhild, and we surmise that on the level of symbolic values her "vroeliche muot" must be taken to owe its origin to something more than her pride in being this splendid man's wife. By virtue

24 Mowatt and Sacker, *ibid.*, note on 829, speak of Kriemhild's "strange *action* of marrying Siegfried" (italics added), though it is more accurate to say that she is bartered to Siegfried (cf. chapter VI, p. 108).
25 W. Fechter, "Ueber die Vergleiche in der fünften Aventiure des *Nibelungenliedes*," ZfdA, LXXXIX (1958/59), 91–99.

of the repeated moon simile Kriemhild and Siegfried become a unit, each other, one, in symbolic language.

The identity of the similes not only illustrates the close bond between the Santeners, but also enhances the mutually reflecting presentations of Kriemhild and Siegfried as we come to know them in the first and second *Aventiure*. The two persons portrayed in them correspond to each other in such a manner as to belong together inalienably and by nature, the one being a male replica of the other. From these two *Aventiure* we learned what we now find verified and explicitly indicated by means of parallel images: Kriemhild and Siegfried were destined for each other; they are "moon-crossed" lovers.

It is true of course that with Siegfried what comes from within, "von sin selber muote" (23), makes him eager for life, to prove his royal manhood; Kriemhild, on the other hand, we see shy away from an important facet of life as it is to be lived in her sphere, at least according to Ute (14 ff.). The very mirrorlike relation between the first and second *Aventiure* reveals one of the basic differences between Kriemhild and Siegfried.

Kriemhild's strophe on Siegfried comes after her boast that he is worthy of Gunther's realm (815), and derives its poignancy from its location: strophe 817 claims that Kriemhild is worthy to be queen of the Burgundians not only because she is Siegfried's wife, but also because of the double moon simile. Thus Brunhild is given a double challenge from the outset, and whatever she may claim regarding Gunther's superiority over Siegfried (and by implication regarding her own over Kriemhild), her reaction to Kriemhild's boast must do without the support of a double moon simile or any other parallel images uniting Brunhild and Gunther on the level of symbolic language.

Thus understood, the moon similes – or the very lack of them for Brunhild and Gunther – provide an example of the self-revealing and self-referential patterns in the *Nibelungenlied*, for the similes provide the briefest and most immediately convincing "inside" explanation of why Kriemhild's former determination to keep aloof from love (15 ff.) vanishes, turns out to be but a "wint" (47), once Siegfried moves into her life and she, faced by the man who was to dominate her, "dem si wart sider undertan" (46), loses the liberty to adhere to her former resolve. For whereas she wants to avoid love in order to avoid suffering – knowing it to be a law of life that the one follows from the other as naturally and inevitably as night follows the sunset – Kriemhild is fated. Hers is Isolde's situation: she might as well have drunk a love potion.[26]

All this is not to say that for the present investigation Fechter's suggestions regarding classical allusions – detectable in the moon similes – are of no consequence. On the contrary, his findings are highly important, since his is one of the persuasive arguments to date[27] that the poet of the *Nibelungenlied* somehow stands in the classical tradition. This tradition makes it possible to read in a new light Kriemhild's falcon dream and the following conversation with her mother. For whereas the attempts to interpret Kriemhild's dream and the fervor of her determination not to love have been many, none of them has yet been fully persuasive, since all fail to do justice to Kriemhild's bearing during her conversation with Ute. Kriemhild's reaction to her mother's advice to welcome love carries a hue of vehemence that does not seem to blend at all harmoniously with the Kriemhild of the first *Aventiure*.[28] It is therefore small wonder that in Weber's view, for instance, Kriemhild in this conversation displays a self-centeredness, a hard core, that ultimately may grow into something bigger, may come to occupy and possess Kriemhild completely, thereby destroying her.[29] It is the best Weber can do on his premises. And to be sure, the question of why Kriemhild should be so vehement when she proclaims she will never fall victim to love *is* disconcerting and riddlesome...until it comes to mind – in connection with Fechter's article on classical influences at work in the *Nibelungenlied* – that Kriemhild is thinking of love as

26 For reasons too elaborate to detail here it would seem that just as interesting as Fechter's remark is the similarity between the first encounter of Kriemhild and Siegfried and the episode in *Tristan* in which Isolde is imaged by means of falconry lore (10996 ff.). This similarity, incidentally, is but one of the many that urge a comparative study of motifs in *Tristan* and the *Nibelungenlied*.

27 See also Panzer, *Das Nibelungenlied*, passim; G. Eis, "Die Hortforderung," *GRM*, xxxviii (1957), 209–23; J. Bumke, "Die Eberjagd im Daurel und in der Nibelungendichtung," *GRM*, xli (1960), 105–11; Curtius, *Europäische Literatur*, p. 192.

28 G. Nordmeyer, "Source Studies on Kriemhild's Falcon Dream," *GR*, xv (1940), 298, speaks of the incongruity of Kriemhild's bearing in the first *Aventiure* and ascribes it to a source in which Brunhild had the dream. On Kriemhild's dream, cf. also F. R. Schröder, "Kriemhilds Falkentraum," *Beiträge*, lxxviii (Tübingen, 1956), 319–48.

29 Weber, *Das Nibelungenlied*, pp. 55 f.

that tragic madness which plunges otherwise sane persons, usually women, into crime and disgrace. This is the sort of love a Medea, a Phaedra, or a Dido falls prey to, and the love against which maidens pray that the gods may protect them. Such love must be avoided at all cost, its effects being too appalling to contemplate. It is this – perhaps only obscure – awareness that places Kriemhild with those figures in the epic who *know* about things, though at times only darkly.

From this point of view, Kriemhild's falcon dream and resulting determination do not acquire all the values that have been detected in this scene. Kriemhild's "taming her falcon" has nothing to do with her exerting a refining influence on Siegfried, as has been suggested,[30] but is an allusion to king Siegfried becoming a slave of love.[31] What ensues from the falcon dream – if seen as a reflection of tragic motifs in classical literature[32] – and the talk following is the view that Kriemhild's resolve and her mother's argument are based on different concepts of love. Whereas Kriemhild is preoccupied with the notion of love as possible tragic madness in which reason is suspended, Ute thinks of a love that bears domestic comfort in its wake. Such love may bring its pangs, but it is on the whole comfortable. It is the love of a Penelope, who is content to be cherished by Odysseus together with the other possessions constituting his household. This love, though assailed at times, is never really endangered – and it is never dangerous. It provides a protective shield for the faithful wife. Though the partner in such love may wander about, ultimately he is expected to come home again. Ute, for all we know, is propagating the double standard in the conduct of love.

Mother and daughter, then, think of different types of love and, since they do not define their terms, they talk past each other. What their concepts share is the age-old tradition in which they run parallel. That views of love can be so different within one family is also shown by Gunther. His is a merry celebration of the joys of the senses. It is unproblematic and – within the sphere in which it is practiced – seemingly to be regarded as innocent and perhaps even wholesome. Gunther's view, too, has an old tradition behind it, running parallel to those of his mother and sister. Ute of course has had her day and is

30 Sacker, "Irony and Symbolism," p. 277.
31 This matter will be treated in chapter VI.
32 See in this connection E. Ploss, "Byzantinische Traumsymbolik und Kriemhilts Falkentraum," *GRM*, VIII (1958), 218–26.

of an age at which she can be expected to adhere to her established way of thinking. But Gunther and Kriemhild could be different. They could have an inkling of "romantic" – or at least pre-romantic, that is, courtly – love.

This latter type of love seems too new for the members of Worms' royal family to be very familiar with. They know of its outward gestures, but they have not yet been able to make its philosophical base and implications their own. If they had, they would know that such love is positive in value since, in so far as it is capable of developing into "romantic" love, it may ennoble and refine the person who experiences it, and it is therefore not to be dreaded. Given Gunther's cheerful and superficial sensuality, he would not be interested in the intrusion of such effects upon his love. His is not a philosophy of love.

What about Kriemhild then? She evidently thinks of the tragic effects of love and its ability to warp and make ugly and cause sufferings. The love to which she refers when talking with Ute makes its victim incapable of exercising rational control or of asserting his will. But though love, if it comes to her, may eventually acquire some of the courtly trappings and manifestations, it will likely have very little else in common with the new type of love, particularly if it is to lead to marriage, as both Kriemhild and Ute assume it will.

In this connection it bears pointing out that after he is married Siegfried no longer displays towards Kriemhild any reverence that could claim to be of courtly orientation.[33] While the moon similes testify to their deep and true love for each other, the courtliness of which Renoir speaks[34] amounts to little more than a display of pleasant manners, and is only detectable up to the time they marry. After that, "reality" prevails. For instance, when Kriemhild attempts to settle her inheritance rights (691 ff.), Siegfried seems annoyed. The poet does not say why, but there are several indications in the *Nibelungenlied* that marriage is a doubtful venture for a woman, and that she may do well to take with her whatever wordly goods she can.[35] Siegfried's annoyance at seeing Kriemhild insist on her rights may very well stem from his apprehension that she might be less tractable than a wife without independent means.

33 Cf. Mowatt and Sacker, *The Nibelungenlied*, p. 15.
34 A. Renoir, "Levels of Meaning in the *Nibelungenlied*: Sifrit's Courtship," NM, LXI (1960), 353–61.
35 See chapter VI, pp. 114 ff., on the position of women in the epic.

And then there is the moment in the fourteenth *Aventiure*, after the quarrel between the queens and after Gunther has declared Siegfried innocent, when the latter says:

861   ... "Geniuzet et min wip,
      daz si hat ertrüebet   den Prünhilde lip,
      daz ist mir sicherlichen   ane maze leit,"
      do sahen zuo zein ander   die guoten ritter gemeit.

      "Man sol so vrouwen ziehen,"   sprach Sifrit der degen,
      "daz si üppecliche sprüche   lazen under wegen.
      verbiut ez dinem wibe,   der minen tuon ich sam.
      ir grozen ungefüege   ich mich waerlichen scham."

      ... *"If my wife went unpunished after having insulted Brunhild,*
      I should be very sorry indeed." The good knights exchanged
      glances.

      "One should train women so," said the warrior Siegfried, "that
      they refrain from thoughtless talk. Forbid your wife; I'll forbid
      mine. I am truly ashamed of her great breech of courtesy."

To my knowledge, there has been no exception to the view that Siegfried's listeners look at each other in astonishment and dismay because his courtliness turns out to be but skin deep. And indeed, skin deep it is, but that lack of courtly finesse is not the cause of the glances mentioned in strophe 861. The passage shows that ten years of married life have not made Siegfried and Kriemhild more refined. If anything, Kriemhild's courtliness has deteriorated even more than Siegfried's: we surmise that she tells Hagen with a certain amount of smugness about the beating Siegfried has given her:

893 "Vil lieber vriunt Hagene,   gedenket an daz,
      daz ich iu gerne diene   und noch nie wart gehaz.
      des lazet mich geniezen   an minem lieben man.
      er'n sol des niht engelten,   hab' ich Prünhilde iht getan.

      "Daz hat mich sit gerouwen,"   sprach daz edel wip.
      "ouch hat er so zerblouwen   dar umbe minen lip;
      daz ich iz ie geredete   daz beswarte ir den muot,
      daz hat vil wol errochen   der helt küene unde guot."

"Dear friend Hagen, bear in mind that I gladly serve you and never hated you. Let my dear husband benefit from that. He should not be held accountable if ever I insulted Brunhild.

"I have learned to rue that," the noble lady said, "He has beaten my body blue for saying things that came to weigh on Brunhild's mind. The bold and good knight has punished me severely for that."

From this point of view, Kriemhild's becoming Siegfried's "undertan" (46) reflects a change in the courtly bearing of both towards each other. Her love for him has had no ennobling effect.

From the moment she married Siegfried, the effect of Kriemhild's love has been rather profound, not on him, but on herself. There is, for instance, precious little of the courtly lady about her when she tells Brunhild during the quarrel that it was Siegfried who overcame Brunhild in the bridal chamber. The remark, intended to hurt Brunhild, and used to cap a specious argument – though not specious in Kriemhild's mind in the same manner in which the reader knows it to be specious – reflects on Kriemhild's own position. During that night – only the second of her wedded life – Kriemhild hardly enjoyed the status of a lady on a pedestal, however metaphorical that pedestal be. She had to go to bed alone, to wonder why Siegfried sneaked away from her during the banquet, and her remark to Brunhild:

839 "Kundestu noch geswigen,   daz waere dir guot.
　　du hast geschendet selbe   den dinen schoenen lip:
　　wie möhte mannes kebse   werden immer küniges wip?"

"If you could only be silent; that would be better for you! You yourself have brought disgrace upon you. How could a vassal's paramour ever become the wife of a king?"

relies on the boast that he went away that night in order to spend time in a strange bed.

With these considerations, it becomes less likely that the knights, hearing Siegfried speak of reprimanding wives, are in fact dismayed and amazed because Siegfried's words are out of place in this environment. If there is dismay and amazement – the poet says nothing about that – it may well be due to the discord that has obviously come to prevail among the members of the royal family. After all, knights were indeed amazed about the discord between the queens in the fourteenth *Aventiure* (834); this world is accustomed to seeing those in high places attempt again and again to retain peace and harmony (cf. chapter I, p. 21), and now the kings' own wives defy this perpetual attempt. It is more likely, however, that the looks mentioned in strophe 861 are not those of dismay and amazement, but of approval, in the nature of Giselher's following suggestion (866) that it was a women's quarrel to which no more attention should be paid than Gunther and Siegfried are willing to pay to it, and that it had best be settled quickly and effectively, in the manner suggested by Siegfried.[36]

It is this Kriemhild – who had the terror of the falcon dream, whose determination not to love turned out to be as unstable as the wind, who inadvertently reveals herself in thoughts, words, and actions, who attaches importance to outward semblance and equates it with innate qualities, and who after her marriage does not enjoy the status of the courtly lady – it is she who puts on the ring and belt when she prepares to meet Brunhild in front of the minster. And it is this Kriemhild who in the end demands the hoard from Hagen in a situation where he cannot possibly be expected to accommodate her request. Though the hoard plays a role of consequence in the *Nibelungenlied* (cf. chapter VII, pp. 130 ff.), Kriemhild's request for it at this moment can only have symbolic value. To say it with Schröder:

> Nun steht Hagen vor ihr als Gebundener, und ihre erste Frage
> lautet: "Welt ir mir geben widere   daz ir mir habt genomen"
> (2367). Sie zielt vordergründig auf den von ihm geraubten
> Nibelungenschatz, hintergründig auf Sivrit selbst. Den Geliebten,
> den er ihr genommen hat, vermag Hagen ihr nicht zurückzugeben,
> es könnte sich nur um *eine symbolische Wiedergutmachung*
> *handeln.*[37]

36 Weber, *Das Nibelungenlied*, p. 69, suggests that the court's reaction is one of surprise due rather to Gunther's words than to Siegfried's, since the former's professed conviction that Siegfried is innocent meets with skepticism in those who have witnessed the quarrel and have heard Brunhild declare that the ring and belt were hers. General belief, however – as indicated by Giselher (cf. 866) – does not hold Siegfried guilty of having violated Brunhild's honor.

37 W. Schröder, "Tragödie," p. 154. Italics added.

Schröder's passage shows why the hoard at this moment is significant to Kriemhild. What with her tendency to confuse semblance and intrinsic value, the hoard is for Kriemhild a piece of Siegfried, *is* Siegfried. It is ironic that her request to Hagen hinges on the outward rather than the "personal" symbol of Siegfried's essence.[38] Siegfried himself had seen things differently: he had left the hoard in the land of the Nibelungs, never to make use of it until he gave it to Kriemhild as *Morgengabe*, and had taken only the *Tarnkappe* with him.[39] Kriemhild, we must gather, never quite understood the essence of the man she married. She and Hagen – whose insight into Siegfried is keener than hers – struggle for a power which they are unfit to possess. The chapters on Hagen will delineate the how and why of this struggle.

38 See in this connection the rather complex relation between the hoard and the *Tarnkappe* as delineated in chapter VI, pp. 104 ff.

39 Cf. Mowatt and Sacker, *The Nibelungenlied*, note on 1124.

iv

BRUNHILD:
THE KINGSHIP MOTIF

THE FOLLOWING CITATIONS of critical views are fairly representative of the evaluations made about the Brunhild figure. Schneider observes, "Brünhilds Triebe sind ungebändigt, ihr Treiben hat einen materialistischen Anstrich, ihr Leben ist unheroisch, unritterlich, unköniglich."[1] Weber conceives of her as "eine überkraftvolle nordische Jungfrau, wir würden etwa sagen, vom isländischen Landadel – von etwas grobschlächtiger Schönheit."[2] De Boor sees Brunhild as a person who "diesem Dichter wenig zugänglich ist. ... Sie ist ihm nur noch ein nötiger Hebel der Handlung."[3] Mueller thinks of Brunhild in these terms: "Of crude disposition, she is presented as a creature of monstrous strength and freakish, masculine behavior. Her bridal night is centuries apart from Kriemhild's."[4] Heusler says, "Siegfrieds Trug an dem fremden Weibe empfindet [die Welt des *Nibelungenliedes*] nicht als Makel: nur gegen den Schwertbundene hatte er Pflichten."[5]

1 H. Schneider, *Die deutschen Lieder von Siegfrieds Tod* (Weimar, 1947), p. 50.

2 Weber, *Das Nibelungenlied*, p. 35.

3 De Boor, *Geschichte*, p. 162.

4 W. A. Mueller, *The Nibelungenlied Today: Its Substance, Essence, and Significance* (Chapel Hill, 1962), p. 4. By way of contrast, it was urged previously (chapter I, p. 3) that the poet is not at all interested in pulling his epic apart by emphasizing characters as "centuries apart" or "of different cultural strata" (Mueller, p. 5).

5 A. Heusler, *Nibelungensage und Nibelungenlied* (Dortmund, 1955), p. 16. On Brunhild's role, see also, for example, G. Schutte, *Sigfrid und Brünhild: Ein als Mythos verkannter Roman der Merowingerzeit* (Kopenhagen-Jena, 1935); K. von See, "Die Werbung um Brünhilt," *ZfdA*, LXXXVIII (1957/58), 1 ff., and "Freierprobe und Königinnezank in der Sigfridsage," *ZfdA*, LXXXIX (1958/59), esp. 164 ff.

In contrast to all this is the claim made in the previous chapter according to which Brunhild is a self-confident figure whose self-assurance issues from her innate awareness that she is all queen. As such she differs from Kriemhild, for whom kingship relies on the display of pomp and splendor. Whereas for Brunhild the attributes of kingship are attached to the person wearing the regalia, for Kriemhild the essence of kingship lies with the regalia themselves.[6] For that matter, Kriemhild's brother also confuses the semblance of kingship with its innate substance:

396 Ir waren niwan viere, die komen in daz lant,
     Sifrit der küene ein ros zoch uf den sant;
     daz sahen durch diu venster diu waetlichen wip.
     des duhte sich getiuret des künec Guntheres lip.

There were just the four of them arriving in the land. Brave
Siegfried led a horse ashore; that was seen through the windows
by the fine ladies, and king Gunther felt himself enhanced by it.

In addition, Gunther's claim to his kingship is based on the fact that he has inherited the kingdom (112), and somewhat vaguely he argues that the "riterschaft" which he and his men practice would be in poor shape if he were to allow Siegfried to take the kingdom by force:

112 "Wie het ich daz verdienet," sprach Gunther der degen,
     "des min vater lange mit eren hat gepflegen,
     daz wir daz solden vliesen von iemannes kraft?
     wir liezen übele schinen daz wir ouch pflegen riterschaft."

"How did I deserve," said the bold Gunther, "that what my father
so long honorably maintained we should now lose by anyone's
force? It would be poor proof that we practice chivalry."

Gunther speaks of "we," circumspectly countering the "I" of Siegfried's proposal of a confrontation to see who is the more worthy claimant to the throne of Worms (cf. 110). Brunhild, too, thinks and speaks in terms of "I." To be sure, she too is said to have inherited her kingdom (518), but she has been prepared, and still is, to display her

6 Cf., for contrast, Mowatt and Sacker, *The Nibelungenlied*, note on 118.

right to Islant's crown by placing it in the balance against anyone wishing to challenge her in the games. These games have borne testimony
to the validity of her claim to be the strongest in the realm and therefore the warranted bearer of the crown.

Brunhild is not the only one who thinks that strength is kingship
and that kingship comes with strength. Not only is Siegfried of that
opinion (cf. below), but his fellow Santeners are also. Kriemhild's
opening statement in her confrontation with Brunhild shows her to be
of the same view:

815   "ich han einen man,
    daz elliu disiu riche   ze sinen handen solden stan."

"I have a husband who is fit to rule over all these kingdoms."

Hagen's reminiscing speech upon Siegfried's first arrival in Worms
implies the acknowledgment that might is right (cf. chapter VII, p.
123). Alberich explicitly states that Siegfried owed to his strength his
right to kingship over the land of the Nibelungs (cf. 500). That kingship entails certain obligations is also evident. One of the main functions of crownbearers is to retain peace and harmony (cf. chapter I, p.
21). Liberality, too, is an indispensable mark of kingship (cf. chapter VI,
pp. 101 ff.). Even Gunther feels certain obligations: when seeing at the
casement of Isenstein the lady whom he would love if he were not
already committed to wooing queen Brunhild (392 ff.), Gunther realizes that kings have their duties as to alliances by marriage. Santen is
of the same opinion (cf. 48), and so is Etzel (1149).

In this manner, given the premises upon which Brunhild views
the nature of kingship, no other person in the *Nibelungenlied* has established the right to a crown more convincingly than she. Brunhild in
this regard is ahead of Siegfried who, precisely because he shares her
view of what constitutes a true and rightful king, thinks it expedient
and necessary to show the validity of his candidacy by first proving
his kingly qualities:

55"Waz mag uns daz gewerren?"   sprach do Sifrit.
    "swaz ich friwentliche   niht ab in erbit,
      daz mac sus erwerben   mit ellen da min hant.
      ich triuwe ab in ertwingen   beide liut unde lant."

"What do we care?" said Siegfried. "Whatever I do not acquire by
friendly requests my valor will get me. I can take their lands and
their people from them."

58"Des enist mir niht ze muote,"   sprach aber Sivrit,
  "daz mir sulen recken   ze Rine volgen mit
  durh deheine hervart   (daz waere mir vil leit),
  da mit ich solde ertwingen   die vil waetlichen meit."

"I don't like it," said Siegfried, "That warriors should accompany
me to the Rhine as if on a warlike expedition (I should indeed
regret that) with which to acquire the beautiful girl."

109"Ich bin ouch ein recke   und solde krone tragen.
  ich wil daz gerne füegen daz si von mir sagen
  daz ich habe von rehte   liute unde lant.
  dar umbe sol min ere   und ouch min houbet wesen pfant."

"I, too, am a warrior, and entitled to wear a crown, but I want to
see to it that people will say of me that I own my people and lands
by right. On this I stake my head and my honor."

Brunhild and Siegfried also share the view that the right to kingship
depends on physical prowess, and it is the awareness of possessing this
power that lends each of them his self-assurance.

It may be said that in her victories over suitors Brunhild has frequently shown herself more of a "man" than any of them. It is this
quality that presents her as a person rather than as a woman, eye-
catching less for her femininity than for her courage and ability in the
games. Though she is said to be beautiful, we may gather that her
appearance lacks something which Kriemhild is thought to possess by
those experienced in such matters:

593 Die vrouwen spehen kunden   unt minneclichen lip,
  die lobten durch ir schoene   daz Guntheres wip.
  do sprachen da die wisen,   die hetenz baz besehen,
  man möhte Kriemhilden wol   für Brünhilden jehen.

The judges of women and of beautiful bodies praised Gunther's
wife for her beauty, but the experienced who were more discerning
opined Kriemhild was more beautiful than Brunhild.

Brunhild may be dazzling, but she is queen before she is woman. Perhaps we are intended to consider hers a beauty with a gloss of regality subduing the pure feminity that is Kriemhild's. It is this kingly bearing that leaps to the eye of Gunther (392) – who habitually looks for outward appearance without wondering whether it harmonizes with inward substance – and renders her most desirable to him, whereas Siegfried prefers Gunther's sister.[7]

These remarks come close to a suggestion that Gunther and Kriemhild both have a disastrous propensity to marry outside their class,[8] but it must be remembered that Kriemhild is completely passive in the procedures leading to her marriage, and that the active part is played (though with lapses) by Siegfried. In fact, it could be argued that it is a piece of sheer luck for Kriemhild that she is bartered to a man of her liking (cf. chapter VI, p. 108).

It is of consequence for the correct evaluation of things that Brunhild's crown is safeguarded by her virgin strength upon which she has made that crown dependent. By that token, retention of her virginity is for Brunhild not the all-important thing it has been suggested to be: her *kingship* is all-important, and it will not do to speak of Brunhild's "Virginalitätswahrung"[9] if by that is meant a resolution never to marry. If that is Brunhild's aim, she simply could refuse ever to marry, could abolish the games and remain the virgin queen. Actually, for all we know, Brunhild may be avid to marry, but this readiness is subservient to something more important, the necessity that a prospective husband be able, with a display of strength, to assert his right to kingship and thus do justice to her status. Brunhild's view of marriage is therefore anything but sentimental. Wishing to avoid a misalliance, she is rational and pragmatic, ready to strike a utilitarian bargain which will do honor to her kingship.

These considerations lead to the conclusion that Brunhild and Siegfried share a similar view of kingship. For them, kingship relies

---

7 Cf. *ibid.*, note on 48: "Although Sifrid and Gunther behave correctly in selecting their wives according to general report, without personal acquaintance, they still make their choice to suit themselves rather than the needs of inter-state diplomacy. They may be concerned only with the type, and not with the individuality of the women of their choice, but the types they choose are nevertheless very revealing for their characters. ... Etzel's is the more statesmanlike approach."

8 See Mowatt, "Studies," p. 266.

9 Weber, *Das Nibelungenlied*, p. 26.

not on outward semblance but on the holder's ability to defend it with physical strength. They have the knowledge, born of past experience, that they *are* the strongest. Whereas Siegfried's strength and consequent right to wear a crown are based on the *Tarnkappe* – "... die truoc alle zite der schoenen Kriemhilde trut" (1119) – with Brunhild strength and crown are inextricably united by virtue of her virginity – symbolized by the belt "den si umb ir siten truoc" (636) – and a (for the time being, hypothetical) conqueror will and must have not only her virginity but also her crown.

If the phrase which in the *Nibelungenlied* is used to characterize Siegfried is applicable to anyone else, then it applies to Brunhild. With Brunhild, too, demeanor and code of conduct emanate from her own disposition, "von [ir selber] muote" (23). It is part of Brunhild's philosophy of kingship that she must be taken by force, as it is Siegfried's philosophy – *if* he can be said to have one – to take a wife or a crown by force. Each of them is ever ready to exert himself. Siegfried does so in the Saxon war, Brunhild in the games. Siegfried and Brunhild would be like Hagen in this respect – that is to say, *if* Nagel were right in seeing in Hagen the typical Germanic hero whose heroism can never be at rest but is driven on to ever renewed self-exertion.[10]

Siegfried, then, is just the man Brunhild has been looking for, and though she has never seen him before (cf. below), she greets him before she greets Gunther despite his subservience in the horse-landing scene (396 f.), which Brunhild *may* have observed, and despite the fact that they both go in royal white. This greeting testifies to Siegfried's undoubtedly striking appearance; he alone in the epic is occasionally "recognized" by someone who has never seen him before (see chapter I, p. 22). Brunhild takes for granted that it is Siegfried who has come to woo her, and not that other man. Siegfried gives her the biography of Gunther (420 ff.), because she has not heard of the king of the Burgundians before; that is to say, not in terms related to the frame of reference (physical strength and prowess) in which she is accustomed to thinking of kings. Gunther is not in her class.

The relationship which Brunhild herself has established between marriage and kingship is not without contradictions, and it is charged with potentially ironic consequences, of which she herself ultimately becomes the victim. For while the condition which she stipulates serves

10 Nagel, "*Das Nibelungenlied*, p. 287.

to lure a *worthy* suitor, whom she presupposes to be of the same view as herself (in that he will not be prone to become the slave of passion but will be king also in the realm of this nebulous thing called love), in effect she lures Gunther, who displays his lack of *maze* by allowing wine to spill (804), and who generally seems to give in to the appetites of the flesh.

The argument conducted so far has implications for the problems with which many critics of the *Nibelungenlied* have occupied themselves: Brunhild's double refusal to submit to Gunther, and the double deception practiced on her, first in the Islant games, then in the bridal chamber. Some studies endeavor to smooth the plot of the epic in this regard as much as assumed borrowing from multiple sources permits. They are based on the axiom that the poet attempts to do the best he can with a bad thing – his best not being quite good enough, since he acquiesces in the redundance of Brunhild's refusal and the consequent double deception. In addition, the "confused" motivation for the decision that Siegfried must die is seen as the inevitable result of the poet's endeavor to do justice to different sources, so that the decision cannot be attributed unilaterally to either Brunhild or Hagen.

Regarding Brunhild's repeated refusal to submit to Gunther, critics have claimed that she has no choice because she is (still) what she once was. So, for instance, Schneider: "Natürlich, die Brunhild, die als Schildmaid, als Berufskämpferin unterlegen war, verteidigte mit der letzten ihr gebliebenen Kraft ihr Magdtum. Eines besonderen Anlasses, einer Verstimmung bedurfte et nicht erst, sie ihrem Freier gegenüber halsstarrig zu machen."[11] Others have it that Brunhild is aware in an occult sort of way that something is wrong,[12] or that she can be fooled "optisch, aber nicht psychisch."[13] Still others – and they have turned the misunderstanding of the *Nibelungenlied* into a high art – find that the poet is not really interested in a well motivated plot development, and that he rides roughshod over the details to get to his main purpose as quickly as possible, whatever that main purpose may be. None of these attempts to explain the composition of the episodes involved has been fully persuasive. They acquiesce in the theory that there is a double plot because there is a plurality of sources, which the poet fails

11 Schnieder, *Lieder*, p. 23.
12 Weber, *Das Nibelungenlied*, p. 36.
13 Nagel, "*Das Nibelungenlied*, p. 287.

to fuse and rather leaves undeveloped, with the result that the attentive reader cannot help but be bothered by seams showing.

It would seem, however, that the poet, while using materials from several sources, makes these materials his own by combining them into an admirable unity. To this purpose he uses a device which does not exactly leap to the eye but which, once indicated, is astonishing in its simplicity and clarity, and makes perfecty logical, indeed inevitable, the repetition of Brunhild's refusal to submit to Gunther.

The device involved hinges on the number twelve, the number that is also of consequence for Siegfried (cf. chapter VI, pp. 104 ff.). The poet uses this number to provide a gauge of Brunhild's virgin strength and the relation of that strength to Siegfried's. During the preparations for the contest in Islant twelve men have difficulty hauling the stone which is to be used by Brunhild and her suitor (449). Not only is Brunhild able to pick up the stone unaided, she also throws it over a distance of twelve *Klafter*. It is no wonder that so far no one has been able to outdo Brunhild in the games, and it is no wonder that she "knows" that this time, too, the strength of this unknown Gunther will be far insufficient to acquire her. Not only is the number twelve used in explicit testimony of Brunhild's strength, but her shield and spear also testify to her physical prowess (437 ff.). She awes Hagen, who can only curse her as a devil (438, 450).[14] Even Siegfried, for the first time in the epic, is said to be afraid (451), and well he may be, as he sees that Brunhild's strength is greater than that of twelve men and therefore comes perilously close to equalling his own.

When Brunhild is then beaten in the games, it is not simply that she is psychologically incapable of acquiescing in a change of status from virgin queen to queen consort of a man whom she never expected to meet her standards; she also finds it impossible to believe in his real superiority. And thus, given Brunhild's past experiences with suitors, she has no choice but to determine whether the unbelievable must be believed, or whether there was a fluke in the play. The second test touches the very core of her power and claims to an eminent husband: the test in the bedroom. Though that test deserves some scrutiny, for the moment it suffices to say that not only to us, the readers, but also to Brunhild herself it is now quite clear that she has lost. It is also clear to her, however, that her subduer has not found

14 The reason for this curse is discussed in chapter VII, p. 126.

the going easy and that the manner in which he won justifies in retrospect her decision that a second test was necessary.

On that day of insults, ten years later, the confused argument between Brunhild and Kriemhild seems to settle little or nothing. Only the belt speaks a language which is meaningful to Brunhild, but it is for the moment a moot question how she understands this language, and all we know is that she is in agony. Gunther's expressed belief in Siegfried's innocence (860) is meant to assuage her grief and is ostensibly a public retraction of a public insult. In this connection Bumke observes:

> Weil der Frauenzank nicht die Enthüllung des Werbungsbetrugs
> gebracht hatte, ergab sich kein Ansatzpunkt, von dem die Rache-
> handlung ausgehen konnte. Vielmehr wird in der Eidszene die
> Unwahrhaftigkeit des Münstergezänks erwiesen und damit der
> Faden zwischen dem Streit der Königinnen und der Ermordung
> Sigfrids zerschnitten.[15]

It is true that the oath scene does belie the validity of the queens' quarrel and the veracity of the assumptions through which it develops; it does undo the public aspect of the insult as a possible reason for Siegfried's death; and it does give the lie to the *Kebse* insult, leaving only one thing certain: Brunhild was not Siegfried's *Kebse*. For, Brunhild reasons, would not Gunther come to the defense of his queen's honor, if only to defend his own, if there were the slightest doubt about Siegfried's innocence? And is not Gunther in the best position to judge whether he himself consummated the marriage, or had a lieutenant perform for him? Having been married to Gunther for ten years, Brunhild may have discovered that he does not mind having delegates act for him, but she also has come to know him as a man who does not like to be inactive if he can indulge the joys of the senses.

And yet Brunhild decides that Siegfried must die, not because of the ruse practiced on her in the Islant games – they are never mentioned again and for all we know Brunhild never learns about that deception[16] – but because of the role he played in the royal bedroom at Worms. He did have a function in that room, as the belt testifies. And that is exactly why Siegfried is guilty: to have had a function, to have gone

---

15 Bumke, "Quellen," p. 19.

16 See below for comments on the games and the reason they are not mentioned again.

so far, and no further. His was the right, indeed, the duty as king to take her, but he refrained from doing so. Within her code of honor and values, Brunhild turns out to have been insulted, not because Siegfried vanquished her – she only minded being vanquished by the wrong man – but because he did not do more than that, and because at the decisive moment he stepped aside for Gunther. That is Siegfried's guilt as borne out by the belt and Gunther's statement in the oath scene regarding Siegfried's innocence: not to have done what he was in a position to do. When the situation is thus developed, it is seen to be full of grim irony. It is irony, for instance, that Gunther's very declaration of Siegfried's innocence tells Brunhild of Siegfried's guilt. And so the quarrel between the queens confronts Brunhild with a state of affairs the awful insult of which is intolerable.

Bumke is correct of course that the oath scene proves the false basis for the queens' quarrel, but it does not follow that there is no connection between this quarrel and Siegfried's death. As we have seen, it is only on the surface of things – from the point of view of Worms, but not of Brunhild – that the whole argument in front of the minster can be forgotten once Gunther asserts Siegfried's innocence. And the missing link which Bumke discovers between quarrel and oath scene, on the one hand, and the council scene meandering into the decision that Siegfried must die, on the other, is not a missing link at all. Nobody in Worms – except Brunhild of course – is aware of the true nature of the insult because it is so flagrantly and diametrically opposed to the assumed insult. The world of Worms has no conception of the magnitude of the crime as experienced by Brunhild.

Ten years after the bedroom episode, then, Brunhild learns from the belt, and from Gunther's statement, that Siegfried let an opportunity go by to do what he should have done. And so, she discovers, her life over the past decade turns out to have been a lie, and therefore an insult, not to her honor as a woman – or rather, not to her honor as Worms would define it – but to her status as queen. She has been disdained by the only true, because strongest, king, who cheated her into marrying a second-rate king and caused her, the crownbearer of Islant, to become guilty of violating the code by which kings must live.

Brunhild's retrospective view of the state of affairs is supported by the internal parallelism of some of the episodes in the *Nibelungenlied*. On the symbolic plane this parallelism leads Sacker to claim that a comparison of the horse-landing scene with the scenes in the bridal room and at the fountain where Siegfried finds his death brings out

Siegfried's habit of stepping aside and allowing Gunther to go first, whereas by virtue of his own qualities he could be expected to assert his own priority.[17] To quote Schröder, who, however, used the words with a somewhat different thought in mind: for the sake of Kriemhild "verleugnet Siegfried vor Brunhild seine königliche Würde."[18]

Regarding Sacker's denial that his study is historical, King finds it "historical in another way, since it bears unmistakably the stamp of its period: only in a sex-obsessed age or society would a serious article give such prominence to sneering references to Siegfried's 'morals' or vaginal-phallic symbols."[19] To this it can be claimed that sex and its symbols had achieved consequence in the minds of people long before the *Nibelungenlied* was written. Its poet deals with love at a time when the age-old culture of love is beset with a new problem, that of courtly love.[20]

Brunhild, of course, does not become involved with courtly love, but falls prey to multiple deceptions. Though the first deception is not important enough for the poet to bring it up again, Brunhild knows in the end all she must know to wish Siegfried's death. Hagen, putting in a visit,

864 ... vragete was ir waere,   weinende er si vant.
do sagte si im diu maere,   er lobt' ir sa zehant
daz ez erarnen müese   der Kriemhilde man,
oder er wolde nimmer   dar umbe vroelich gestan.

He asked what the matter was finding her weeping. She told him
the story. He promised her immediately that Kriemhild's husband
would have to pay for it, or he himself could never again be happy.

It has been suggested that in this one anemic strophe the motivational force in the *Nibelungenlied* is suddenly twisted Hagen's way.[21] On the basis of the suggestions advanced in these pages, however, it is more accurate to say that this strophe fuses two motivational forces.

17 Sacker, "Irony and Symbolism," pp. 271 ff.
18 W. Schröder, "Epische Konzeption," p. 197.
19 King, "Message," pp. 541 f.
20 See chapter VI for comments on courtly love.
21 See, e.g., Bumke, "Quellen," pp. 18 f.; P.B. Salmon, "Why Must Hagen Die?"
GLL, XVII (1963/64), 10.

The "double plot" which critics have again and again attempted to unravel – often with interesting and important side results – is thus not at all a double plot, but a double motivation, one motive issuing from Brunhild, the other from Hagen who now has an opportunity to advance his own interests (cf. chapter VII, pp. 124 ff.).

Dealing with the brief statement of Hagen's visit with Brunhild, Salmon is correct in saying that "this strophe carries a heavy burden since at this point Brunhild ceases to be important, while Hagen becomes a central figure."[22] But it does not follow that "this is a clue that the Siegfried-Brunhild relationship is less important for the *Nibelungenlied* than is generally held." On the contrary, it is *more* important than is generally held. For now we have a situation in which Siegfried chooses, from Brunhild's point of view, the wrong woman to love, even though he came close to leaving his mark where, as the strongest king, he should have left it. Thus seen, the Siegfried-Brunhild relationship becomes all-important, even though Brunhild retires from the public scene once Siegfried is condemned to pay for the consequences of the thoughtless choice he has made. And Siegfried's guilt is now suggested to be not quite so much the violation of the dignity of the woman Brunhild[23] as the violation of the principle of kingship. Gunther (and perhaps other kings) are of a different caliber from Brunhild; only Siegfried is of her mold. He should have recognized the validity of the principle represented (and propagated) by her. Perhaps he did recognize it, but chose to ignore it. In Willson's words, Siegfried stepped out of the "ordo," to which, together with Brunhild, he was ordained.[24]

It is clear by now that, whereas the present line of reasoning supports or at least in no way invalidates some of the valuable interpretations dealing with Brunhild, it does turn others topsy turvy. It hardly needs pointing out, for instance, that von Kralik's claim must be rejected: "Der Reinigungseid Siegfrieds macht auf Brunhild keinen Eindruck, hält sie doch auch diesen Schwur für erlogen."[25] Precisely be-

22 Salmon, *ibid.*, p. 10.

23 King, "Message," p. 545.

24 B. Willson, " 'Ordo' and 'inordinatio' in the *Nibelungenlied*," *Beiträge*, LXXXV (Tübingen, 1963), 83 ff.

25 D. von Kralik, *Die Sigfridtrilogie im Nibelungenlied und in der Thidreksaga* (Halle/Saale, 1941), pp. 694 f.

cause Brunhild believes Gunther's statement – for good reasons of his own Gunther makes that statement before Siegfried actually swears an oath – the scene provides her with the key to Siegfried's guilt. Indeed, the more emphatically and convincingly Siegfried's innocence is proclaimed and made acceptable to Worms – cf., for instance, strophe 870[26] – the more certain becomes his guilt from Brunhild's point of view. That, too, is irony, and of no mean order!

Bumke (to return to him) finds the quarrel of the queens doubly lamentable:

> Wenn es richtig ist – und alle andere Fassungen bestätigen das – dass es die Funktion der Zankszene war, den an Brünhilt begangenen Betrug ans Licht zu bringen, dann hat die Szene im Nibelungenlied ihr Ziel verfehlt. Denn der Werbungsbetrug bleibt im Nibelungenlied unaufgeklärt, kommt niemals zur Sprache. Statt dessen zanken sich die Frauen mit Argumenten, die unwahr sind, bewusste Lügen oder bestenfalls hartnäckige Irrtümer.[27]

From the vantage point presented in this chapter the poet of the *Nibelungenlied* is seen to say everything there is to say, and to leave unsaid only that which has no immediate bearing on the nature of the real insult. Indeed, the queens' quarrel and the scenes following furnish together one of the most fascinating examples in German literature that in spite of "bewusste Lügen oder bestenfalls hartnäckige Irrtümer" the truth will out, provided the right key is used. That key, we gather, is held by Brunhild, even though de Boor finds that "ihre wahrhaft heroische Szene, die Frau, die die Männer zum Werkzeug ihrer Rache zu machen versteht, der Dichter Brunhild genommen [hat]."[28] Though it is quite true that "der Zank der ragende Fels durch alle Zeiten ist,"[29] it does not follow that the poet of the *Nibelungenlied* did not shift and alter the core of its purpose. In this connection also, Bumke's elucidations as quoted in these pages constitute a demonstration that

26 Not only Giselher (866) but many in Worms remain attached to Siegfried (cf. 872, 882, 1039).

27 Bumke, "Quellen," p. 13.

28 De Boor, *Geschichte*, p. 162. See also note 3 above.

29 S. Beyschlag, "Das *Nibelungenlied* in gegenwärtiger Sicht," *WW*, III (1952), 194.

the traditional interpretations of Brunhild's role in the epic tend to run up against blank walls because motivations are wanting and essential details lacking.

It is true, as Bumke says, that in the *Brunhildlied* the *Kebse*-reproach was justified. It does not follow, however, that in the *Nibelungenlied* "das Wort zur Verleumdung [wird], weil der Dichter die Voraussetzungen geändert hat."[30] The poet did change "die Voraussetzungen," but in a manner totally different from that alluded to by Bumke. It is also true that the word *Kebse* is used by Kriemhild to put Brunhild in her place. But it has already been pointed out that in her anger Kriemhild thereby insults herself by her own code – if she adheres to one with any consistency – by telling all the world that as early as the second night of her wedded life Siegfried spent time in an alien bed. Though it may be claimed that Kriemhild in her anger does not realize that one of the implications of the intended insult reflects on herself, it still does not mean that Brunhild takes the *Kebse* reproach to be insulting in the manner Kriemhild means it to be. Of course, from *within* this world in which the position of women is open to improvement, such self-deprecation cannot be taken too seriously. Indeed, there may be a type of satisfaction in Kriemhild's accusation other than that of hurting Brunhild, and issuing from the proud assumption that her Siegfried could give Brunhild virile treatment. Kriemhild's now exhausted willingness to regard her "knowledge" as intimate and confidential (842) supports the notion that in her mind there is little appalling about Siegfried's assumed erstwhile intimacy with Brunhild. Thus it becomes possible to infer that the quarrel does not even give vent to jealousy in the realm of love on the part of *Kriemhild* (see chapter v, p. 97), and that for her, too, it hinges exclusively on *Brunhild's* notion of what is of consequence. With this, a peculiar light falls on the suggestion advanced by Nagel in *Das Nibelungenlied* (p. 186) that the epic, with Kriemhild at its center, "den Roman einer Liebe darstellt."

To be sure, in the course of the quarrel Brunhild proclaims (also in anger) her intention to bring Siegfried to an end (845), but that, as I read it, only because of the publicity given to her alleged intimacy of a decade ago with an *Eigenmann*. Before investigating this *Eigenmann* motif, however, another consideration must be advanced; it is self-

30 Bumke, "Quellen," p. 13.

revealing and self-referential in its implications, and deals with the fact that during and after the queens' quarrel the Islant games are never mentioned. This "omission" has left many readers wondering why the poet "forgot" these games. The answer is simple from the vantage point taken in this chapter: the deception practiced in the games has nothing to do with Brunhild's decision that Siegfried must die, since Brunhild as *queen* – willing and eager to be outdone by the strongest king only – was *not* deceived in Islant. Siegfried *did* exert his kingly strength in the games – though on the basis of unkingly thinking. Brunhild, *if* she thinks about the games in retrospect and draws the correct conclusions concerning Siegfried's role in those games, cannot but approve of a king who asserts his strength. In the bedroom, however, he failed to do so, and thereby violated the principle by which kings must live.

Like Kriemhild (chapter III, p. 52), Siegfried displays a "gradual fall": kingly action without kingly thinking in the Islant games degenerates into unkingly inaction in Brunhild's bridal chamber. To put it differently: a comparison between the Islant deception and that in the bridal chamber tells us once again that what matters to Brunhild is not so much deceptions practiced on herself (as a woman) as the deception practiced on kingship.

In this connection also, when Brunhild finds out that it was Siegfried who vanquished her in the bedroom, she realizes automatically that Gunther was involved in the crime against kingship. This insight is of some consequence since it evokes the question of why she does not punish Gunther together with Siegfried. The answer to this question indicates that Brunhild is "representationally" rather than psychologically developed: Gunther is incapable of being an aspirant to kingship as Brunhild conceives of it. He therefore cannot violate it either, and only such a violation must be punished.

V

BRUNHILD:
THE EIGENMANN MOTIF

BECAUSE the evaluation of the Siegfried-Brunhild relationship in the previous chapter differs fundamentally from the other interpretations known to me, it may be worthwhile to scrutinize the *Eigenmann* motif. As I understand it, this motif goes to the very core of Brunhild's problem in the quarrel episode and the scenes following.

Several critics have had their say about this motif of Siegfried's vassalage. Attention has been drawn to the stubborn fashion in which Brunhild adheres to the view that Siegfried is subservient to Gunther. Her tenacity has been put down as an indication that the poet of the *Nibelungenlied* does not mind less than perfect verisimilitude of portrayal so long as he has a good story to tell, and that he refuses to worry about obscure details or even inconsistencies. Schneider, for instance, thinks that the poet himself "mit dem Motiv der Vasallität keinen Rat weiss."[1] Wachinger says, "Die Frage, die auf den ersten Blick die wichtigste zu sein scheint, will ausgeklammert werden, weil sie wahrscheinlich überhaupt nicht ganz befriedigend beantwortet werden kann: die Frage, warum Brünhilt solches Gewicht auf dieses Motiv legt."[2] Bumke states:

> Viel grössere Bedeutung hat im Nibelungenlied ein dritter Betrug:
> Siegfried erscheint vor Brünhild als Gunthers *man*. Das scheint
> ein harmloser Betrug zu sein, und ein ärgerlicher zudem, weil man
> nicht einsieht, was die Verstellung bei der Werbung nützen soll.
> Der Dichter muss sein Gewicht viel schwerer empfunden haben, als
> wir es heute vermögen. Dass ein freier König sich als *man* ausgibt,

---

1 Schneider, *Lieder*, p. 33.
2 Wachinger, *Studien*, p. 105.

das ist mehr als ein harmloser Scherz in einer Welt, die den gött-
lichen *ordo* auch in der irdischen Hierarchie der Gewalten ver-
wirklicht sah.[3]

Bumke, I think, sees the problem keenly and puts it cogently.

Brunhild's stubbornness about Siegfried's subservient status has
also been interpreted as a desperate effort to overcome or keep subdued the personal feeling she has for Siegfried, a feeling that comes
to carry the hue of love-hate.[4] Generally, the *Eigenmann* motif is
thought to have been obscurely applied, to be in want of significance,
and to confuse matters.

It is possible, however, to suggest for the scenes in which the
Eigenmann motif occurs a manner of reading which shows the development of events, as evaluated by Brunhild, to be fully consistent with
the references and allusions to Siegfried's alleged vassalage – particularly as they occur in the queens' quarrel and the scenes following.[5]
Therefore, though on the surface the *Eigenmann* motif is but an inconsequential bit of nonsense in the quarrel between two fury-blinded
women, I should like to review the various instances in which it
occurs in order then to deal once again with the reason Brunhild wants
Siegfried's death.

The first time the *Eigenmann* motif occurs, Siegfried himself suggests that he pass as Gunther's vassal:

3 Bumke, "Quellen," p. 34.
4 Nagel, "*Das Nibelungenlied*," p. 237. Against Nagel, cf. Wachinger, *Studien*, p.
109, note 3: "Nagel bezieht Siegfrieds Minne als 'Minnefatum' von Anfang an
gegensätzlich auf die 'natürliche Partnerschaft' zwischen Siegfried und Brünhilt
und leitet daraus die Tragik ab. Das wäre sehr schön, wenn die 'natürliche
Partnerschaft' Siegfrieds und Brünhilts gesichert wäre."
5 Bumke, "Quellen," pp. 7 ff., has dealt with the multiple values to be attached
to the various terms that in this chapter are subsumed under the term *Eigenmann*,
since in Brunhild's mind there is no ambiguity about Siegfried's status. In this
connection, the argument presented by Mowatt and Sacker in *The Nibelungenlied*,
especially notes 620, 724, 725, 730, 802, 815, 816, 817, 821, 822, 825, 841, 864,
hinges on a manner of reading the text that has little in common with the "naive"
manner of perusal followed in the present work. The latter method cannot seek
to be persuasive by adopting the abstracting and startingly modern technique
followed by Mowatt and Sacker.

386 "So wir die minneclichen   bi ir gesinde sehen,
　　　so sult ir, helde maere,   wan einer rede jehen:
　　　Gunther si min herre,   und ich si sin man,
　　　des er da hat gedingen,   daz wirdet allez getan."

　　"When we see the lovely lady with her retainers about her, you,
　　noble knights, must abide by this one story: That Gunther is my
　　lord, and I am his vassal. In this manner all his aspirations will be
　　fulfilled."

He then acts out this subservience in the landing scene:

396 In waren niwan viere,   die komen in daz lant,
　　　Sifrit der küene   ein ros zoch uf den sant;
　　　daz sahen durch diu venster   diu waetlichen wip.
　　　des duhte sich getiuret   des künec Guntheres lip.

　　　Er habt' im da bi zoume   daz zierliche marc,
　　　guot unde schoene,   vil michel unde starc,
　　　unz der künic Gunther   in den satel gesaz.
　　　also diente in Sifrit,   des er doch sit vil gar vergaz.

　　There were just the four of them arriving in the land. Brave
　　Siegfried led a horse ashore; that was seen through the windows
　　by the fine ladies, and king Gunther felt himself enhanced by it.

　　He held the bridle of his fine steed for him, trusty and handsome,
　　big and strong, until king Gunther sat in the saddle; thus
　　Siegfried served him – a service later completely forgotten.

Whereas there is no evidence that this scene is observed by Brunhild
herself, she recognizes Siegfried (411 and 419) despite the presence
of that other figure clad in royal white, who looks exactly like Siegfried (399). Brunhild takes for granted that it is Siegfried who intends
to woo her:

416 Do sprach diu küneginne: "nu brinc mir min gewant.
　　　unt ist der starke Sifrit   komen in diz lant
　　　durch willen miner minne,   ez gat im an den lip.
　　　ich fürchte in niht so sere   daz ich werde sin wip."

*Then the queen spoke: "Bring me my robes. If strong Siegfried has
come to this land for the sake of my love, his life will be at stake.
I do not fear him enough to become his wife voluntarily."*

This strophe is of consequence. It does not present an inconsistency
in the Siegfried-Brunhild relationship, but it clarifies it, for it shows
that Brunhild does *not* know Siegfried. She only knows *of* him (and
of his strength).[6] Her very words tell us that she has never experienced
this prowess of his. If she had, she would know that he (with *Kappe*)
is stronger than she. She knows only from hearsay that his power is
impressive – the way he knows about her frightful ways, her "vreisliche sit" (330). Furthermore, there is not the slightest hint in strophe
416 that Brunhild is angry with Siegfried because of his (assumed) intention to make her his. All she says is "ez gat im an den lip." But
this line does not mean that Brunhild wishes to kill Siegfried because of
his audacious interest in her, as if she were some reincarnation of
Moloch, unceasingly hungering for male flesh! All Brunhild actually
says is that Siegfried will have to go through the contest games since
she will not and cannot become his or anyone's wife without putting
the candidate to the test. As has been suggested in more general terms
(cf. chapter IV, p. 73). Brunhild may actually be glad to see Siegfried, happy finally to meet a suitor whose reputation leads her to
think she is about to encounter the man she has been waiting for. By
that token, Brunhild's assumption that Siegfried wants her may be an
eager rather than an angry one. That he will have to show his prowess
and that, if he loses, he must die, is but the inevitable condition posed
to safeguard herself as the principle of kingship personified. Siegfried,
if he really is what she thinks he may turn out to be, will understand
such reasoning, since he, too, is then the personification of kingship
par excellence.

The second time Siegfried pretends to be Gunther's vassal (420),
he perpetuates in words the deception that he initiated by pantomime
in the landing scene, and Brunhild accepts his explanation without dis-
belief. We may wonder, in the light of the above, whether she is dismayed, but she does not demur. Instead she is immediately prepared
to confront Gunther, intending that he shall go through all the experiences – including the last one – of her previous suitors.

6 Cf., for contrast, Nagel, "*Das Nibelungenlied,*" p. 289, as well as the comment
on strophe 331 made by Mowatt and Sacker in *The Nibelungenlied.*

The following reference to Siegfried's vassalage comes from the queen of Islant herself: " 'ist er din herre   unt bistu sin man' "/" '*If he is your lord and you are his vassal*' " (423). Couched in the form of a conditional clause which serves as an introduction to her reminder that any suitor must subject himself to a series of tests, the *Eigenmann* reference is of little consequence. At most it constitutes the slightest of hint that Brunhild *is* disappointed to find Siegfried in vassalage to another man.

And why should she not be? She has just experienced a keen loss of hope because she is confronted once again with a suitor who she has no reason to think will be able to live up to the standards of kingship she has set. Gunther will surely die, and once again she will be waiting. It is Brunhild's preoccupation with kingship, together with her eagerness to encounter a worthy suitor, that supplies the explanation why she threatens not only Gunther, but also his companions with death. Her disappointment, however, has nothing to do with any frustrated *personal* feelings for Siegfried (cf. below).

An indirect reference to Siegfried's status comes from the king of the Burgundians at a later moment, when Siegfried returns to Islant with the thousand Nibelungs. Gunther's claim that they are his men (509) tells Brunhild once again that their leader, though higher in the hierarchy than his followers, is subservient to Gunther.

The welcoming scene following is generally thought to constitute a snub of Siegfried by Brunhild[7] – "Sifride mit dem gruoze   si von den anderen schiet" "*With her greeting she singled Siegfried out from the others*" (511) – but it is not at all clear why this should be so. In fact, it makes not sense to read a snub into the verse. After all, it is perfectly possible, and more than plausible within the context,

---

7 Weber, *Das Nibelungenlied*, p. 36; Bumke, "Sigfrids Fahrt ins Nibelungenland: Zur achten Aventiure des *Nibelungenliedes*," *Beiträge* (Tübingen), LXXX (1958), 254 and 263; de Boor's translation in Sammlung Dietrich, – "Nur Sifrit mit dem Grusse   sie von den anderen schied" – is as vague and noncomittal as the original verse, though the addition of "nur," if not used merely to fill out the meter, seems to favor the view that Brunhild does snub Siegfried. And in his note to the strophe in his edition after Bartsch in *Deutsche Klassiker*, de Boor finds that Brunhild greets Siegfried "anders als die übrigen, und zwar unfreundlicher, weil sie ihn für einen unfreien Lehnsmann hält." De Boor does not explain why Brunhild should greet the Nibelungs under the command of a snubbed leader. See also Mowatt and Sacker, *The Nibelungenlied*, note on 511.

that the verb on which the meaning of the line hinges – "scheiden" – has a selective rather than an excluding quality adhering to it, and that Brunhild is understood to bid the Nibelungs welcome by welcoming their commander.

And again, why should not Brunhild greet Siegfried as the representative of the Nibelungs? She takes him to be an *Eigenmann*, has accepted Siegfried's own statement to that effect, and is completely in the dark about the true state of affairs. Siegfried's own words and actions, Hagen's explanation of Siegfried's whereabouts during the games (473) – suggesting that Siegfried was not important enough to make his presence at the games mandatory – and Gunther's declaration that the Nibelungs are his men, all serve to implant and confirm in Brunhild's mind the notion that Siegfried is Gunther's vassal.

The situation emerging is clear: Brunhild was interested in Siegfried only as long as she thought of him as her would-be suitor (cf. 416, 419). As soon as she learned that he was not, she lost all interest in him. And she had no reason to hold anything against him because he turned out to be an *Eigenmann*. As Brunhild sees it, Siegfried's fame abroad before their meeting had led her to take for granted that he was a king. Now she knows that he is not and has therefore forgotten about him as a candidate for her attentions. It was all a mistake, a logical one, but now forgotten and leaving not a vestige of resentment. Siegfried is only a vassal, one of the best no doubt – otherwise Gunther would not have entrusted to him the task of procuring troops from the land of the Nibelungs – but he is no more than that. And so Brunhild greets Siegfried as the leader of the arriving Nibelungs. She is the queen engaging in a required bit of protocol, as indicated by her question to Gunther about the advisability of a greeting (510).[8]

As a result of Siegfried's service as a messenger to Worms to announce the approach of the royal couple (ninth *Aventiure*), his subservient status, as far as Brunhild is concerned, is once again an observable fact, and confirms her view of Siegfried as an *Eigenmann*. So also does her observation of Siegfried leading Kriemhild's horse (cf. 582).

In light of this evaluation of the *Eigenmann* motif, it comes as no surprise that Brunhild is upset when she sees that Siegfried marries

8 See A. T. Hatto, *The Nibelungenlied: A New Translation* (Baltimore, 1965), p. 73, note 1.

Kriemhild (620).[9] Gunther's explanation of Siegfried's position (623) fails to undo Brunhild's anxiety about Kriemhild's marriage to a man who does not belong in the royal family into which Brunhild herself also marries. She does not want just anyone for a brother-in-law; little good can come of such an alliance.

And why should Brunhild be convinced by Gunther's glib explanation? The oral and visual evidence of Siegfried's subservience has been too abundant to be outweighed by the one brief statement made by Gunther, who with other things on his mind, is scarcely likely to spend his wedding day informing his bride of the hierarchical values in Worms. To him, Brunhild's problem is a nuisance, because an obstacle to the fulfilment of his eager desires. To her it must be resolved. Even if she accepted Gunther's explanation and came to believe in Siegfried's kingship, that he is in fact "ein künic riche," (623), it would still be possible for her to think of Siegfried as inferior and subservient to Gunther, in the manner that much later a queen is said to be served by twelve kings (1391). Brunhild will learn that one king's kingship is not necessarily on a par with that of another when she finds out that Gunther is not greater than Siegfried, but vice versa.

That she meanwhile, despite Gunther's explanation, continues to think of Siegfried as an *Eigenmann* becomes evident ten years after her wedding day, when she urges Gunther to invite the Santen couple for a visit to Worms (724, 728). Having decided that the family tie with Siegfried does indeed constitute a cloud, however small, on her blue horizon – after all, it is only fit that Siegfried should render service – she resolves to set the matter straight, since Gunther is too easygoing. In fact, Brunhild may feel that Gunther has little or no backbone. The very manner in which he first opposes her suggestion that the Santeners be invited (726 f.), and then suddenly gives in by saying that he is as eager as she to see the relatives (731), provides what is perhaps not her first experience of his tendency to succumb quickly when someone proclaims views differing from his own.

However that may be, the *Eigenmann* motif, evoked by Siegfried himself, perpetuated by Gunther, and carried further into the narrative by Brunhild, becomes the bone of contention in her quarrel with Kriemhild. We need to observe the quarrel once again to see how it is

9 D.R. McLintock, "Les larmes de Brünhilt," SN, xxxiii (1961), 307 ff., also deals with the possibility that Brunhild is upset because of Kriemhild's marriage to an *Eigenmann*

affected by this motif. For one thing, Brunhild's unshaken belief that Siegfried is Gunther's vassal indicates that she has been content – if not as a woman, then as queen – to live by the code which she believes is meant for kings worthy of the name. For another, Kriemhild's opening statement in the conversation leading to the quarrel is in essence a denial of Brunhild's evaluation of Siegfried's status:

815   "ich han einen man,
        daz elliu disiu riche   ze sinen handen solden stan."

"I have a husband who is fit to rule over all these kingdoms."

With this, Kriemhild declares her adherence to the view that the strongest must be king, and that Siegfried is the strongest.

There seems to be no compelling reason to attribute conscious or unconscious designs to Kriemhild when she speaks these words. They are merely the sentiment of a loving and proud wife in a bubbly mood. This suggestion is supported by the assumption that Kriemhild does not wear the belt and ring until she has dressed for the confrontation with Brunhild. Only then is she planning to hurt Brunhild. With this view, it can be suggested that in strophe 815 we have a prime example of how the use of language may entangle its speakers and lead to their ultimate doom – cf. chapter IX, p. 159.

Kriemhild's boast constitutes a challenge to Brunhild, to the complacency to which she has become accustomed during the past decade, and to her erstwhile determination to marry the strongest. Her reply, though ostensibly referring to Gunther's political rank and power, suggests that it is she, Brunhild, who married the strongest:

816   "wie kunde daz gesin?
        ob ander niemen lebte   wan sin unde din,
        so möhten im diu riche   wol wesen undertan.
        die wile lebt Gunther,   so kundez nimmer ergan."

... "How could that be? If no one were living but he and you, these realms might be subservient to him. But that will never happen as long as Gunther lives."

Presently the *Eigenmann* motif enters into the verbiage and things deteriorate rapidly.

Now, one of the most interesting and important features about the *Eigenmann* motif is that it suddenly becomes of no consequence in the confrontation between the queens, or rather, that it is no longer used by Brunhild after Kriemhild has called her Siegfried's *Kebse*.[10] Before that, Brunhild alludes to Siegfried's status over and over again to argue her view of the matter at stake. Once the word *Kebse* has fallen, she no longer makes mention of Siegfried's rank. Instead it is now Kriemhild who in angry irony keeps referring to Siegfried's alleged subservience after she has flung into Brunhild's face the accusation of her intimacy a decade ago with an *Eigenmann* (839 f.).

Brunhild's ensuing tears *after* her honor has been publicly restored by Gunther have been the subject of many discussions, but none of them has managed satisfactorily to clarify the obscurity which traditionally shrouds the quarrel episode and the scenes following. Actually, the obscurity is not an obscurity at all; the poet has supplied us with sufficient indications of the directions in which we should look for answers, as much by what he tells us as by what he leaves unsaid. The true importance of the *Eigenmann* motif lies in the fact that in Brunhild's mind it is the counterpart of the kingship motif. They are the two sides of one coin. Embedded within this pair of parallelistic motifs is the concept that an *Eigenmann* cannot be the strongest. That would be contrary to the code of kingship as Brunhild adheres to it. Similarly, the strongest cannot be an *Eigenmann*. That, too, would undermine the kingship philosophy. This, then, is Brunhild's shattering experience: Siegfried's subservience to Gunther becomes an impossibility in her mind as soon as Kriemhild shows her the belt. This much is now clear to Brunhild: Siegfried has vanquished her! The how and why of this truth do not crowd in upon her at the moment. All she knows is that the symbol of the belt speaks[11] – the magic of its web!

When Gunther himself then declares Siegfried innocent of having made Brunhild his *Kebse*, Brunhild receives another blow, much heavier still, for only now, after the belt and after Gunther's testimony,[12] does it come home to her that Siegfried vanquished her but

10 Wachinger, *Studien*, p. 113: "Brünhilt ist im *Nibelungenlied* schon von dem Augenblick an sehr zurückhaltend, da sie das Wort 'mannes kebse' hört."

11 Hans Naumann, "Brünhilts Gürtel," *ZfdA*, LXX (1933), 47.

12 *Ibid.* "Als ob man der Magie des Symbols mit der Magie des Schwures begegnen könne." But cf. chapter VI, p. 113.

did not possess her. She, who for a decade has lived as Gunther's queen, satisfied that she has been true to her calling, that is, has upheld the sanctity of the kingship code according to which the strong allies with the strong, turns out to be the wife of the weaker king who, significantly, has always tended to think of kingship in terms of outward display. The strongest, Brunhild now knows, cannot be Gunther's vassal. He is the true king, but he abstained! Not until this flash of insight comes to her does Brunhild burst into tears again. They are tears shed for the sake of a dispensation that was brought to ruin ten years ago. Brunhild now knows that the code of morality for kings has been her code alone, and that long since it has been a code without substance. And so, Brunhild, the only one with judgment unimpaired in a world with decayed kingly values, though she cannot undo the awful crime, takes upon herself to blot out the criminal, the violator by abstention.

Brunhild's kingship philosophy constitutes fervent adherence to an order, the core of which is the principle of hierarchy backed by power.[13] It is part of Brunhild's tragedy that with the discovery of Siegfried's misdeed comes the discovery that the order which she has professed is irreparably damaged, cannot be re-established, and has no future. From her vantage point it is inevitable that chaos will ultimately prevail. Small wonder then that, no longer able to contribute to order as she has believed in it, she withdraws within herself.[14] Her refusal to meet Etzel's minstrels (1485) is a refusal to re-enter the scene in which kings have become mere figureheads and are no longer the personifications of established order.[15]

And so Brunhild's affinity for Siegfried was not the affinity of a

13 From this point of view it is unlikely that Hagen and Brunhild have a bond of loyalty prevailing between them (see chapter VII, p. 128).

14 This in contrast to the prevailing opinion that Brunhild is *reduced* to nothing – so, e.g., Mowatt and Sacker, *The Nibelungenlied*, note on 406.

15 This does not invalidate the view that Brunhild, speaking through Volker, indicates that she wishes no communication of any sort with Kriemhild or her messengers. Cf. Bostock, "Realism," pp. 228 f. Incidentally, this is as good a moment as any to draw attention to Weber's dictum in *Das Nibelungenlied*, p. 41: "Wie eine Kriemhilt im Ganzen zu zerstören ist die Brünhilt-Natur nicht. Das ist ihr versagt." Weber's sentiment emanates from what may perhaps best be designated as "the psychological phallacy."

woman for a man, as Nagel suggests[16] – and many with him – but of the queen for the strongest king. This is not to say that Nagel's evaluation is null and void. In fact, no one has stated the importance of the results of the Siegfried-Brunhild relation (as seen by Brunhild) more convincingly:

> Am auffälligsten bezeugt sich Brünhilds unaufhebbare partner-
> hafte Bindung an die Person Siegfrieds darin, das mit dessen
> Tode auch Brünhild aus der Handlung ausscheidet. Ohne anderen
> ersichtlichen Grund bricht an dieser Stelle ihre Rolle jählings
> ab. Dieses unvermittelte Sinken ins Nichts, dieses Erlöschen
> des persönlichen Daseins vergegenwärtigt noch einmal,
> dass die individuelle Erfüllung dieses Lebens an die Existenz
> Siegfrieds geknüpft war, dass es überhaupt nur in dieser
> polaren Spannung gelebt werden konnte, hingegen zu einem
> blossen Schemen verdorren musste, sobald der Gegenpol ausge-
> schaltet war. Dieses – im Wortsinn "beziehungslos" gewordene –
> Leben Brünhilds hat der Nibelungelied-Dichter mit einer
> bis zur Unwahrscheinlichkeit gehenden Drastik bewusst gemacht.[17]

Nagel is quite correct about Brunhild's life becoming "beziehungslos" – not with the death of Siegfried, but with the discovery that he violated kingship. However, by seeking to establish in Brunhild a love-hate tension with regard to Siegfried, Nagel's acute insight is pulled awry. If adapted to the suggestions made in these pages, however, the cited passage becomes awesome in its impact.

The surest refutation of Brunhild as a love-thwarted woman is found in these strophes:

> 724 Nu gedaht' ouch alle zite   daz Guntheres wip:
> "wie treit et also hohe   vrou Kriemhilt den lip?
> nu ist doch unser eigen   Sifrit ir man;
> er hat uns nu vil lange   lützel dienste getan."

> Diz truoc si in ir herzen   unt war ouch wol verdeit.
> daz si ir vremde waren,   daz was ir harte leit,
> daz man ir so selten diente   von Sifrides lant.
> wa von daz komen waere,   daz hete si gerne bekant.

16 Nagel, "Das Nibelungenlied," pp. 284 ff.   17 Ibid., p. 287.

All the time Gunther's queen kept thinking, "How is it that lady
Kriemhild has such lofty demeanor? After all, Siegfried her
husband is our vassal; He has long since done us no service at all."

This she carried in her heart, and kept it well hidden, for it
chagrined her that they remained aloof from her, and that she
received so little service from Siegfried's land. She wanted to know
why that should be so.

In these lines we find the true motivation for Brunhild's decision that
Siegfried and Kriemhild should be invited to Worms. For it is one thing
to doubt the veracity of what the various characters in the *Nibelungenlied* say, but it is another to doubt what the poet tells us they are
thinking. In the former case we may, and should, be wary: all the
characters in the epic, Brunhild included (cf. 725 f.), feign at times, or
tell lies, whether deliberately or inadvertently. But to doubt the veracity
of what we are told they are thinking is to rewrite the epic as we think
the poet should have written it. Such interpretations, ingenious as they
may be at times, tend towards *Systemzwang*.[18] In Nagel's case, the
interpretation must be psychologized into, under, and between the
lines. Witness, for instance, the "translation" of the scene in which –
as Nagel sees it – Brunhild snubs Siegfried upon his return from the
land of the Nibelungs:

> Es ist höchst bezeichnend, dass sich Brünhild diesem Siegfried
> gegenüber eigentümlich unsicher fühlt und Gunther fragen
> muss, wie sie sich zu Siegfried verhalten soll, und welche Art des
> Grusses hier angebracht sei. Den stärksten Ausdruck jedoch und
> einen ganz persönlichen Akzent gewinnt diese innere Betroffen-
> heit Brünhilds daran, dass sie – gegen Gunthers Wunsch einer
> herzlichen Begrüssung Siegfrieds – "ob wir si sehen gerne   daz
> si daz wol verstan" (511) – diesen betont unfreundlich grüsst.[19]

18 Such *Systemzwang* is at work in the c* version, as when Brunhild in a few lines
altered in strophe 813 is depicted as driven by the devil to wait for an opportunity to show Kriemhild's inferior status.
19 Nagel, *"Das Nibelungenlied,"* p. 285.

Nagel's interpretation is not acceptable, not because it goes counter to the interpretation of this scene as given above, but because it makes the situation "richer" and more complicated than it actually is, and issues from a particular way of reading the strophes involved: Brunhild does *not* ask Gunther how she must greet Siegfried, but how the Nibelungs should be met. Gunther's answer indicates that he understands that question as Brunhild asks it: they both talk about the Nibelungs rather than about Siegfried — to greet whom is a matter of course to both of them if any greeting at all is to take place. Brunhild simply asks about an item of protocol and Gunther simply tells her what Worms' customs in such a situation demand. In other words, here, too, Brunhild's thoughts are of kingly conduct, not of love-hate towards Siegfried.

Strophe 724, just quoted, and several other references, show Brunhild's interest to be centered on Kriemhild rather than Siegfried. Of Gere, who returns from Santen, she asks:

771 "nu sagt mir, kumet uns Kriemhilt?   hat noch ir schoener lip
       behalten iht der zühte,   der si wol kunde pflegen?"

"Now tell me, is Kriemhild coming? has her beauty retained any of
the elegance that she was capable of displaying?"

After the arrival of the guests,

799 under wilen blicken man   Prünhilde sach
      an vroun Kriemhilde,   diu schoene was genuoc.

Now and again Brunhild was seen glancing at lady Kriemhild,
who looked very lovely.

There is no indication in these references that Brunhild's interest has anything to do with Siegfried as a man — though she is fond of him: "si was im waege" (803). Instead, this scrutiny of Kriemhild is an attempt to verify what Brunhild has "known" long since: marriage to an *Eigenmann* cannot have failed to register its effect on a princess of the blood royal. There is thus a type of parallelism between this expectation of Brunhild and Kriemhild's assumption after her falcon dream that she will remain beautiful if she does not marry. Moreover, these citations, when compared with strophes 724 and 769, tell us something about the position of women: men inquire after men, women inquire (only) after women.[20]

To repeat, Brunhild's affinity for Siegfried – until the moment she "discovered" he was an *Eigenmann* – was that of a queen for a king, not of a woman for a man. Not only is there nowhere in the epic a hint of a personal feeling by Brunhild for Siegfried, the very adherence to this suggested love affinity leads to a hopeless contradiction:

> Ist aber Brünhilt, wie sich eindeutig nachweisen lässt, auf die
> Gattin Siegfrieds eifersüchtig, so verliert das Argument der Vasal-
> lität seinen Sinn. Eifersucht auf die Frau eines Eigenmannes
> ist für die Königin Brünhilt gegenstandslos.[21]

Precisely, and since the *Eigenmann* motif lies at the core of the quarrel which brings the truth to Brunhild rather than obscures it, it is not the Eigenmann motif which becomes pointless – at least, not in the sense in which Nagel means it – but Brunhild's alleged jealousy in the realm of love. To paraphrase: it is true that the *Eigenmann* motif becomes pointless, but that does not happen until Brunhild discovers that Siegfried is not an *Eigenmann*, and its pointlessness does not emerge from her jealousy in the realm of love, but from the appearance of the truth about Siegfried's status. If there is to be talk of jealously at all, it relates to the manner in which Brunhild guards the dignity of kingship and established order.[22]

20 The following citation is of interest: "What is certain is that where a Germanic race reached its maturity untouched by the Latin spirit, as in Iceland, we find nothing at all like courtly love. The position of women in the Saga is, indeed, higher than that which they enjoy in classical literature; but it is based on a purely commonsensible and unemphasized respect for the courage and prudence which some women, like some men, happen to possess." From C.S. Lewis, *The Allegory of Love* (New York, 1958), p. 9.

21 *Ibid.*, pp. 291 f.

22 Seen in this light, the quarrel between the queens is quite correctly interpreted by Mergell, *"Nibelungenlied,"* 312: "Im tiefsten Grunde geht es nicht um Rang und Würden im höfischen Sinn, sondern um ihrer aller Existenz, die sich in der Beziehung zum Dasein Siegfrieds entscheidet und sich entscheidet am Geheimnis seiner Individuation" – provided "Individuation" is taken in a "representational" rather than a psychological, a unique, sense.

We have arrived at the same conclusion reached in the previous chapter by a different approach; the investigation of the Brunhild-Siegfried relationship through the scrutiny of the *Eigenmann* motif offers a checking device that bears out and supports the suggestions made in the kingship study. I suggest that the interlocking significance of the kingship and *Eigenmann* motifs is one of the most important examples of what in the first chapter was called the self-revealing and self-referential pattern in the *Nibelungenlied*, and that therefore the *Eigenmann* motif is an all-important and consequential link in the development of the epic.[23]

If some of the suggestions made in these pages have begun to seem redundant, the reason is a concern that the *Nibelungenlied* be read correctly, a concern that makes it difficult to avoid restatement. How difficult it sometimes is to retain one's balance can perhaps be shown advantageously with the help of a specific example. The verb "rüe-men" occurs four times in the parts of the epic just investigated. Bumke has said interesting things about the way in which the poet "purpose-fully" beclouds matters by using the "ambiguous" verb "rüemen":

> In Brünhilds Mund hat [das Wort rüemen] einen anderen Klang
> als bei Gunther: "hat er sich es gerüemet,   ez get an Sifrides lip"
> (845). In Gunthers Sinn müsste das heissen: "Wenn Sifrid die
> Verkebsung lügnerisch behauptet hat, wird er es büssen." Aber
> Brunhild kann nicht wissen, dass es eine Lüge ist (sie spricht die
> Worte vor der Eidszene). Für sie muss es heissen: "Wenn Sigfrid
> es getan und Kriemhild gegenüber auch noch damit geprahlt
> hat ... ." Aber der Dichter will gerade solche Unterscheidungen
> vermeiden, indem er alle von *rüemen* sprechen lässt.[24]

Bumke's reasoning regarding Gunther's and Brunhild's use of the verb "rüemen" is unacceptable. The cause of my recalcitrance here is of course my view that Siegfried must die precisely because he did *not* possess Brunhild. What, then, about the verb "rüemen" in Brunhild's line? Does it continue to be ambiguous despite the entirely different

23 McLintock, "Les larmes," 313, calls the motif "sans doute le point plus faible du récit."

24 Bumke, "Quellen," p. 22.

understanding gleaned from the verse? I suggest that it does not, and that its use is now crystal clear and without the slightest ambiguity. For, as already stated, Brunhild does not take offense at the alleged boast of Siegfried as the readers know him, but at the boast of Siegfried as *she* knows him up to this moment, that is, of Siegfried as *Eigenmann*. And it is this type of boast only, and not any sort of implication as read from it by Bumke – "das kann nur heissen, weil er sie besessen hat"[25] – that constitutes the insult. For at this very moment (i.e., as Bumke observes, before the belt and oath scenes inform her of the true state of affairs) Brunhild still "knows" that Siegfried did not vanquish her, since he could not, and he could not because he was, as she thinks, not strong enough. That lack of sufficient strength accounts for his status as a mere *Eigenmann*. Both Brunhild and Gunther, then, use "rüemen" in the sense of "maintain falsely," and whatever ambiguity seems to prevail issues not from different values attached to "rüemen" by Brunhild and Gunther – or so Bumke believes – but from the fact that Brunhild still thinks of Siegfried as an *Eigenmann*, whereas Gunther knows better.[26]

Ironically, whereas Brunhild's line issues from a false assumption regarding Siegfried's status, its central idea – Siegfried must die – remains valid, and there is no way out of the entanglement in which Brunhild's language traps him. Either he must die if he (as *Eigenmann*) has boasted about something he has not done and was incapable of doing, or, as it turns out by the time Brunhild puts two and two together upon seeing the belt and learning from Gunther that Siegfried is "'innocent," he must die if he (as king), though capable, did not do anything.

To refer once again to the theory that two or more stories are combined in the *Nibelungenlied*: though historically correct, the fact is of secondary importance, since it has little effect on the strain of motivational forces that are set to work in the epic. For the poet now uses motivations in such a manner as to amalgamate them in Hagen (cf.

25 *Ibid.*

26 Hagen's use of the verb "rüemen," viewed by Bumke as deriving its meaning from Brunhild's use of it (as evaluated by Bumke) – "weil [Siegfried Brunhild] besessen hat" – constitutes a deliberate misunderstanding of the recent events, it being to his advantage not to understand anything, and to remain uninformed (see chapter VII, p. 129).

chapter VII, passim), while at the same time he has the opportunity to show what from one point of view – Brunhild's – is wrong in Siegfried's love for Kriemhild.

It is evident that the Brunhild emerging from these pages resembles in some respects the Brunhild emerging from Beyschlag's study,[27] and the question arises whether we may draw the same conclusion about Siegfried and Hagen after we have studied them in some detail. Though the present study – and those preceding – have already made some suggestions about them, at least with respect to Siegfried these statements are in the main Brunhild's way of looking at him, and it remains to be seen how he looks when viewed without her bias. For of course, Brunhild's opinions do not necessarily constitute the objective truth. Besides, she refrains from stating explicitly her reasons for wishing Siegfried's death. The result is that – for instance – Kriemhild has no inkling what is going on in Brunhild's mind. This being so, it will be well to check Siegfried through the eyes of others, in an attempt to arrive at a somewhat more commonly prevailing opinion.

27 S. Beyschlag, "Das Motiv der Macht bei Siegfrieds Tod," GRM, xxxiii (1951/52), 95–108.

vi

SIEGFRIED

FROM THE POINT OF VIEW of many people Siegfried as a candidate for kingship has much to recommend him. Like all the crown bearers in the *Nibelungenlied* – and some of their emulators as well, Rüdeger, for instance – Siegfried is liberal in giving. Such liberality is an attribute indispensable to kings:

309 In der hogezite   der wirt der hiez ir pflegen
mit der beste spise.   er hete sich bewegen
aller slahte scande,   die ie künec gewan.

> *During the feast the king regaled them with the choicest foods; he had placed himself beyond all such criticisms as kings may incur.*

It does more than create good will; it creates honor as well. Indeed, these abstract goods are bought by giving, as though they are commodities available for cash on the market place. Sieglind "buys" honor and popularity for her son this way:

29 Von der hohgezite   man möhte wunder sagen.
Sigmunt unde Siglint   die mohten wol bejagen
mit guote michel ere;   des teilte vil ir hant.
des sach man vil der vremden   zuo z'in riten in daz lant.

> *One could speak marvels of the splendid feast. Siegmund and Sieglind knew how to acquire much honor with the great gifts they dispensed. In consequence many strangers traveled to their land.*

38 Swie vil si kurzwile   pflagen al den tac,
   vil der varender diete   ruowe sich bewac.
   sie dienten nach der gabe   die man da riche vant.
   des wart mit lobe gezieret   allez Sigmundes lant.

   Der herre der hiez lihen   Sivrit den jungen man
   lant unde bürge,   als er het e getan.
   sinen swertgenozen   den gap do vil sin hant.
   do liebt' in diu reise,   daz si komen in daz lant.

   Diu hohgezit werte   unz an den sibenden tac.
   Siglint diu riche   nach alten siten pflac
   durch ir sunes liebe   teilen rotez golt.
   si kundez wol gedienen   daz im die liute waren holt.

*However much amusement they brought throughout the day,
many minstrels refrained from resting. They served for the sake
of gifts which were abundant there, so that Siegmund's entire
realm was adorned with their praise.*

*The king commanded the young Siegfried to bestow land and
castles, as he himself had done in the past. Siegfried's hand gave
richly to his companions, so that they were much pleased with
their journey to this land.*

*The festivities lasted until the seventh day. The wealthy Sieglind,
according to ancient custom, distributed red gold in honor of her
son. She well knew how to win the favor of the people for him.*

Kriemhild buys loyalty with gifts, thereby arousing Hagen's anxiety
and wrath (1127 ff.), a sign of the efficacy of the means employed.
Hagen himself buys Eckewart's confidence (cf. chapter VIII, pp. 135 f.).

Liberality in giving being an indisipensable attribute of kingship,
on a par with the ability to display magnificence, all the kings give
gladly. This is not to say that they give for the mere sake of giving.
Their giving amounts to striking a bargain: I give you this, you give me
that (loyalty, honor, praise, friendship, *et al.*), and the ultimate purpose
of such giving is to strengthen the position held.

From this point of view emerges the possibility that Brunhild is not miserly. Her objection to Dankwart's spendthrift behavior at her cost (cf. 515 ff.) may issue from her confidence as a queen. Unlike others, she has no need to give more than custom makes mandatory; she has no need to buy anything with gifts, either honor, loyalty, or friendship. She may feel that she already has those goods in sufficient abundance, or she may not desire them. If, like Kriemhild on two occasions (691 ff. and 1280), she wants to take treasures along in order to establish herself in a new land, it is perhaps because, confident as queen of Islant, she is aware of the fickleness of fortune and realizes that as queen of the Burgundians she may do well to have the means to buy whatever she may need.

What, then, about Siegfried's liberality as a mark of kingship? An instance of it is his insistence that Kriemhild not demand the full share of the wealth that is hers by right (694 ff.). The mere display of Kriemhild's brothers' liberal intentions to give her everything to which she has a claim is evidently enough to earn them Siegfried's liberal refusal to accept their offer. That at this early moment in her wedded life Kriemhild's will is already subservient to Siegfried's reflects on their relationship and accords with the comments to be made later about the position of women in the *Nibelungenlied*.

All in all, however, Siegfried's manner of giving does not differ much from that of other kings. Though he displays liberality, he does not practice it on a gigantic scale, except for the hoard – if a *Morgengabe* can be said to constitute a gift. If Siegfried's eminence as a king is factual, more trustworthy manifestations must be found elsewhere. In this connection it is of consequence that we have the poet's own word that Siegfried exercises justice (714). In addition, in a manner of speaking, the hoard comes to him as a result of the sense of fairness which the kings of the Nibelungs know to be part of him. It is this sense of fairness that causes them to ask him to preside over the division of the hoard (91).

Siegfried's qualities are clearly indicated from within the world of Santen: the court wishes him to accept the crown, and Siegmund believes the land will do well with Siegfried as king. These opinions issue from considerations relating to indispensable kingly qualities which those around him believe Siegfried has.

One other fact about Siegfried is mentioned again and again by those who mold public opinion. All the important characters in the *Nibelungenlied* indicate, explicitly or implicitly, that strength and wealth as possessed by Siegfried are *the* ingredients for kingship (chapter IV, p. 71). And to be sure, in a world in which kings must give gifts to strengthen their position, the qualities of strength and wealth become the marks of kingship, make for the *right* to kingship. In Siegfried's case these marks are represented by the hoard and the *Tarnkappe*.

With these considerations we must touch upon an intriguing phenomenon, that the value of the hoard-*Kappe* complex is twofold. It is valuable in so far as its wealth constitutes power, and on a more symbolic plane it fuses itself to its owner, as it were, with the *Kappe* as the symbol of that fusion. The poet himself does not distinguish clearly between these two values, and moves readily from the one to the other, causing them to overlap and to become difficult to distinguish. Strophe 118, for example – " 'jane dörften mich din zwelve   mit strite nimmer bestan' "/" '*Indeed, twelve like you could not stand up to me in battle*' " – leaves undecided whether twelve Ortwins would be incapable of overcoming Siegfried *an sich*, or Siegfried with *Kappe* donned. Whether this confusion is deliberate or not seems a moot question, but the way the poet uses the number twelve indicates that he knows what he is doing. This number lies close to the essence of the hoard and becomes a means of conveying symbolically and not too covertly its value and significance. These are the salient features about the hoard as it relates to the number twelve. To acquire the *Tarnkappe*, and with it the hoard, Siegfried kills twelve giants (94);[1] Gernot and Giselher use twelve carts – making three trips daily for four days – to get the hoard to the ship that will take the gold to Worms (1122); Kriemhild, when preparing to depart for Gran, manages to take twelve trunks of the gold with her (1280), as though to symbolize her inalienable rights to the hoard at large.

Not only is the number twelve of consequence with respect to Brunhild also (cf. chapter IV, p. 76), but it lies close to the essence of Siegfried's power on a more personal basis as well. Before acquiring the *Kappe* and hoard, he has a penchant for doing things on his own, "al eine an' alle helfe" (88); afterwards, as though to dramatize his ownership of the *Tarnkappe* – which, donned, lends him the additional strength of twelve men – he travels to Worms with twelve com-

---

1 Note the confusion here, too, between the two values of the hoard-*Tarnkappe*: the giants are killed without the aid of the *Kappe*.

panions (64). It is revealing that none of these ever appears individually or ever says a word, and that they remain anonymous to a man. They are all shadowy figures indeed – almost, one would venture to say, as if they were the ghostly remnants of the twelve giants that succumbed to Siegfried in the land of the Nibelungs. In addition, when accompanied by these twelve, Siegfried makes no use of the *Tarnkappe*, and when he does, the twelve are not mentioned. Furthermore, it would seem that the number of knights accompanying Siegfried and Kriemhild on their visit to Worms – there are twelve hundred of them at the banquet (803) – relates to the importance of the number twelve as an indicator of Siegfried's power. Since it is the number twelve a hundred times, Brunhild wonders about Siegfried's power (this is the first time she receives any visible indication of it) and about the discrepancy between this display of strength and Siegfried's assumed vassalage.

About the *Tarnkappe* in relation to the number twelve Panzer says:

> Wenn der Tarnkappe an unserer Stelle ausser der Kraft
> unsichtbar zu machen noch die Verleihung von zwölf
> Männerstärken zugeschrieben wird, so ist auch diese Angabe
> dringend verdächtig, eine Erfindung des Dichters ad hoc
> zu sein. Sie bedeutet ja gewiss keine organische Eigenschaft
> des Gegenstandes, und es wird, so viel mir bekannt ist, diesem
> Zaubermantel niemals ein solches Mana zugeschrieben. Man
> verdankt die Angabe wohl nur der Fürsorge des Dichters, der
> sich verpflichtet fühlte, einigermassen begreiflich zu machen,
> dass Siegfried im Weitsprung noch König Gunther mit sich
> durch die Luft trägt.[2]

But the poet of the *Nibelungenlied* is not at all in the habit of attempting to make the impossible believable (cf. chapter 1, p. 3), and this invention is not ad hoc at all, the poet having carefully distributed allusions to the number twelve throughout his narrative.[3] Precisely

2 Panzer, *Das Nibelungenlied*, p. 327.
3 That the writer of the c* version had no eye for the significance of the number twelve has been inadvertently indicated by Morgan, "Numbers," 20: "For this passionate fondness of the poet [of the B* version] for the number twelve I have

because the *Tarnkappe* has this strength-lending quality in no other known version of the *Nibelungenlied*, its importance in the B* text is perfectly evident. Rather than making believable Siegfried's ability to carry Gunther with him in the jumping contest, the number twelve serves to connect as closely as possible Siegfried's and Brunhild's strength, on the one hand, and Siegfried and the hoard, on the other, by means of the *Tarnkappe*. The *Kappe,* as Schröder has suggested, is thus raised to the status of a natural symbol.[4]

With these considerations, it is small wonder that Siegfried is quite confident that he has all the necessary qualities of a king. His refusal to accept the crown of Santen as long as his father lives (42 f.) does not stem from self-doubt, but from filial respect, from his wish to show first that he is worthy of the crown – and perhaps from his playfulness. Nor does it imply a feeling of inferiority regarding kingship; in fact, his self-confidence may strike those whom he encounters as reprehensible. A (temporary) lack of confidence comes only *vis-à-vis* Kriemhild, for something happens to this highly qualified candidate for kingship when he encounters Kriemhild.

At first glance Siegfried is a schizophrenic lover. One moment his demeanor is overbearing, the next abject. In the beginning he sets out to acquire Kriemhild, by force if need be, indeed preferably by force – against the advice of his parents, who favor the approach common in the arrangement of any marriage which entails political consequences. This approach is used by Etzel later (twentieth *Aventiure*). In Siegfried's case, neither the advice given nor his own view of the procedure to be followed falls into the category of courtly methods (if seeking marriage is possible at all in the frame of courtly love). Siegfried's proposed way of doing things is suitable, rather, to a king as envisioned by Brunhild.

It has been said that Siegfried's love for Kriemhild before first sight is one indication of a love in the courtly tradition.[5] True as this may be, the suggestion is not necessarily of great consequence in

---

no explanation and find no analogy. Lacking any further evidence, we must regard this as a personal foible of the poet." See also M. Schwarze, "Die Frau in dem *Nibelungenlied* und der *Kudrun,*" *ZfdP,* XVI (1884), note 1.

4 W. J. Schröder, *Das Nibelungenlied,* p. 20, note 2.

5 W. Schröder, "Tragödie."

the context of the *Nibelungenlied*: Gunther's experience with Brunhild is very similar, but few readers would suspect him of attuning *his* love to the courtly mode,[6] except that he may adopt an occasional (outward) courtly gesture. In this connection, Mergell's critique of Dürrenmatt's book on the courtly theme in the *Nibelungenlied* comes to mind:

> Im ganzen lässt sich gegen N. Dürrenmatts Auffassung von
> höfischer Dichtkunst einwenden dass Darstellung höfischer
> Lebensformen allein noch keinen Massstab für die Beurteilung
> ihrer tieferen Gehalte abgibt: Dass sie allenfalls ornamentale,
> nicht aber wesenhafte Bedeutung hat. In diesem Punkte bedürfte
> unsere Gesamtanschauung vom Wesen "höfischer Dichtung"
> einer ernsthaften Ueberprüfung.[7]

This dictum, if applied to love, holds true not only for Gunther but also for Siegfried. Until he marries, Siegfried is a lover with a curious mixture of self-assertion and longing in the true courtly fashion, to which a third ingredient is added. For the "hohe minne" on which Siegfried is said in strophe 47 to set his mind is equated in the following strophe with "staete minne":

47 Do gedaht uf hohe minne   daz Siglinde kint.
ez was ir aller werben   wider in ein wint.
er mohte wol verdienen   scoener frouwen lip.
sit wart diu edel Kriemhilt   des küenen Sivrides wip.

Im rieten sine magne   und genuoge sine man,
sit er uf staete minne   tragen wolde wan,
daz er dan ein wurbe   diu im möhte zemen.
do sprach der küene Sivrit: "So wil ich Kriemhilden nemen."

Then Sieglind's son began to think of noble love. Against him, the courting of all others was as nothing. He was well able to win lovely women and in due time the noble Kriemhild became the wife of brave Siegfried.

6 Weber, *Des Nibelungenlied*, p. 124, speaks of Gunther's "zarte Liebe" for Brunhild.
7 Mergell, "*Nibelungenlied*," p. 307.

His kinsmen and many of his retainers advised him, since he had
set his mind on constant love, to woo a lady becoming to his
station. Then the bold Siegfried spoke: "In that case I shall take
Kriemhild."

Thus "straete minne" is in turn equated with the marriage state which
Siegfried decides to enter on the advice of his – policitally motivated –
environment. Indeed, it is political considerations advanced by those
seeking to direct his affairs that lead Siegfried, *after* he has set his mind
on love, to choose Kriemhild as its object.

When Siegfried finally gets to see his lady, having despaired
meanwhile of ever attaining her (285), love is mutual, but its manifestations must remain secret.[8] When then Siegfried asks for Kriemhild's
hand in marriage, he proposes a political bargain: I help you, you help
me (333). When arrangements are made, it does not seem to occur to
anyone, least of all Siegfried, that Kriemhild's will could be a relevant
factor. Only a passive role is expected of her. Asked into the circle
(610 ff.), she blushes properly and gives her consent – without yet
knowing to which man Gunther intends to give her. The whole scene
is out of tune with the ideals of courtly love. Actually, we are in a
world in which women are the mute objects of gifts and barter, in the
eyes not only of brothers, but also of lovers.

It could be argued that Siegfried's behavior loses all its ambiguity
if we consider that the courtly manners of which he is capable are
natural and a matter of course in his relation to Kriemhild whenever
the existence of her environment – Worms, and more specifically, her
brothers – does not have to intrude upon his words or actions; when
he does not have to be "practical," but is in a position to think exclusively of his beloved; when he can afford to act as Kriemhild's
swain. This is but another way of saying that Siegfried's courtly bearing towards Kriemhild is of the same consequence as Gunther's towards Brunhild. As stated, the non-courtly facets of Siegfried's demeanor pertain to instances in which he communicates with Kriemhild's environment. After his initial plan to acquire Kriemhild by force
has been evaporated, Siegfried behaves towards her brothers like any
suitor whose position and that of the desired lady command a practical
– in this case, a political – approach. Neumann has it "dass die Gestalten

8 Renoir, "Levels of Meaning."

des Nibelungenliedes ihre alte Art [behalten], soweit diese durch die Grundfabel verlangt wird. Sie nehmen die Haltung der höfischen Ritter und Ritterdamen an, wenn ihnen die Kernhandlung nicht die Gebärden vorschreibt."[9] Neumann, then, sees a duality which arises from the attempted fusion of different orientations rather than from within the characters as they adapt themselves to circumstances. But in actual fact, courtliness comes quite naturally to Siegfried whenever he is with Kriemhild and can enjoy being simply in her presence (cf. 294). In this connection, it will not do to speak of courtly Worms and courtly Kriemhild and to refer to Siegfried as of a different, presumably uncourtly, order.[10] The seeming discrepancy between courtly and not so courtly does not lie with Worms in contrast to Santen, or with Kriemhild in contrast to Siegfried, but in the fact that the lover Siegfried cannot avoid being a political figure. To Kriemhild he may speak of love in any manner he deems fit; to her brothers he must speak and act as a responsible suitor, and therefore politically. Understood in this manner, Wachinger is correct: "In der Welt des Nibelungenliedes sind die Schichten ... der höfischen Form und der politisch-ritterlichen Realität tatsächlich nicht zu trennen."[11] This is not to deny that the courtliness of Siegfried or Kriemhild – or, for that matter courtliness in the epic in general – is but skin deep. Courtliness, while "natural," is shallow because the characters are "hollow" (cf. chapter IX, p. 154).

The instances in which courtliness in the Siegfried-Kriemhild relationship becomes manifest are but minor compared to those in which the non-courtly aspects reveal themselves. Nevertheless, we have been taught – and convinced – by Renoir[12] that the poet of the *Nibe-*

---

9 F. Naumann, "Schichten der Ethik im Nibelungenlied," *Festschrift für Eugen Mogk* (Halle/Saale, 1924), p. 129.

10 Willson, " 'Ordo' and 'inordinatio.' " Willson's argument carries itself to destruction. Claiming that Siegfried has an uncourtly effect on Kriemhild, he suggests that she joins him in his *ordo*, that of Santen, and outgrows that of Worms. Willson has no choice but to overlook the fact that after Siegfried's death she decides to stay in Worms. Actually, Kriemhild does not need to refine Siegfried, and Siegfried does not need to "decourtify" Kriemhild. Each of them is capable of displaying courtliness or the lack of it, depending on whether the position in which they find themselves at a given moment is "courtly" or not.

11 Wachinger, *Studien,* p. 108.

12 Renoir, "Levels of Meaning."

lungenlied is perfectly informed of the courtly mode of conduct in love, and that he incorporates into his materials more of the manifestations of courtly love than are apparent at first sight. Indeed, the courtly aspects that do not leap to the eye outnumber and are more important than those that do. This fact by itself is of consequence since it suggests that the poet deliberately *mutes* his presentation of Siegfried as a courtly lover, and of Kriemhild as a lady of courtly love. For that matter, it may be suggested that the poet wishes us to pay no more attention to the love of these characters than is strictly necessary. In so far as he deals with it, he introduces love in a multiplicity of forms (cf. chapter III, p. 63, and below), but that does not mean that these various forms are of great intrinsic interest to him.[13] The various views of love are of importance only to the persons holding them, and the very multiplicity of types of love prevents love from becoming pre-eminent as the main motif in the epic. These loves may affect individuals directly and in the core of their existence, but they do not directly touch the structure of the society in which they exist. This society does not meet its doom because its main characters love or fail to love, but because they have the power to affect the lives of masses of people.

There is good and inevitable reason why the poet of the *Nibelungenlied* refrains from embroidering heavily on those manifestations of Siegfried's love for Kriemhild – and hers for him – that can be labeled courtly. To emphasize these facets would pose for the poet the problem of how to deal with them by the time Siegfried marries Kriemhild. For that reason the spiritual ecstasies of *Frauendienst* receive only slight attention – if any at all. Because of the marriage, the poet must also provide for the physical ecstasies of passion.[14] If he had his

13 Nagel, *Das Nibelungenlied*, p. 186, finds that the epic, with Kriemhild at its center, "den Roman einer Liebe darstellt," and on p. 185 he speaks of the "so eindringlich geschilderte Liebe" of Siegfried and Kriemhild. F. Ranke, "Die höfisch-ritterliche Dichtung," in: *Deutsche Literaturgeschichte in Grundzügen* (Bern/München, 1961), p. 58, finds that the poet works primarily "mit Kräften aus dem höfisch-ritterlichen Bildungsbereich seiner Seele. Seine Liebe gehört dem reinen Paar Siegfried und Kriemhild, dessen Geschichte er, soweit der Stoff zulässt, aus dem verfeinerten Empfinden seiner Zeit heraus neugestaltet."
14 In his note to strophe 47 in *Deutsche Klassiker*, de Boor speaks of Siegfried's (potential) "entsinnlichte Liebe" for Kriemhild; Sacker, "Irony and Symbolism,"

way we should believe that these spiritual and physical ecstasies reach their apex, fully harmonized and fused, on the wedding night. Marriage is to bring about a synthesis of, and stand duty for, the different types of love that in the *Nibelungenlied* lead up to it. This attempt at fusion is an attempt to achieve what it took the poetry of love some two hundred years after the courtly period to accomplish: the synthesis of passionate, courtly and married love, in which the latter is to stand for the ingredients that are now expected to harmonize in it. The poet of the *Nibelungenlied* is, if you like, an early student of "romantic" love.

Before the poet's attempt at synthesizing passion, married love, and *Frauendienst*, they were kept apart with a firmness that at times bordered on cynicism. But the poet's predecessors — poets as well as scholastic thinkers — had had little choice, since the medieval view of passion had little in common with passion as defined and understood after its synthesis with other ingredients had been realized in the poetry of romantic love. As conceived under the influence of neoplatonism, passion ennobles those who experience it, works an essential change upon appetite and affection, and turns each into a different thing. About passion in this sense the medieval thinkers have nothing to say, just as they have nothing to say about electricity. They have not heard of it. It was only coming into existence when the *Nibelungenlied* was being written, and it found its first expression in the poetry of courtly love.

The medieval counterpart of this "modern" passion is something quite different. Instead of allegedly producing positive values, it is negative in its effect, is to be avoided, even if the object of it is one's own spouse. If a man once yields to this emotion he has no choice between guilty or innocent love; he has only the choice of repentance, or else of different forms of guilt, that is to say, guilt inside or outside marriage. To medieval man, passion has nothing purifying or ennobling about it. Instead it degrades, since its victim's reason cannot prevail. Married love stands in contrast to such passion, as it stands in contrast to courtly love. Marriage is a contract, arranged by one's guardians, and

gleans from the same strophe that there is something disreputable about Siegfried's experience with women. The strophe in actual fact is a verbal sleight of hand surreptitiously making the transition from a general reference to "hohe Minne" to the prediction of Kriemhild's becoming Siegfried's wife.

calling for a certain amount of sobriety and at least in theory assuming a degree of disinterest on the sexual plane. It is this medieval view of marriage that makes a synthesis between married love and courtly love so tenuous. For far from being a natural channel for courtly love, marriage is the drab background against which that love stands out in all the contrast of its tenderness and delicacy. The situation is a simple one, and not unique in the Middle Ages. And though it took a long time before the synthesis succeeded in producing "romantic" love, attempts at harmonization are found as soon as the phenomenon of courtly love becomes of consequence. Chrétien de Troyes, for instance, with an exception for his *Lancelot*, attempts "courtly marriage" in all his works.

It is this excursion[15] into the realm of "romantic" love as it is beginning to emerge at the time of the *Nibelungenlied* that highlights – because of the contrast – the nature of the Brunhild-Gunther relationship. For with Brunhild we conceive of a framework of thought emptied of that ideal of "happiness" – a happiness based on successful romantic love. Brunhild does not expect such love, and no such love comes her way. But if she is to be pitied for missing such love, she can be pitied only by standards that are not her own.

These remarks about the diverse types of love combined in the marriage state are of consequence for the Siegfried-Kriemhild relationship, as becomes evident when we consider that from an unexpected corner beyond the horizon of the *Nibelungenlied* – the world of the scholastic thinkers – there is a parallel to Brunhild's view of Siegfried's failure to exercise reason in love. Brunhild defines this failure as a failure to adhere to a king's way of abiding by values; scholasticism defines it as a failure to keep love from the sin of passion.[16]

There is support available within the epic for the contention that Siegfried's falling in love is accompanied by a suspension of his

---

15 E. Trojel (ed.), *Andreae Capellani regii Francorum de amore libri tres* (Kopenhagen, 1892) serve as background material. See also F. Schlösser, *Andreas Capellanus: Seine Minneauffassung und das christliche Weltbild um 1200* (Bonn, 1960); D. de Rougement, *Love in the Western World* (New York, 1940).

16 J. K. Bostock, "The Message of the *Nibelungenlied*," MLR, LV (1960), 205, at one point of his argument puts it this way: "The contemporary public of the *Nibelungenlied* would recall the tradition that love made fools of Aristotle and Solomon."

(kingly) reason. His acceptance of the crown of Santen after his marriage is a prostitution of his more kingly statement of a former day
when he refused the crown for the duration of his father's life (43).
By accepting the crown now, he makes his kingship subservient to
his love. And the hoard, which lies close to the essence of his kingly
strength, he gives to Kriemhild for love's sake, making it subservient
to his love as well.

Furthermore, Siegfried's violation of kingship is discovered by
Brunhild because he violated a symbol: under the circumstances prevailing he allowed the belt to "tell" Kriemhild that he took Brunhild's
virginity (cf. chapter III, p. 58). The nature of this unspoken boast
is in itself a violation of kingship, his own as well as Brunhild's. To this
transgression is added the perversion of the testimonial power of the
belt. This, too, is a grave trespass, for in a world where warnings go
unheeded (cf. chapter VII, passim), advice is scorned, and people talk
past each other (cf. chapter III, p. 63, and chapter IX, p. 159),
language is an inadequate tool of communication, and symbols are
the only things with abiding and binding value on which one can rely.
Woe unto him who wrongs them; he is an enemy of a society one of
whose lifelines is the adherence to symbols. If neglected or mistreated,
such symbols will have their revenge.

In this connection, there is a revealing irony detectable in the belt
and oath scenes, one which vindicates the power of symbols. This irony
– and the ensuing vindication – lies in the fact that the oath scene is not
actually an oath scene at all; it does not need to be. When Siegfried expresses his willingness to make an oath and is interrupted by Gunther's
hurried declaration of his innocence, Gunther's non-oath turns out to
be sufficient to gainsay the mistreated testimonial power of the belt –
and to reveal the truth to Brunhild. Hence Naumann's dictum as cited
previously – "Als ob man der Magie des Symbols mit der Magie des
Schwures begegnen könne" (chapter v, note 12) – should be para-
phrased to accommodate the true state of affairs: "Als ob man der
Magie des irreführenden Symbols nur mit einem leicht gesprochenen
Worte zu begegnen brauche."

It is with these considerations in mind that we must see Siegfried's
love for Kriemhild as inordinate.[17] Whether such inordinance consti-

17 Willson, " 'Ordo' and 'inordinatio,' " 93. The approach used by Willson is
unfortunate. It pits persons, societies, and cultures against each other, and

tutes guilt in any objective sense is a different matter. Indeed, with respect to Siegfried, too, we can say that "Schuld Schicksal ist und Schicksal Schuld,"[18] Siegfried being as fated as Kriemhild. As we have seen (chapter III, p. 60), this inevitability of his love for Kriemhild is indicated by the moon similes applied to them.

Nor is the Kriemhild-Siegfried relationship after their marriage (cf. chapter III, p. 64) – when courtly ingredients are lost to sight – to be interpreted as a waning of this love. Rather, if we look at the position of women in general, it becomes evident that Kriemhild's position is typical.[19] For one thing, there is Brunhild after her marriage. Though a queen in her own right, once she is married her influence is close to non-existent, and her personal wishes, laments, and regrets are of little or no consequence to the people around her. Gunther himself is the first to treat her woes offhandedly. Hagen, who pays a visit (863 f.) immediately after Siegfried's advice to punish wives who talk before they think, seems to be an exception – but cf. chapter VII, p. 128.

In addition, Brunhild's dismay at Dankwart's liberal manner of disposing of her gold before her departure from Islant (515 f.) may gain significance. Dankwart's offer to do the giving – it was not Brunhild's idea that he function as her representative – may be politically motivated. Independent wealth could be vitally important to Brunhild, as it could be to Kriemhild at the times of her marriages, when she attempts either to settle her inheritance rights (chapter III, p. 64) or to take with her whatever worldly goods she can. For who is to say, in a world in which marriage is a doubtful venture for a woman, when she may need financial means? No wonder Hagen and Gunther laugh at Brunhild's concern regarding Dankwart's liberality at her expense

identifies now one, now another character as belonging to one order or the other. Willson's nomenclature could be gainfully employed to juxtapose the general interest of the characters in retaining order and harmony with their proneness to misunderstand and to talk past each other, thus causing disorder and disharmony. As it is, Willson at one moment, for example, associates the allegedly inordinate Brunhild with the devil, whereas Siegfried – equally inordinate – is said to display features reminiscent of Christ.

18 Nagel, "Das Nibelungenlied," p. 279.

19 Mowatt and Sacker, The Nibelungenlied, p. 14, speak of the "limitations imposed on women in a man's world."

(521): Dankwart helps to render Brunhild dependent before she is Gunther's wife in fact.[20]

There is also the moment when Rüdeger proclaims, not even in Etzel's name, the necessity for Kriemhild to take gold with her (1273 ff.). Such gold would render Kriemhild more independent than Etzel might like. In addition, Rüdeger's reaction reflects favorably on himself perhaps, or is intended to,[21] and it certainly is meant to reflect favorably on Etzel's tremendous wealth and consequent honor and power.

And there is Giselher's engagement to Rüdeger's daughter. As with Kriemhild, the girl is not asked what she thinks of the plan suggested by Hagen and then discussed in detail by those present. Not until the question of dowry has been settled is the girl called in. As with Kriemhild, it is the good fortune of Rüdeger's daughter that she is yoked to a man apparently to her liking. Later we hear from Giselher that the marriage plan was attractive to him mainly because of the prospective father-in-law.

Elsewhere Siegfried has thoughts that fall squarely within an uncourtly view of women. His reaction to Brunhild's defeat in Islant is "simply the commonplace opinion that women should be feminine and obedient."[22]

474"So wol mich dirre maere,"   sprach Sifrit der degen,
   "daz iuwer hohverte   sint also hie gelegen,
    daz iemen lebet   der iuwer meister müge sin.
    nu sult ir, maget edele   uns hinnen volgen an den Rin."

"This is good news indeed," spoke Siegfried the warrior, "that your pride has been thus lowered, and that there is someone alive who can master you. Now, noble maiden, you must come with us to the Rhine."

At a moment when Siegfried has scant leisure to think peripheral thoughts of little or no consequence, there is a strophe that lends cre-

20 Bumke, "Sigfrids Fahrt," p. 265, gives a different interpretation of the scene, but his view does not invalidate the evaluation here presented.
21 G. F. Jones, "Rüdiger's Dilemma," *SP*, LVII (1960), 205.
22 Bostock, "Message," p. 205.

dence to the view that women should occupy a specific place, a position
that bears little relation to that of the courtly lady:

> 673 "Owe," gedaht' der recke   "sol ich nu minen lip
>   von einer magt verliesen,   so mugen elliu wip
>   her nach immer mere   tragen gelpfen muot
>   gegen ir manne,   diu ez sus nimmer getuot."

> *"Alas!" thought the warrior, "if I should lose my life on account
> of a maiden, all women might in time become overbearing towards
> their husbands, though otherwise they would never act in this
> manner."*

In this strophe Siegfried sees himself as the champion, once and for
all, of male domination in marriage; all wives will revolt if he does
not win this one event.

As a last example of the position of women there is Kriemhild's
statement about the way Gunther asks her help in the preparations for
the trip to Islant:

> 356 "Ir sult mich, riter edele,   niht sorgende bitten,
>   ir sult mir gebieten   mit herlichen siten.
>   swaz iu von mir gevalle,   des bin ich iu bereit,
>   unt tuon ez willecliche."

> *"You must not, noble knight, ask me with such diffidence. You
> must command in lordly fashion. Whatever you wish to ask of me,
> I am prepared to do it, and do it willingly."* ...

There may be some courtly polish about this speech, but it also
carries the thought of a woman accustomed to subservience rather than
to breathing in the atmosphere of refined *Frauendienst* – Kriemhild's
words are very similar to those in which she tells Gunther she will
gladly marry whatever man he deems suitable (cf. 613). It is of consequence that Gunther's reaction to Kriemhild's reminder to speak in
lordly fashion begins with a command corresponding to a more im-
perative bearing on his part: " 'ir sult vil rehte merken   was ich iu,

23 See Mowatt and Sacker, *The Nibelungenlied*, note on 356.

frouwe, sage' " / " 'Now mark what I tell you my lady' " (360).[23] It must be annoying to Gunther that Kriemhild has to remind him that a king must act in kingly fashion.

As we have seen, once married, Siegfried reverts to the orientation in which Kriemhild's position is as subservient as that of other women in the epic. She reverts with him in the sense that she readily adapts to a marriage state in which courtly ingredients are lost to sight. Prior to this change, Siegfried accepts the crown of Santen for Kriemhild's sake and attaches importance to the outward mark of kingship, not for that kingship's sake, but for love's. He will pay for that lapse, that momentary – and momentous – failure to assert his kingship, since it occurs at a time when the queen is crossing his path.

vii

HAGEN
IN RELATION
TO SIEGFRIED

IT IS THE PURPOSE of this chapter to see whether our understanding of Hagen would benefit from the intra-comparative evaluation that in the preceding chapters was considered a valid and rewarding way of reading the *Nibelungenlied*. This procedure does not attempt a full-scale study of Hagen, but seeks to delineate aspects of his character that have received little or no attention in literary criticism. Hence, through the accumulation of circumstantial evidence a figure may emerge whose evaluation falls beyond the mainstream of prevailing opinions.[1]

The first time we hear of Hagen, he is a mere name:

9 Daz was von Tronege Hagene   und ouch der bruoder sin,
  Dancwart der vil snelle,   von Metzen Ortwin,
  di zwene marcgraven   Gere und Ekkewart,
  Volker von Alzeye,   mit ganzem ellen wol bewart.

  Rumolt der kuchenmeister,   ein uz erwelter degen,
  Sindolt und Hunolt,   dise herren muosen pflegen,
  des hoves unt der eren,   der drier künege man,
  si heten noch manegen recken,   des ich genennen niene kan.

  Dancwart der was marschalk,   do was der neve sin
  truhsaeze des küneges,   von Metzen Ortwin.
  Sindolt der was scenke,   ein uz erwelter degen.
  Hunolt was kameraere,   si kunden hoher eren pflegen.

1 As some of the following notes indicate, the delineation of Hagen by Mowatt and Sacker in *The Nibelungenlied*, though quite different from the one suggested here, is also very much beyond this mainstream.

That was Tronje's Hagen, and also his brother Dankwart the
valiant, Ortwin of Metz, the two margraves Gere and Eckewart,
Volker of Alzei, his courage without blemish.

Rumold the cook, an exquisite hero, Sindold and Hunold, these
lords upheld the court and its honor and were in charge of the three
kings' retainers. They had many other men whom I cannot name.

Dankwart was marshall, there was his nephew, Ortwin of Metz,
the king's steward. Sindold was cup-bearer, an excellent warrior.
Hunold was chamberlain. These were [quite] able to maintain the
high honor [of the court].

Whereas Hagen is the first mentioned of these nine important Burgundians, we learn nothing about his or Volker's positions at court. Since
they turn out to be the most important among the kings' men, it is
striking that the poet has nothing to say about Hagen, and about
Volker only that he is courageous, "mit ganzem ellen wol bewart." Of
the other seven we learn immediately their functions at court and in
the realm, even though their roles, with the exception of Dankwart's,
remain extremely limited. This lack of information about Hagen and
Volker makes it possible for the reader to become acquainted with
them in their own words and acts. The poet allows us to "see" them
with our own eyes.

We hear Hagen's name again when Siegmund warns his son
against going to Worms: Siegmund *knows* Gunther and his men (51),
and Hagen himself is awe- and fear-inspiring (54). Weber suggests:
"Man sieht [Hagen] zum erstenmal in Siegmunds hellsichtig warnen-
der Beleuchtung, und sogleich fällt des treffsichere Stichwort: 'Hagene
der degen,/der kan mit übermüete der hohverte pflegen'(54)."[2] But
Siegmund's fear, typical of all the characters in the *Nibelungenlied*
who are led to think or speak of alien parts and persons (cf. chapter I,
pp. 18 f.), is for the moment only an expression of a subjective opinion
and may well turn out to be unwarranted.

This reserve on the reader's part is perfectly justified, since we are
dealing with an epic in which at some time or other practically all the
characters of consequence err, lie, cheat, or sail under false flags by

2 Weber, *Das Nibelungenlied*, p. 43.

disguise or pretense. Besides, their deliberate fostering of misconceptions and their inadequate clarification of things constitute two salient features of the structure of the *Nibelungenlied* (cf. chapter IX, pp. 159 f.).

Only when Hagen's name is mentioned a third time are we able to "see" him. Called to the court, he identifies the visitors in the yard as Siegfried and his companions (85 ff.). Hagen's advice that Siegfried be treated cordially (101 ff.) seems to classify Siegmund's warning as superfluous and invalid: it is upon Hagen's explicit advice that Siegfried is received hospitably and it is Hagen who in effect helps to attach him to the court of Worms.[3]

It is true that Hagen's advice constitutes by implication as much warning against Siegfried as does Siegmund's advice to Siegfried against Hagen: there is room for mutual distrust between Siegfried and Hagen from their first encounter onward. But it is equally true that Hagen's demeanor during this encounter is impeccable. Instead it is Siegfried whose behavior can bear improvement when Gunther and his men converse with him. Brazen and cocky, Siegfried rather than Hagen plays "mit übermüete der hohverte" (54), the proud, arrogant fellow. Siegfried's bearing accords with his reaction to his parents' advice regarding his proposed trip to Worms (51 ff.) and with the way he decides to woo Kriemhild (52 ff.), once more against his parents' suggestions. Knowing from his father the dread which Hagen should inspire, Siegfried belittles this warning by reacting to Hagen with a boldness that hardly bespeaks any degree of diplomacy. Just as he prefers to gain Kriemhild by force rather than by diplomatic activity, so he now prefers to taunt Hagen (and Worms in general) rather than adopt a conciliatory tone. Siegfried is sure of himself, perhaps from the point of view of Worms obnoxiously so, and it is surprising that everyone likes him once he has established himself at the court (cf. 128), unless – and here is the rub – Worms finds Siegfried's behavior perfectly normal and acceptable, and only objects because such an objection is also normal and a matter of course. Such behavior on each side would accord with the commonly prevailing opinion that might is right.

Hagen meanwhile has adopted the policy that silence is better than words, even though in doing so he disappoints Gunther (119).

3 Panzer, *Das Nibelungenlied*, p. 239.

Having just reviewed Siegfried's past deeds of prowess, Hagen is quite aware of the potential danger in this foreigner. For as Hagen has just stated, Siegfried has a *Tarnkappe*, which not only makes him invisible when it is donned, but also lends him the additional strength of twelve men (337).

The courtyard scene between Siegfried and the Burgundians furnishes another example that in the *Nibelungenlied* words are often spoken to no avail. Just as in Santen Siegmund's advice to Siegfried falls on deaf ears, so in Worms Hagen's listeners in the recognition scene hear but do not make the information received their own. It does not affect their words or actions. Not only does Gunther's disappointment at Hagen's silence show this failure to grasp the warning implied in Hagen's advice to treat Siegfried politely, but Ortwin's behavior also shows that Hagen's report on Siegfried's past has served no purpose. Whereas Gunther's disappointment betrays his habitual reliance upon Hagen, thus indirectly telling us something about Hagen's function at court, Ortwin's angry words and Siegfried's reaction to them put the finger on the very reason for Hagen's caution:

116   ... "disiu suone   diu ist mir harte leit,
      iu hat der starke Sivrit   unverdienet widerseit.

    "Ob ir und iuwer bruoder   hetet niht die wer,
    und ob er danne fuorte   ein ganzez küneges her,
    ih trute wol erstriten   daz der küene man
    diz starkez übermüeten   von waren schulden müese lan."

    Daz zurnde harte sere   der helt von Niderlant.
    er sprach: "sich sol vermezzen   niht wider mich din hant.
    ich bin ein künec riche,   so bistu küneges man.
    jane dörften mich din zwelve   mit strite nimmer bestan."

"This appeasing tone distresses me. The strong Siegfried had no warrant to harrass you.

"If you and your brothers did not have defensive means and if he came with a whole royal army, I should dare to fight so that the rash man would have good reason to stop his overweening arrogance."

That greatly angered the hero from the Netherlands. He said:
"Your hand shall not boldly be raised against me. I am a powerful
king, and you are no more than a vassal. Indeed, twelve like you
could not stand up to me in battle."

In Weber's evaluation of the encounter scene, Hagen, when he finally speaks, bitterly rejects Siegfried's taunts.[4] But Weber's discussion relies on a somewhat obscure reading of the sequence in which the various characters speak. Actually, when Hagen speaks his words do not carry the belligerence and anger that Ortwin's do in strophe 116 f.

121   ... "uns mac wol wesen leit,
allen dinen degenen, daz er ie gereit
durch striten her ze Rine. Er soltez haben lan.
im heten mine herren sölher leide niht getan."

 ... *"We, all your knights, have good reason to regret that he ever*
 came riding to the Rhine in a warlike mood. He should have
 refrained. My lords would never have provoked him in such a
 manner."

In fact, Hagen's speech is mild. In addition, like Ortwin he refers to Siegfried in the third person, as though his words were addressed to the Burgundians surrounding him, or else he mutters under his breath without the benefit of a specific interlocution. But whereas Ortwin speaks of opposing Siegfried alone, Hagen, as if to avoid running the risk of confronting Siegfried by himself, circumspectly speaks in the first person plural (and from within the protective circle of the Burgundians). Siegfried then taunts the very man against whom his father warned him specifically, and not until then does Gernot impose silence upon the Burgundians so that Siegfried's following taunt

125"War umbe bitet Hagene und ouch Ortwin,
 daz er niht gahet striten mit den friwenden sin,
 der er hie so manegen zen Burgonden hat?"

4 Weber, *Das Nibelungenlied*, p. 43.

*"Why is Hagen hesitating, and Ortwin with him, and why does he
not rush into battle with his friends of whom he has so many here
in the land of Burgundy?"*

remains unanswered and leaves the reader in doubt as to how Hagen
would have reacted to Siegfried's words had not Gernot intervened.
Hagen, for once, deems it good and wise to obey a king's order.

When we think of Hagen's caution in the courtyard and look
back on his speech, from which the reason for this caution was
gleaned, it becomes evident that Hagen recognizes a king – even
though a king not yet crowned – when he sees one. And if in the
courtyard Hagen is careful not to arouse Siegfried's enmity and seems
to go out of his way to avoid a confrontation, the question arises
whether he is merely prudent because he is aware of Siegfried's
formidable potential as a foe. Nothing prevents him from realizing
Siegfried's equally formidable potential as a friend and as a king.[5]
Hagen's manner of reporting on Siegfried's past leaves ample room for
the inference that Siegfried is stronger than, and by far outdoes,
Gunther. And so, what with the view of the characters in the epic that
the strongest man has the right to be king (cf. chapter IV, p. 71, and
chapter VI, p. 104), Hagen's cautious and neutral attitude is ambiguous. All we know for certain is that Hagen's bearing issues from his
determination not to aggravate Siegfried because he knows he is not
a fit match for Siegfried. Hagen may also know it to be a law of life
that sooner or later Siegfried's superiority is bound to assert itself.
He is correct: no sooner have the Burgundians begun to converse with
Siegfried than he challenges Gunther.

With these suggestions, it is questionable whether Hagen's loyalty
("triuwe") is of a high order, idealistic and not blemished by self-
interest.[6] Hagen may very well be "der völlig bedenkenlose Realpolit-

5 Mowatt and Sacker, *The Nibelungenlied*, go further and find in their note on
strophe 13 that Hagen may initially envisage establishing a homosexual relationship with Siegfried; and in note 976 they wonder whether the hunt scene is a
"homosexual hunt, with Hagen and Siegfried the two wild boars of Kriemhild's
dream ... and fatal penetration from the rear Siegfried's punishment for not caring
for Worms."
6 Bostock, "Realism," p. 206.

ker" that Dürrenmatt suggests,[7] and Beyschlag thinks he is.[8] For now Hagen is not necessarily a faithful vassal, but may serve Gunther's interests only in so far as they tend to advance his own.[9] In fact, Hagen by implication becomes a potential traitor to Gunther as well as to Siegfried.[10] The interpretation of Hagen's "disinterested loyalty" is also difficult to maintain in view of the fact that Hagen foresees and yet deliberately brings about Gunther's decapitation. Or would Bostock claim that Hagen in the final *Aventiure* sees it as his duty as a disinterested and loyal vassal to protect Gunther's honor against Gunther himself by helping him to die a hero's death?[11] The closing scene of the epic does not allow the suggestion that Hagen's fidelity lies with Gunther the man, or with Gunther the king. It lies with an obsession centering around himself in relation to the hoard and the *Tarnkappe* (cf. below).

To return to the first encounter between Hagen and Siegfried, there is not the slightest hint that Siegfried's poor manners excite Hagen's wrath. Once Siegfried has settled down and has become a member of Gunther's circle, his relationship with Hagen is smooth. In the following *Aventiure* it is Hagen who suggests that Gunther ask Siegfried for help against the Saxons (151). Hagen himself seems perfectly content and thinks it quite proper and logical that in that war he will function under Siegfried's command. Siegfried as a matter of course hands the prisoner Liudegast over to Hagen for safekeeping. And when on the battlefield the might of the Saxons becomes too overpowering after Siegfried's riding gear fails (210), Hagen comes to his aid – to be sure, not by himself, but in the protective company of Gernot, Volker, and Dankwart. Hagen and Siegfried rely on each other for help, and their relationship is untarnished by any apparent un-

---

7 Dürrenmatt, *Das Nibelungenlied*, p. 264.

8 Beyschlag, "Das Motiv der Macht," pp. 95 ff.

9 Cf. King, "Message," p. 546: "No one is likely to challenge the contention that Hagen is entirely loyal to his master ... as long, that is, as his master's interest demands the death of Siegfried."

10 Stout, *Hagene*, p. 326: "[Hagen] ist der 'vil ungetriuwe'; nicht nur Siegfried und Kriemhild, sondern das ganze Wormser Königshaus hat er verraten. Die xxv. Aventiure soll diesen Eindruck festigen und verstärken."

11 Hans Kuhn, "Der Teufel im Nibelungenlied: Zu Gunthers und Kriemhilds Tod" *ZfdA*, xciv (1965), 288, observes, "Es ist Hagen, der angeblich treueste Vasall, der Schuld am Tode seines Herren wird."

favorable opinion towards one another. Whether this mutual reliance is equatable with mutual trust is a different matter, though for Siegfried it seems to be so.

It is only in the sixth *Aventiure* – *after* Siegfried has met Kriemhild – that Hagen's words and actions relating to Siegfried acquire a different type of ambiguity. Whereas in the encounter scene Hagen was careful around the foreign visitor, he is now in favor of running the danger against which Siegfried warns when telling Gunther of Brunhild's "vreisliche sit" – another instance of an unheeded warning. In fact, Hagen's advice that Siegfried accompany Gunther to Islant (331), immediately following Siegfried's advice not to go, makes it seem that Hagen in effect confirms Gunther's plan to go. His attitude is all the more striking when we remember that before the beginning of the war against the Saxons Hagen had counseled prudence and caution, and in so doing countered and outmaneuvered Gernot, who did not wish to spend time on deliberations and preparations (151).

331"So wil ich iu daz raten," sprach do Hagene,
  "ir bittet Sivride   mit iu ze tragene
  die vil starken swaere,   daz ist nu min rat,"

"In that case," said Hagen, "I advise that you ask Siegfried to share with you the very great perils ..."

Hagen's statement has been interpreted as a reluctant assent to Gunther's plan. Nothing is further from the truth. This "acquiescence" is altogether different from Hagen's acquiescence at a later day when, after warning the Burgundians not to go to Gran (1485 ff.), he decides to join them, and takes it upon himself to lead them. As far as the trip to Islant is concerned, Hagen simply is aloof from its possible dangerous consequences. At this moment he has no reason to take for granted that he is to participate in this Islant adventure. Later there is indeed an occasion on which Hagen stays behind as caretaker; the kings go off and Hagen uses the opportunity to take the hoard from Kriemhild (1136 ff.). Regarding the Islant trip, it is Siegfried who suggests that Hagen come along *after* Gunther has been more firmly committed by Hagen's persuasion to make the trip.

Of course, Hagen's quick and effective intervention in the discussion between Siegfried and Gunther is no sign he does not think highly of Siegfried's ability to give effective aid. Physical skill and bravery are all-important for the Islant trip. If Gunther is successful and picks up an additional kingdom when acquiring Brunhild for his queen, Hagen cannot possibly lose by that. On the other hand, if Gunther is not successful and fails to return, a wealth of possibilities will become available to the caretaker in Worms.

Thus when Hagen finds out that he, too, is to go to Islant, his agile mind does not find it difficult to make its peace with this disposition of his own immediate future. For when he hears that he is to accompany Gunther (342), he has already learned that Siegfried loves Kriemhild (333), and this love presents an even greater wealth of possibilities, at the potential cost no longer of Gunther only – who may very well suffer the experiences of Brunhild's former suitors, including the last one – but also of Siegfried. Because of Siegfried's love, Hagen no longer needs to be concerned about Siegfried as a potential friend and king, or as a potential enemy. This king in love is not a desirable ally; nor is he a dangerous individual who must be placated or treated circumspectly. Instead he is now more useful than ever to further one's own (private) schemes. With this new awareness, Hagen proceeds to arrange matters as he sees fit: he advises Gunther that not Ute but Kriemhild be asked to prepare the suits for the trip to Islant (346); Hagen foresees Ute's objection that a king simply ought not seek a bride with only three men in his company. Like Etzel and Siegmund, she is of the generation that favors the arrangement of a royal marriage in a politically more orthodox and therefore more acceptable manner. As Hagen sees it, a large number of Burgundians would provide too much safety for Gunther's person.

Given all this, it is small wonder that Hagen curses Brunhild when he sees her perform in the games (438, 450): because of her unexpected threat against the lives of Gunther's companions (423), her brilliant performance in the games drastically crosses all Hagen's plans and expectations.

A little later, Hagen gives Brunhild a glib explanation as to Siegfried's whereabouts during the games. Whatever Hagen knows or suspects about the way in which Brunhild was defeated, he now wants her to be Gunther's bride and Siegfried to be Kriemhild's lover. It is therefore advantageous in Hagen's mind to offer Siegfried the opportunity to see Kriemhild. Such a meeting will further Siegfried's love and thereby enhance the opportunity to keep a check on him and to manipulate him. And thus it fits into Hagen's scheme – now focused on Siegfried and definitely decided, though in details still vague – to become an unobtrusive promoter of Siegfried's cause with Kriemhild by sending him as a messenger to Worms to announce the arrival of the travelers from Islant.

On a different plane, away from the flow of the narrative, Siegfried's service as a messenger constitutes an example of the self-revealing patterns in the epic. Siegfried "acts out" the part in which Hagen correctly typecasts him, precisely because this is the only time when he may be vaguely and uncomfortably aware of his position as a king in love: he is reluctant to go. The fact that he gives in shows that this awareness is not strong enough to cause him to consider his position more carefully, or that he is already enslaved to his love for Kriemhild.

The next possibility that Hagen has some private thought in relation to Siegfried occurs when messengers display the riches they have received from Siegfried, whom they invited to visit Worms. Seeing the gifts, Hagen speaks of Siegfried's desirable wealth and – for the first time – expresses the hope that the hoard may come to Worms (774). It is a moot question whether Hagen has allowed himself to speak the wish only because his kings are absent.

Aside from a brief mention of Hagen's function at court on the occasion of Siegfried's and Kriemhild's arrival (796), his name is not mentioned again until he and Brunhild meet after the queens' quarrel:

864 Er vragete waz ir waere,   weinende er si vant.
    do sagte si im diu maere,   er lobt' ir sa zehant
    daz ez erarnen müese   der Kriemhilde man,
    oder er wolde nimmer   dar umbe vroelich gestan.

He asked what the matter was finding her weeping. She told him the story. He promised her immediately that Kriemhild's husband would have to pay for it, or he himself could never again be happy.

Though we are left uninformed what exactly is said during that interview (cf. chapter IV, pp. 79 f.), we know that in the following council meeting Hagen's argument hinges on the claim that Brunhild has been insulted. This Gunther himself refutes by pointing out that Siegfried has brought Worms nothing but honor (868 ff.). Giselher is of the same opinion (866), and nobody aside from Hagen and Ortwin (cf. 870) claims that Siegfried must die.

The conclusion is clear: Hagen's reason for wishing Siegfried's death has nothing to do with his professed conviction that Siegfried

insulted Brunhild. Whatever Brunhild tells Hagen during their interview, the fact remains that Hagen did not care for Brunhild in the past
and may never have changed his mind.[12] She is the first person in the
epic who qualified for the epithet "devil" and that designation came
from Hagen's lips. Besides, Brunhild in Islant insulted Hagen with her
nonchalant and mocking look over the shoulder (447), and – in a world
in which people bear grudges for decades on end – Hagen is the least
likely person to forgive and forget such an insult. Furthermore, if we
remember Beyschlag's suggestion that the epic deals with the celebration of the court nobility,[13] then it is precisely Brunhild – as delineated
in the preceding chapters – who best represents authoritative kingship
backed by power. Against her, Hagen, the main representative of the
self-assertive nobility, would wish to take care of his own interests.[14]
The only subsequent use Hagen makes of his interview with Brunhild
is to advance reasons for wishing Siegfried punished, but the reasons
are confused and somewhat contradictory. One moment it is that
Siegfried has become too powerful and dangerous (993); the next,
that Kriemhild insulted Brunhild (1790). Over against these specious
claims made by Hagen (why after all should he kill Siegfried who
after the visit would return to Santen and thus pose no danger for
Worms, or why should Siegfried die for the insult which Kriemhild
had flung into Brunhild's face and which had been vindicated by
Gunther?) the poet's own statement indicates explicitly that Brunhild
counseled Siegfried's death (917).[15]

In addition, Hagen himself does not believe in Siegfried's guilt regarding Brunhild, no matter what she tells him when relating "diu
maere." If Gunther has claimed Siegfried's innocence, why should
Hagen doubt it? Would not Gunther be the first to defend his own
honor, no matter how weak and inconsequential his attempt? He did
not make such an attempt, but instead vindicated Siegfried in public,
thus providing Hagen – as well as the rest of the court – with the sound-
est proof against this ridiculous suspicion the whole court was talking

12 It is generally thought that by becoming Gunther's queen Brunhild automatically acquires Hagen's loyalty. See, e.g., Mueller, *The Nibelungenlied Today*,
p. 15.
13 Beyschlag, "Ueberlieferung," pp. 211 f.
14 See, e.g., Singer, "The Hunting Contest," pp. 177 f.
15 See also strophes 1001, 1610, 1785.

about. (It is this vagueness regarding Hagen's awareness – or lack of it – of what happened in the Islant games and in Brunhild's bedroom that indicates the poet's sovereign manner of rearranging old story motifs into a new pattern with new meaning.) But Hagen needs no proof of Siegfried's guilt or innocence; he wants none. The less he hears explained, the better. Explanation is impossible in the first place; and in the second, troubled waters make for good fishing. By hearing less about the quarrel, Hagen has at least the semblance of correctness when he leaps to the "defense" of Brunhild and proclaims his conviction that Siegfried must be punished.[16]

Thus seen, Hagen's rhetorical question, "suln wir gouche ziehen?"/"*Shall we raise bastards?*" (867) asks precisely what it seems to ask. "Gouche" does not refer to Siegfried but to his possible future bastards – it is none of Hagen's concern that the question casts a dubious light on Brunhild (from the point of view of Worms).[17]

Hagen's scheme leads him to a second and more persuasive argument why Siegfried must die. For, Nagel's opinion to the contrary,[18] it is not the court but Hagen who makes that decision and after some effort persuades Gunther. Hagen is aided only by Ortwin, who has his own reason for getting rid of Siegfried (cf. chapter IX, p. 159). But, like his proclaimed intention to defend Brunhild's honor, Hagen's reminder that Siegfried's death would gain territorial power for Gunther (870) is but a smoke screen to hide his private intentions.

In this connection, Singer's suggestion comes to mind: "Our poet deliberately employs a Hagen with little reason to kill Siegfried and less to play with him beforehand. This Hagen becomes an instrument, helping fate to a triumph which abysmally undermines those of which a courtly Siegfried is capable."[19] It is true that Hagen is an instrument. In fact, there is ample room for the contention that he is an instrument in much the same way Siegfried is. Like Siegfried – who "playfully seconds fate in its game with him" – Hagen, too, in the end helps fate

---

16 Wachinger, *Studien*, p. 115, also believes that Hagen does not *want* to know the truth.

17 See in this connection L.L. Hammerich, "Zu *Nibelungenlied* 867," *Neophilologus*, XVI (1931), 96 ff. Mowatt and Sacker, *The Nibelungenlied*, note 870, see matters somewhat differently.

18 Nagel, "Probleme," p. 64.

19 Singer, "The Hunting Contest," p. 180.

to work itself out, also against himself (cf. chapter VIII, p. 148). In this connection also, it is good to remember that – to paraphrase Singer[20] – the subtlety of thought inherent in the design of the *Nibelungenlied* is beyond Hagen, and this subtlety arises from the poet's own grand conception of his work. It does not follow, however, that "the poet fully intends the irrational element to dominate our impression of the murder"[21] by failing to provide Hagen with a good reason to kill Siegfried.

Nor does it follow, however, that Hagen's antagonism towards Siegfried is fed by a *personal* hatred, as Naumann suggests: "Hagen greift zu, der geringfügige Anlass, an dem sich sein verstockter Hass entzünden kann, ist endlich da."[22] In this regard too, Hagen "simply does not care"[23] – this is his demonic nature.

Hagen's first mention of the desirability that the hoard come to Worms (774) is not followed in the council meeting by a reference to the gold. This is startling: Hagen speaks to Gunther of territorial gains but does not say a word about the tremendous wealth that could come Gunther's way. And then we remember that it is Hagen rather than the Burgundian kings – who are never closely associated with the hoard – who manages to get the gold to Worms by manipulating the aid of Gernot and Giselher. Salmon says: "It is not clear why Hagen takes the treasure; he must have foreseen how Kriemhild would use it once it had been brought to Worms: the brothers were safe from revenge once they were reconciled to Kriemhild, and Hagen was safe in their protection."[24] To this we can say that Hagen is not only a clever schemer, he is also a careful one, and he would not take steps for the hoard to come to Worms on the outside chance that Kriemhild's use of it would give him reason to urge the kings that it should be taken from her. Instead, he gets the hoard to Worms because he is the grand manipulator of people as well as events,[25] fully confident that he can create a situation in which he can take the hoard unpunished.

20 *Ibid.*, p. 176.

21 *Ibid.*, p. 180, note 49.

22 Naumann, "Brünhilts Gürtel," p. 48.

23 Singer, "The Hunting Contest," p. 179.

24 Salmon, "Why Must Hagen Die?" pp. 6 f.

25 This in possible contrast to Singer, "The Hunting Contest"; Hagen manipulates not only Siegfried but up to a point (cf. chapter VIII, pp. 140 ff.) everybody and everything.

The poet of the *Nibelungenlied* has supplied two explicit indications of Hagen's position in relation to the hoard. Having sunk the gold into the Rhine, he is said to hope that he can make use of it in the future, but it is a vain hope: "des enkunde niht gesin" (1137). Three strophes later we hear that Hagen and the kings swear to keep the whereabouts of the hoard secret until only one of them remains alive, "unz ir einer möhte leben." Does strophe 1137 indicate that Hagen is prepared to break the oath mentioned in 1140? Or does 1140 suggest that Hagen is confident that the three kings will die before him?

However that may be, a few strophes earlier Alberich speaks a few interesting lines:

1120"Nu ist ez Sifride   leider übel komen,
        daz uns die tarnkappen   het der helt benomen
        unt daz im muose dienen   allez ditze lant."

"Unfortunately, Siegfried ended badly because he took the cloak away from us, so that all these lands had to serve him."

According to Alberich, the *Tarnkappe* was the cause of Siegfried's death. De Boor interprets this strophe as referring to Siegfried's function in the bridal chamber,[26] but his interpretation solves nothing, since for all we know only Siegfried knew of the role which the *Kappe* played in that event. Besides, as we have seen in the previous chapters, Siegfried did *not* die as a consequence of helping Gunther in the bridal chamber, and the Boor's view does not explain Hagen's systematically provoking Kriemhild's hatred after Siegfried is gone (cf. below). Read as it is written, however, Alberich's strophe simply states that Siegfried died because he had become the owner of the *Kappe*. Siegfried, then, died because someone else wanted the *Kappe*. And now, the mosaic of Hagen's seeming confusion about his reasons for wishing Siegfried's death becomes meaningful. It explains why in the council meeting Hagen does not say a word about the hoard and the *Kappe*, even though we know that from his first encounter with Siegfried his words and actions have been colored by an awareness of these possessions. We now understand why Hagen, who again and again acts contrary to his kings' wishes, and does it with impunity, this time needs a semblance of correctness: his true motivations for wishing

26 De Boor, *Deutsche Klassiker*, note to 1120.

Siegfried's death are not to the benefit of his kings, and he wishes them to remain unknown. We now realize also that what Hagen had to say in the recognition scene was of consequence not only for the presentation of information about how Siegfried acquired *Kappe*, hoard, and invulnerability, but also for the presentation of Hagen himself in so far as his speech reveals (in retrospect) his immediate and lasting preoccupation with the *Kappe* and the hoard.[27]

From Alberich's strophe it follows that for Hagen the *Tarnkappe* constitutes and represents the essence of the hoard. Hagen is not the only one to view the *Kappe* in this manner. When Gernot and Giselher come to fetch the hoard, Alberich tells his comrades that he is willing to surrender the gold because it belongs to Kriemhild by right, and particularly because the *Tarnkappe* is gone anyway:

1118 "Wir turren ir des hordes   vor gehaben niht,
    sit sin ze morgengabe   diu edel küneginne giht,

  "Doch wurdez nimmer,"   sprach Albrich, "getan,
  niwan daz wir übele   da verlorn han
  mit samt Sifride   die guoten tarnhut,
  want die truoc alle zite   der schoenen Kriemhilde trut."

"We cannot keep the hoard away from her, since the noble queen received it as her Morgengabe.

"Yet," said Alberich, "it would never happen, if we unfortunately had not lost, together with Siegfried, the good cloak, for the beauteous Kriemhild's beloved wore it all the time.

27 Wachinger, *Studien*, p. 99, finds that the hoard is important only in "part II." The present chapter, however, considers the hoard to be important to Hagen throughout the *Nibelungenlied*. Stout, *Hagene*, p. 295, finds that the hoard "als letzte Waffe Kriemhilds, als letztes Drohmittel gegen Hagen, der Sage von Siegfrieds Tod angehängt wurde," and he claims "Hort bleibt Hort, Gold bleibt Gold." But see chapter III, p. 67, for the symbolic significance the hoard acquires in the closing *Aventiure*. See also chapter VI, p. 104, for the twofold value acquired by the hoard-*Tarnkappe* complex. On the hoard, see Hilda S. Ellis, "The Hoard of the Nibelungs," *MLR*, XXXVII (1942), 466–79; Hans Kuhn, "Kriemhilds Hort und Rache," in: *Festschrift für P. Gluckhohn und H. Schneider* (Tübingen, 1948), pp.

This strophe tells us that for Alberich the hoard without *Kappe* is no more than a tremendous heap of gold – to which Kriemhild is welcome. Though it is still of consequence – after all, it incorporates the wishing rod (1124) – it is no longer the same hoard as when it was owned by the possessor of the *Kappe*. Siegfried, too, had considered the *Kappe* more important than the hoard (cf. chapter III, p. 68).

It is thus Hagen's perpetual concern with the *Kappe* and the hoard that suggests his attitude towards Brunhild as well as to his kings in the council meeting. And the utter brevity of the strophe in which Brunhild is said to tell him "diu maere" (864) is no longer of any consequence in so far as our understanding of Hagen's role in this meeting is concerned. By hindsight we learn from it that Hagen's loyalty to all of Worms' royal family is doubtful and that his interest in the hoard is strictly personal and not for the sake of his kings.

It is the implication of these remarks regarding Hagen's determination to make the *Tarnkappe* and the hoard his own that provides the only plausible explanation why Hagen is as adamant towards Kriemhild as he was against Siegfried. That Kriemhild would hate him violently after he had killed Siegfried is natural, but this does not explain why Hagen systematically and deliberately provokes her hatred after Siegfried is gone. Now, in connection with the hoard, the reason for this provocation becomes clear: Kriemhild, too, on the basis of her claim to the hoard as her *Morgengabe*, is the owner of a power which Hagen would like to make his own.

This power is visual and "external"; it is not identical with the invisible power accompanying the ownership of the *Kappe* (cf., in this connection, the twofold value of the *Kappe* – hoard complex as delineated in chapter VI, pp. 104 ff.). The invisible power is of greater magnitude and desirability. The difference is of consequence in revealing why Hagen – who prefers to remain "unknown" (cf. chapter VIII, p. 136) – is preoccupied with the *Kappe* as well as the hoard. On a different plane, this difference constitutes an allusion to Kriemhild's tendency to attach importance to outward display and to identify it with innate qualities.

Hagen, then, may be able to handle and manipulate Gunther and

84 ff.; H.W.J. Kroes, "Die Sage vom Nibelungenhort und ihr mythischer Hintergrund," in: *Festgabe für Th. Frings* (Berlin, 1956), pp. 323-37; G. Eis, "Die Hortforderung"; W. Schröder, "Tragödie"; and Weber, *Das Nibelungenlied*, pp. 13 ff.

his brothers, and he may have done his share to relegate Brunhild to the sideline long before she tells him "diu maere," but Kriemhild, like Siegfried,[28] is a different matter. The latter was an imposing rival due to his ownership of the *Tarnkappe*; Kriemhild is formidable because she owns the hoard. This supplies the most plausible reason why the poet – once again treating his sources freely to suit his own purposes and designs – has the hoard figure as Siegfried's *Morgengabe* to Kriemhild. With the hoard in her possession, given Hagen's desire for it, he becomes inevitably her implacable enemy.

And so we must conclude that Brunhild's and Hagen's reasons for wishing Siegfried's death, though very different, issue from the same discovery: each of them sees Siegfried as a king whose error is his love for Kriemhild and his consequent failure to assert his status as the strongest king. This discovery leads Brunhild to the decision that Siegfried must die because he violated kingship, and it leads Hagen to the same conclusion because Siegfried's death will facilitate the acquisition of the hoard. That this common decision does not constitute a close alliance – mutual understanding and help and "triuwe" – between them is indicated by the fact that Hagen, after he discovers Siegfried's love for Kriemhild, fosters that love as much as he is able in order to benefit his own purposes, whereas Brunhild – in retrospect and in order to serve kingship – would rewrite history in order to blot out that love. From this point of view also, Siegfried's love for Kriemhild inevitably determines that he be destroyed by the grinding mill of Brunhild's and Hagen's inadvertent and accidental cooperation.

28 There is no contradiction here with Singer's view in "The Hunting Contest" that Siegfried dances to Hagen's tune. The view of Siegfried as an impossible opponent relates only to the fact that he has the *Kappe*.

viii

HAGEN
IN RELATION
TO MINOR
CHARACTERS

FROM THE PREVIOUS CHAPTER Hagen begins to emerge as a figure without redeeming or praiseworthy features. His ability to manipulate makes him a potential traitor to all and everything. That he feels an affinity to traitors becomes apparent in his encounter with Eckewart. The scene between them at the border of Rüdeger's domains is not at all a little idyll introducing the greater idyll of Bechlaren immediately following, but presents a small-time traitor coming into his own when faced with a more exalted member of the guild. The following comments support this suggestion.

Sacker[1] has dealt with Hagen's experiences before and after the Danube crossing, and Bumke[2] has treated Siegfried's trip to the land of the Nibelungs as related in the eighth *Aventiure*. For the present argument the similarities between some of the details in their findings, though resulting from totally different approaches are of interest because they provide several examples of the parallelistic device. Siegfried changes his voice when calling at the castle door of the Nibelungs (487), has his encounter with the giant who is armed with an iron rod, and fears his opponent. He then meets the guard of the hoard, Alberich. Whatever else we learn from these scenes, they emphasize the loyalty of the giant as well as of the dwarf to their master Siegfried.

Hagen also has two encounters. In the first, like Siegfried, he pretends to be someone other than himself (1552) and meets the ferry-man, who turns out to be quite dangerous and manages to give Hagen a blow with his oar. This encounter with the ferryman parallels Siegfried's with the giant, but there is a difference that reflects on Siegfried

1 Sacker, "Irony and Symbolism."
2 Bumke, "Sigfrids Fahrt."

and Hagen: Siegfried taunts his opponent and in the end binds him; Hagen uses at first a friendly approach but in the end kills his opponent.

Hagen's second encounter, with Eckewart, parallels Siegfried's encounter with Alberich. And again there is a reversal in the parallelism. Alberich is alert and unquestionably loyal; Eckewart is less than alert, and it is debatable whether he is unquestionably loyal as Panzer suggests.[3] Eckewart's reaction to the gift proffered by Hagen is cast into relief by the attitude struck by the ferryman – whom Hagen also attempts to "buy," and who is also a border guard. To the ferryman the proffered gift is tempting – for love's sake (cf. 1554) – but does not have the desired effect, since Else's man refuses to betray the trust of his master. True, Hagen says he admires Eckewart for guarding the frontier all alone (1634); presumably he also admired the ferryman whom he killed for carrying out that same duty alertly and faithfully – but the fact remains that Hagen finds Eckewart sleeping. The latter, as soon as he has received Hagen's six armbands, warns the Burgundian against going to Gran (1635). The contrast in bearing between the giant, Alberich, and the ferryman on the one hand, and Eckewart on the other, does little to make the reader think highly of Eckewart's faithfulness to Kriemhild at this stage of his career. Panzer's view that Eckewart is "der getreue Eckard" may apply to the earlier Eckewart, but it sheds a glaring light on this warning to Hagen.

Incidentally, there are fascinating implications in the fact that Siegfried first pretends to be unknown in the land of the Nibelungs and then reveals himself. Elsewhere, too, he is recognized: Hagen recognizes him for what he is (after Siegfried has fallen in love), and so does Brunhild. Siegfried himself recognizes neither Brunhild – as the upholder of kingship – nor Hagen " 'het ich an iu erkennet den mortlichen sit ...' "/" 'Had I recognized your murderous intent ...' " (994). He fails also to recognize Gunther's friendship for what it is. In contrast, Hagen pretends to be known to the Bavarian ferryman and turns out to be someone else. Kriemhild thinks also she knows him when she tells him of Siegfried's vulnerable spot; she is grossly mistaken. Hagen himself not only recognizes Siegfried's qualities, but also those of Eckewart. To know and to recognize and to remain unknown; not to know and not to recognize and to be known: these two sets of criteria define to an important degree the interrelationships be-

3 For Panzer, *Das Nibelungenlied*, p. 392, Eckewart is "der getreue Eckard."

tween the characters in the *Nibelungenlied*. Those that apply to Hagen might also describe Iago's relations with Othello and Desdemona.

In the above connection, it is tempting to explain Rüdeger's baffling silence regarding the danger threatening the Burgundians in the land of Etzel by contrasting that silence to Eckewart's lack of reserve. The fact that Rüdeger, like Dietrich, exhorts his retainers not to participate in Gran's joust (cf. 1887) indicates that he is aware of brewing enmity. Is Rüdeger's silence to be interpreted as a type of loyalty to his liege lady, does he not see fit to give a warning that would stamp him as a traitor,[4] and does he hope that somehow peace and harmony will be retained if he says nothing? Rüdeger, we know, painstakingly guards his honor; it has been suggested that this very concern with his "ere" constitutes his flaw and becomes the cause of his death.[5] That Dietrich warns the Burgundians is a different matter; he is a king in his own right, and though he is obliged to his host Etzel, he owes nothing to Kriemhild, who arrived in Gran long after Dietrich had established himself as one of the most important persons in Etzel's entourage.

To return to Hagen, not only his faithfulness, but also his physical valor is less than surface reading suggests. Weber's claim that Hagen is a man "der ohne Waffen nicht zu denken ist,"[6] suggests a figure who will live up to the highest expectations regarding his ability with weapons. And to be sure, the reader, swept along by the ever faster pace of the narrative, *is* left with the impression that Hagen is awe-inspiring. But it is also true that Hagen does not differ in this respect from other Burgundians, and if we refuse to become giddy in the barrage of superlatives applied to Hagen as a warrior, we may begin to wonder whether Hagen is really as awesome as Weber's reading suggests. It turns out that Hagen's stature as a warrior is marred if we allow ourselves to become so steeped in the epic that we can take the narrative for granted and read for the sake of acquainting ourselves with the poet's manner of portrayal, and if we pay close heed to exactly what happens in certain circumstances involving Hagen, how it happens, and why it happens.

4 Kriemhild later does speak of the informer as a traitor (cf. 2228 f.).
5 Jones, "Rüdiger's Dilemma."
6 Weber, *Das Nibelungenlied*, p. 43. Mowatt and Sacker, *The Nibelungenlied*, note 447, agree: "Hagen armed is a threat to any man but Siegfried."

Some remarks in the preceding chapter have made it clear that Hagen feels inferior to Siegfried in skill with arms. Nowhere in the *Nibelungenlied* is this awareness more clearly established than in Siegfried's death scene, in which Hagen not only "acts out" the traitor by fleeing, but also acts out his inferiority, if not cowardice.

In addition, also after Siegfried is gone, Hagen's physical bravery with weapons does not always come through convincingly. In Bavaria, for example, when confronted by Gelfrat, he is unhorsed (1610). Gelfrat apparently dismounts voluntarily so that Hagen in the ensuing struggle on foot is in as favorable a position as his gallant adversary. But as a fighter on foot Hagen is not the best – in contrast to Siegfried in his encounters with the giant and Alberich (cf. 489 ff.), and in contrast to Dietrich in his encounters with Hagen and Gunther (cf. 2348 ff.). Hagen gets into dire straits and must call on Dankwart for help. Dankwart needs only one sword blow to kill Gelfrat (1614). Before that skirmish Hagen was almost killed by the ferryman (1560 f.), though the latter was not conventionally armed. Later, in Gran, it is Volker rather than Hagen whom Kriemhild regards as the more dreadful foe (1768), and the Huns' admiration for Hagen is based on dated feats of valor. It is true that in Gran Hagen manages to kill some outstanding warriors, Iring for instance. Iring also fought with Volker, Gunther, and Gernot without wounding any of them, and he is killed by Hagen not in a face-to-face battle, but by a javelin. Since Iring has his back to his opponent, Hagen's act requires no more valor than when he killed Siegfried.

For that matter, of all the named persons in the *Nibelungenlied* only Siegfried and Iring are killed by spears; Hagen is the killer of each. By way of contrast, one other spear thrown by a Burgundian whom we know by name – aside from the spear used in the Islant games – is Volker's. He picks up a spear and:

2018 Den schoz er krefteclichen   durch die burc dan
     über daz volc vil verre.   den Etzelen man
     gab er herberge   hoher von dem sal.
     sin vil starkez ellen   diu liuten vorhten über al.

He threw it powerfully through the courtyard over the heads of
the crowd, causing the Huns to retreat further away from the hall.
People feared his tremendous strength above all.
murderous Hagen

The impression evoked in this strophe is one of haughty but genuine superiority. And an earlier strophe suggests that the use of spears is an inferior mode of fighting:

1944 Er leidete sich so sere   den Etzelen man
    daz si in mit swerten   torsten niht bestan.
    do schuzzen si der gere   so vil in sinen rant
    daz er in durch die swaere   muose lazen von der hant.

He made himself so hateful to Etzel's men that they did not dare
to oppose him with their swords. Instead they threw many spears
into his shield, until it became so heavy he had to drop it.

All in all, Weber's claim that after Iring's death Hagen stands "un-überwindbar" loads the dice in favor of Hagen.

Hagen, then, is not quite the warrior that a cursory reading suggests. His feats in Gran's banquet hall, because of the circumstances in which the Huns are slain (chapter II, pp. 36 ff.) are of doubtful value. This is particularly so in the strophe that on first reading seems to show him to be fully superior:

1980 Do von Tronege Hagene   die tür sah so behuot,
    den schilt warf do ze rucke   der maere degen guot.
    alrerst begond' er rechen   daz im da was getan.
    do heten sine viende   ze lebene deheiner slahte wan.

When Hagen of Tronje saw the door so well guarded, the splendid
fighting man threw his shield on his back. Now he began in earnest
to revenge what had been done to him, so that his enemies gave
up all hope of living.

It is to a significant degree the Miltonic device that presents a Hagen "der ohne Waffen nicht zu denken ist," but with Hagen particularly the device rings hollow, since his gesture occurs when his opponents are apparently unarmed. As Stout has reminded us: "Ohne Volker wäre Hagen von Kriemhilds 'scar' getötet worden."[7] And yet Hagen manipulates Volker as well, as the following remarks show.

The deepest emotion of which Hagen is capable would seem to

7 Stout, *Hagene*, p. 363.

be his love for Volker. Theirs is the mutual affection of warriors who die together against odds. The intensity of this feeling comes to exclude all other values, and it rises to a prodigality of service. But here is a problem. Whereas some such remarks come close to constituting the evaluation usually made about the relationship between Hagen and Volker, the service rendered is Volker's, and it remains to be seen what he receives in return. It is in this sense that there is a degree of parallelism prevailing between Volker and Siegfried. Siegfried is to Gunther a trusting and trusted friend. Gunther is of course different. And Hagen with respect to Volker?

The first indication of a developing bond between Hagen and Volker is found in the statement that Volker heartily approves of Hagen's destruction of the boat in which the Burgundians have crossed the Danube:

1584 Si fuorten mit in einen   uz Burgonden lant,
     einen helt ze sinen handen   der was Volker genant.
     der redete spaeheliche   allen sinen muot.
     swaz ie begie her Hagene,   daz duht' den videlaere guot.

They had with them one from Burgundy, who was called Volker,
a hero untarnished. He spoke thoughtfully whatever was in his
mind. Whatever lord Hagen did, the fiddler thought it good.

Volker does not express this approval; the poet merely tells us about it. Hagen, we may gather, strikes a haughty pose, unconcerned that as far as he knows nobody approves of his action. Meanwhile, Volker's silence towards "her Hagene" suggests a certain subservience. Their sitting at different tables during the banquet (2005) suggests also a difference in status that is of consequence in the stratified world of Worms. This is perhaps the reason why Weber sees fit to speak of the "Strahlungskraft der Freundschaft" between Volker and Hagen, and can add as afterthought: "Aber doch hat Hagen die Führung [Volkers] fest in der Hand."[8]

There are some details about the relationship as it develops between Volker and Hagen:

8 Weber, *Das Nibelungenlied*, p. 60 f.

1758 Do schieden sich die zwene   recken lobelich,
　　Hagene von Tronege   unt ouch her Dietrich.
　　do blihte über ahsel   der Guntheres man
　　nach einem hergesellen,   den er vil schiere gewan.

　　Then the two heroes – Hagen of Tronje and lord Dietrich – went
　　their individual ways. Gunther's man looked over his shoulder
　　for a comrade-in-arms; he very quickly found him.

Hagen's choice of a comrade-in-arms has fallen on Volker, "wand' er
vil wol erkande   sinen grimmen muot"/"*for he well knew his fierce
courage*" (1759). There is no hint of any particularly warm feelings
on Hagen's part. He merely picks the man who he thinks will suit his
purpose best. That his choice is a good one is indicated by Kriemhild:

1768"Swie starc unt swie küene   von Tronege Hagene si,
　　noch ist verre sterker,   der im da sitzet bi,
　　Volker der videlaere,   der ist ein übel man."

　　"*However strong and brave Hagen of Tronje may be, much*
　　stronger still is the one sitting beside him, Volker the fiddler; he is
　　a terrible man."

Her judgment is borne out by Volker's role as a genuinely able warrior.
　　Kriemhild's approach leads Hagen to propose a bond:

1777"Nu saget mir, vriunt Volker,   ob ir mir welt gestan,
　　ob wellent mit mir striten   die Kriemhilde man?
　　daz lazet ir mich hoeren,   als lieb als ich iu si.
　　ich won' iu immer mere   mit triuwen dienstlichen bi."

　　"*Now tell me, friend Volker, whether you will stand beside me, and*
　　will fight with me against Kriemhild's men. Let me know your
　　answer, by the love you bear me, and I shall stand by you faith-
　　fully forever."

Volker accepts (1778). Hagen's request at this stage amounts to an
endeavor to get someone on his side, even though as far as he knows
(cf. 1776), Kriemhild at first is only interested in killing him. Though
Kriemhild is prepared to view Volker as another enemy (cf. 1768),

Volker and Hagen do not become certain of that until later, when Volker says:

1800   ... "wir haben daz wol ersehen,
        daz wir nie vinde vinden,   als wir e horten jehen.
        wir suln zuo den künegen   hin ze hove gan,
        sone tar unser herren   mit strite niemen bestan."

> ... "we have seen clearly that we shall find enemies here, as we were
> told before. We should go to the kings at court; then nobody will
> dare attack our lords."

In this strophe, incidentally, Volker is more concerned with the welfare of his kings than is Hagen.

Afterwards, having cast his lot with Hagen and becoming most avid to treat the Huns insultingly and with disdain, Volker is the first to enter with Hagen into that realm in which annihilation holds sway, and from which there is no returning. Volker soon is the bloodthirstiest of the Burgundians, eager to rush headlong into battle. It is Volker who becomes angry because the Huns are crowding around them and staring (1820 f.). Such staring occured also in Worms (74), in Islant (408), and again in Worms (768), but there nobody took issue with it.

The general thrust of Weber's discussion on Volker shows that the appeal of Hagen to Volker depends on nihilistic traits. A bond between these two Burgundians can therefore not engage the whole Volker. The artist in him becomes a mere metaphor for destruction and is subservient to the glory of his bloody, smoking sword.[9] Whereas even in Gran, Volker's strings are used to take the dread out of the night (1834 f.), Etzel comes to pronounce judgment over Volker's artistry, and thereby over Volker himself, by linking a satanic quality to his ability to "make music." The contrast evoked with Etzel's "Heil," Dietrich von Bern, turns Etzel's metaphor into more than a metaphor; it lays bare Volker's essence, as Etzel sees it:

2001"Ach we der hohgezite,"   sprach der künec her.
    "da vihtet einer inne,   der heizet Volker,
        als ein eber wilde,   und ist ein spilman,
        ich dankes minem heile,   daz ich dem tiuvel entran.

9 On this point Weber, *Das Nibelungenlied*, pp. 59 f., has a totally different view.

"Cursed be this feast," the king said, "a man called Volker fights in there like a wild boar, and he is a minstrel. I bless my good fortune that I got away from the devil."

Incidentally, Panzer has this view of "Heil": "[Germanische Kontinuität] zeigt sich nicht minder lebendig, wenn den Königen ein vor bösen Schicksalsschlägen sicherndes 'Heil' zugeschrieben wird, das von ihnen auch auf ihre Gefolgsleute auszustrahlen vermag."[10] In the cited strophe, however, it is Etzel, a king, who speaks of his "Heil" at a moment when he has the protective arm of another king around his shoulder. Panzer's definition hardly seems to apply to this particular instance of the "Heil" motif.

Meanwhile, it is Etzel's doom on Volker's artistry that invalidates Schröder's suggestion that the poet reflects himself in his delineation of Volker.[11]

Later, after Volker has been slain, Hagen does not lament the loss of a friend, but says:

2290 "Nune sol es niht geniezen   der alte Hildebrant.
    min helfe lit erslagen   von des heldes hant,
    der beste hergeselle,   den ich ie gewan."

"Old Hildebrand will not outlive this. My helper is slain by the hero, the best comrade-in-arms I ever had."

There is no hint of any particularly warm personal feelings on Hagen's part.

It is true, then, that Hagen's deftness in handling people for his own purposes is evident not only from his visits to Brunhild (863 f.) and Kriemhild (891 ff.), and from the way he manipulates Siegfried, but also in the manner in which he deals with Volker.[12] But what of Hagen's relationship with other persons? Gotelind for instance brings to mind the scene in which we are susceptible to the grace of the receiver that corresponds to the finesse of gesture with which Gotelind's "vil wize hand" (1701) takes Nudung's shield off the wall and gives it to

10 Panzer, *Das Nibelungenlied*, pp. 208 f.
11 W.J. Schröder, *Das Nibelungenlied*, pp. 74 f.
12 Does the loss of Wärbel's hand (1964) constitute an allusion to Hagen's effect on the artistry of Volker as well?

Hagen. This is courtly form at its best and we esteem Gotelind for it, and think highly of Hagen for being such a good receiver. Though not qualified to bear the title in the political sense, Gotelind here is all queen, with true because simple majesty. The rich little scene is one of the most memorable in the *Nibelungenlied*.

And yet, at the core of this scene stands a nagging question. Why does Hagen *ask* for a shield? He is the only Burgundian to do so. And why is his request not for a helmet, a suit of armor, or some other useful piece of equipment? Even though the scene is impressive, the gift of a shield appears repetitive, because we know that a second shield will shortly be given as well, and it is not at all clear how the poet gains by this episode. For the moment he must receive the benefit of the doubt, however, and we must assume that the shield motif, and the fact that in each instance the gift is asked for, is significant rather than a casual repetition within the space of a few *Aventiure*.

Whereas Wapnewski[13] has taught us something about the meaning of Rüdeger's shield gift to Hagen, we have no such evaluations about Gotelind's other than the opinion that it constitutes the most memorable example of the idyll worked into the Bechlaren episodes. It would seem, however, that Hagen's request to Gotelind establishes a bond between himself and Bechlaren, all the more significant because of the feeling which Gotelind has for the shield (cf. 1699 f.). To quote Wapnewski when he speaks of Rüdeger's gift:

> Schenken ist Friede und Bündnis. ... Bei einer solchen Uebertragung aber geschieht mehr als die blosse Ueberreichung eines äusseren Besitzes. Das Geschenk hat eine "Seele," trägt ein Teil dessen in sich, der es besass, und wird diese Seele offenbaren.
> Die Gabe stiftet zwischen dem Gebenden und dem Empfangenden ein innigeres Verhältnis, das gegenseitig verpflichtet. Diese Verbindung vertieft sich und wird offenbar in der Uebertragung der Wesenhaftigkeit des Besitzers.[14]

Wapnewski conveys some of the portent of the scene between Hagen and Rüdeger. Not only Rüdeger but also Hagen is raised to a height of

13 P. Wapnewski, "Rüdigers Schild: Zur 37. Aventiure des *Nibelungenliedes*," *Euphorion*, LIV (1960), 380–410.
14 *Ibid.*, p. 399.

nobility that he does not attain elsewhere, unless in the shield scene with Gotelind. Perhaps we are to view the scene with Rüdeger as a type of conversion scene; Hagen seems to blot out in one titanic self-saving gesture the reprehensible qualities he has displayed heretofore. If this were so, it would be awkward to remember that the gift leaves Rüdeger, who faces a battle for his life, without the protection of his shield. The fact that Rüdeger picks up another shield before rushing into battle, however, indicates that the shield gift to Hagen is important primarily because of its symbolic value. This preoccupation with the symbolic significance leads the poet to be inconsistent on the narrative level – "*den* schilt huop Rüedeger" (italics added).

Hagen, on the other hand, uses the newly acquired shield to protect himself against Rüdeger's men and therefore, though indirectly, against Rüdeger himself. The poet thus moves from the symbolic back to the narrative consequences of this scene. The irony coming to the fore here is more sardonic than that detectable in Rüdeger's death by the very sword he has given to Gernot. Hagen's request for the shield may constitute a type of salvation for Rüdeger, but it also facilitates his death, and Hagen may be said to be partly responsible for it,[15] as he has been said to be responsible for the death of Gernot as a result of his neutrality towards Rüdeger. At any rate, the scene with Rüdeger is ambiguous if we think not only of the symbolic value that renders Hagen's request positive and noble, but also of the concomitant effect it has on Rüdeger's speedy end.

This shift from the symbolic interpretation to that of the level of the narrative flow is warranted, since the poet himself does it consistently. His symbolism, to be sure, is seldom allowed to interfere with the story, but obviously it is at times more important than the narrative itself.[16]

Of course, the difficulty with Wapnewski's view of Rüdeger's shield gift lies with the fact that it assumes Hagen to be susceptible

15 Renoir, "*Nibelungenlied,*" has shown that in addition, with an interpretation leading beyond the *Nibelungenlied,* Hagen may be seen to emerge from the shield scene with Rüdeger as a figure acquiring reprehensible traits.

16 Cf. chapter IX, p. 150. On Rüdeger's shield gift, see also K.J. Jeismann, "Rüedegers Schildgabe oder der Gehalt der Modi: Ein Unterrichtsversuch," *DU,* XIII (1961), 56–62; Hans Naumann, "Höfische Symbolik: Rüedegers Tod," *DVLG,* X (1932), 387–403.

to, and to abide by, the values accompanying the receiving of a gift – as envisioned by Wapnewski. But Hagen may be far from entering into the spirit of such a gift. It is only a small step from his disregard of the crown on Kriemhild's head to the violation of the symbolic power of gifts received.[17]

In this manner, doubt oscillates in our minds because of the ambivalence in Rüdeger's shield scene, an ambivalence emphasized by the fact that the Burgundian kings' appeal to Rüdeger not to fight them hinges on the claim that Rüdeger, because of his hospitality in Bechlaren, is in bondage to them and has the duty of that bondage. As the exchange between the kings and Rüdeger clearly indicates, Rüdeger himself considers the kings' claim valid (cf. 2177 ff.).

If we return to Gotelind's gift we may find in Hagen's request to her implications similar to those rendering the shield scene with Rüdeger ambiguous. For Nudung's shield, too, is a symbol an sich, a symbol of protection, and Gotelind symbolically surrenders that protection, never to see it again, in the same manner in which she presently separates from Bechlaren's protector, never to see him again. Here, too, Hagen's request, symbolically understood (and how else can we evaluate it?), leaves Bechlaren defenseless.

We may also consider Giselher's engagement to Rüdeger's daughter. It is Hagen who proposes the betrothal between the girl and the youngest of the kings (1678 ff.). And what does Hagen think? The poet does not say, though we have been told by some critics to view Hagen's proposal as an indication of his approval of Bechlaren and its inhabitants. But there is in this scene a line that gives food for thought: "Swaz sich sol gefüegen,   wer mac daz understan?"/"Who can oppose what must take place?" (1680). The allusion to the girl's fate suggests that Hagen with his proposal is the agent who brings about the fulfilment of what the poet calls inevitable.[18] The girl herself, as though a mere pawn in someone's game of high strategy, remains nameless.

---

17 Ironically, then, a case of parallelism prevails between Siegfried and Hagen: they both disregard and thereby violate the testimonial power of symbols.

18 Panzer, Das Nibelungenlied, p. 201, discerns in this verse a biblical ring, but on p. 207 he says that "viermal den Bericht eines Vorganges die fatalistische Erklärung, dass dies 'muose also sin' (oder 'wesen'), begleitet," and it is not clear why the reference to fate in strophe 1680 should fall into a different category.

With these thoughts on the various scenes at Bechlaren involving Hagen, it seems possible once again to adopt and paraphrase a dictum advanced by Singer: it is not that Hagen does not care about idyllic Bechlaren: he simply does not care about anything.[19]

Though from the suggestions made in this and the preceding chapters Hagen evolves as a figure with few redeeming features, and certainly with fewer than the critics have granted him,[20] the poet leaves the reader to pass judgment. He comments little; he merely shows. But he seldom makes an imposing figure sympathetic without slipping in something which will show us — if we refuse to be carried away by admiration for picturesque characters — just what we are admiring. Hagen: is he not magnificent to behold? Does he not come to scorn blow upon blow? Is he not splendid in his dark unbending pride? Quite so! He is the man who kills a Siegfried drinking,[21] who decapitates a little child

1961   daz im gegen der hende   ame swerte vloz daz bluot
      und daz der küneginne   daz houbet spranc in die schoz,

so that the blood washed along the sword to his hands, and the
child's head fell into the queen's lap,

and who snatches over the bodies of friend and foe alike at a power which he is not fit to possess. For the *merwip* who have given Hagen — or so he thinks — the gift of knowledge of the future, have taken the future away from him. It eludes Hagen, like the *Tarnkappe* and the

19 Singer, "The Hunting Contest," p. 179.

20 As noted before, a striking exception is Stout, who sees fit (*Hagene*, p. 82) to speak of "die Abneigung des Dichters gegen Hagen."

21 W. Schröder, "Epische Konzeption," p. 199, calls it one of Hagen's greatest heroic moments when he admits to Kriemhild that he slew Siegfried. See also H. Schneider, *Lieder*, p. 55: "Der Mörder wächst ins Heroische, wo er sich der Anklage und einer möglichen Rache ruhig stellt." Whatever the value of these views, they remind us that the poet goes out of his way to *mute* Hagen's reprehensible qualities. This attempt is of consequence for the question of guilt in the epic as well as for the question whether the figures in the *Nibelungenlied* are "representationally" developed.

hoard.[22] By definition, by the fact that the *merwip* already know it, the future is beyond manipulation. Hagen's turning to the *merwip* in order to force them to tell him the naked truth is an effort to impose his type of rationality on what sets itself forth as plainly irrational and beyond reason and manipulation. His attempt to withstand the inevitable future as predicted by the *merwip* – " 'ez muoz also wesen' " / " *it must be thus* " (1542) – helps that future to work itself out.[23] If, then, a demonic quality in Hagen comes to the fore in the scene with the *merwip* – and it could be at least equally well argued that Hagen displays it unabated from the very beginning – we must immediately add that the same scene also defines the limits beyond which this demonic quality cannot operate.

22 H. Drube, "Der germanische Schicksalsglaube im Nibelungenlied," *ZfdB*, xvii (1911), 161, speaks of the Germanic "Drang zur Erforschung des Schicksals, das man wissend gegenübertreten will."

23 Cf. strophes 1574 ff., in which Hagen seeks to destroy the priest, the only one for whom the *merwip* made an exception when they foretold Hagen the end of the Burgundians. From the priest's point of view, of course, Hagen is "ein Teil von jener Kraft, die stets das Böse will und stets das Gute schafft."

ix

CONCLUSION:
STRUCTURAL
DEVICES
AND THEIR
CONSEQUENCES

THE PREVIOUS CHAPTERS have attempted to draw attention to some of the building materials used in the *Nibelungenlied*, and to the nature of their distribution. What the total structure amounts to is a different matter. In order to attempt an evaluation of the epic as a whole, it is necessary to deal with some devices that are akin to that of parallelism, which so far has provided the base from which to view isolated motifs, events, or the functions of individual characters. The task involved demands a survey of the imagery in the epic, of the nature of the symmetry in it, and of pace and action.

The *Nibelungenlied* does little or nothing to meet a demand for "pure" poetry; its integrated structure offers a foursquare resistance to such a search. This does not mean, however, that there is no symbolism in the epic. If we look, as we have done, into the technique of its composition, it becomes apparent that much of the value to be gleaned from it is conveyed by series of parallel images. Some of this imagery is as obvious as the moon similes applied to Kriemhild (283) and Siegfried (817) respectively (chapter III, pp. 60 ff.); some of it is more recondite, and its significance strikes us only when we have immersed ourselves for a time in the epic and begun to notice things which at first may have escaped us in the swift succession of events. Such significance is not so much a matter of the images or symbols themselves as of their placing. It may be compared to the composition of a picture in which a number of objects, more or less significant in themselves, subtly gain added importance from the interrelations of balance and perspective.

A typical example may be mentioned once again to show how the consequences of the poet's arrangements at times hold the key to a correct understanding of the developments. Consider Kriemhild's function in the tailor scene, her statement about Brunhild's having been Siegfried's *Kebse,* and her role in bringing Hagen up to date about Siegfried's vulnerable spot. The interrelation between these scenes provides one of the many examples of how the poet sets his images – whether verbal, pictorial, or otherwise – squarely before the reader and allows them to do their own work.

We have seen how intricate the patterns of parallel motifs can become; the first instance of Kriemhild's "helping" Hagen links with the gem motif which itself occurs in a series and shows a movement that parallels the course of the events. With this way of working with imagery, it is often impossible to strip off the imagery and to present the naked content, for with natural imagery the images *are* the content. It is this phenomenon, the use of natural images, that explains the poet's ease and freedom in shifting from the plane of the narrative flow to that of symbolic significance, and back again. For though the symbolism in the epic seldom interferes with its narrative environment, at times it is more significant than the environment itself. A typical example is encountered when Gotelind gives Nudung's shield to Hagen (chapter VII, pp. 143 ff.). An occasional lapse may occur, as in Rüdeger's shield scene. The inconsistency here (cf. chapter VIII, p. 145) is so striking that it is tempting to interpret it as a deliberate device to draw attention to the symbolic rather than the narrative consequence of the scene.

To put it differently: the imagery and symbolism in the *Nibelungenlied* tend to be strictly functional, even when most pictorial. For it is pictorial: the poet has the eye of a painter and a lightning facility for unforgettably fixing a scene, a look, a movement, in a few words only. For instance, there is Brunhild's look over the shoulder, her ordering that the Burgundians be given their weapons back (477); there is the woman's hauteur and self-assurance, and the insult that look over the shoulder spells for Hagen, who looks even darker than usual, not being accustomed to being put in his place – and by a woman at that! There is the insensitivity of young Dankwart, who is happy to have his weapons back (448) and does not notice the anger of his elder brother. Compare to this another look over the shoulder (1788): Hagen striding across the courtyard, the grouping of the waiting Burgundians, the charged atmosphere. The poet does not tell us all this; he simply shows us and lets his picture produce its own effect. We "see" the slant of Brunhild's or Hagen's face in relief. And by way of another example there is the priest leaning over the church utensils (1575), his hands grasping the gunwale, his capacious habit filled with airpockets that in a moment will help him to stay afloat and gain the shore. Over and over again in such pithy details the poet displays his power to catch and fix a visual impression. And whether he is working on the grand scale or on the small, his images are not only clear, but also consistent; or rather, they are clear because they are consistent. No deviation into philosophy, no express preoccupation with symbolic values seduces him for a moment into taking his eye off its object.

But though the pictorial manner of portrayal is an essential mark of the epic's style, the formation of the materials does not rely solely or even mainly on the poet's "eye." It is his mind that orders the materials, and the mind is reflective rather than speculative. The poet is not philosophically oriented. His reflections do not seek depth; they remain on the surface of things, but they interrelate and refer. This procedure does not suggest a lack of erudition; it merely reflects the poet's psychological make-up.

If the poet requires something useful to his story – some theatrical property, as one might say – he does not falsify the picture by suddenly introducing a strange implement from nowhere. He makes do with what he has. When, for instance, Brunhild's belt is mentioned for the first time (636), it is because something is needed, something detachable, that Brunhild would have at hand as a matter of course to bind Gunther.[1] The belt is the very thing. But look what the poet gains by thus introducing a natural symbol in the most off-hand manner. It is with this belt that Gunther is bridled. Does not the dominance of the allegorical lady Chastity over the allegorical figure Lust come to mind? The narrative thus manages to avoid introducing something totally incongruous, without substituting the symbolic for the pictorial image.

The poet of the *Nibelungenlied*, then, is not interested in making his own imagery and symbols. His interest lies in working with natural ones, those that are ready-made.[2] These symbols are themselves instances of what they symbolize. By simply being what they are, they

1 Whereas the в* text speaks of the belt "den [Brünhilt] umb ir siten truoc" (636), the c* version changes this to "den si alle zite truoc," perhaps to make acceptable the notion that Brunhild would wear the belt in bed. Under the circumstances prevailing, Brunhild would indeed be wise to keep the belt on. Regardless of the difference between the versions, the belt would be close at hand, off or on.

2 Mowatt, "Studies," p. 262.

tell us something about the nature of the greater thing, as protection and safety are greater than the shield symbolizing them, or as the belt is but a visible sign of something more important than itself. The poet arranges such devices in order to add to the richness of his delivery. He does not *make* them meaningful, universal, or always recognizable; they *are* all that. Though they may be old, they are ever new and fresh. The symbolism is therefore not private symbolism, and it resists being called medieval or modern or whatever; such symbolism is of all times and places, and it begs to communicate.[3]

The imagery based on such symbolism displays its universal, because natural, pattern at all levels and in all circumstances, whether or not the poet is or could be conscious of these possible values. We therefore have the right to read from the arrangement of the imagery all the significance we can find, provided, of course, that our interpretation does not involve a degradation of the imagery. With this in mind, we could take any example, great or small, and detect its occasional subtlety and – once we had surrendered to it – its fascination; for instance, the imagery of hands.

Whereas the hand imagery discussed previously (chapter II, pp. 33 f.) pertains to the many instances in which hands are said or implied to carry war gear, five times hands are said to be white; each time the mention of the white hand occurs in "courtly"

---

3 Perhaps Mowatt and Sacker, *The Nibelunglied*, p. 27, mean the same thing when they say that "the literary masterpieces of the Middle Ages ... arrange historically conditioned elements in patterns of universal validity." Even so, symbolism as defined here has little in common with symbolism as understood by Mowatt and Sacker. Witness, for instance, their comment on strophe 909: "In one sense, the bear is Brünnhilde, caught by Sifrid, set loose in Burgundian society, captured a second time by Sifrid, and finally rendered harmless. But whereas Brünnhilde was spared penetration and death (see note 459–461), the bear is less gently treated. In another sense, the bear is Sifrid himself, an uncomfortable guest in Burgundian society, a well-meaning disaster (the bear is only trying to run away), and finally a ritual murder victim. And in so far as Sifrid and Brünnhilde are one composite symbol, the bear is the spark in their relationship that Sifrid stamped out." By definition, of course, natural symbolism cannot be as equivocal as this. In retrospect it may be fair to say that the difference between the thrust of the *Commentary* and that of the present work lies to an important degree in the different definitions of symbolism.

situations.[4] But this courtly aura does not mean that such hands – in contrast to those engaged in warfare – are "reflective." Kriemhild's holding hands with Siegfried, for instance (cf. 294 and 661), is hardly proof that now hand and reason are in harmony. Whether her former unwillingness to welcome a man's love was reasonable or not – her mother thought it was not – Kriemhild's decision was at least based on a type of reasoning, whatever its soundness. Now her gesture of intimacy in holding hands with Siegfried is proof that her determination to remain uninvolved with love was but a "wint" (47), and the mention of her white hand, while suggesting a little idyll, is proof that reason has been suspended. So also when Kriemhild's white hands lift the head of the dead Siegfried to give him a last kiss (1069): her sorrow is measureless, "unmaezlichen groz" (1066).[5]

In Bechlaren, Giselher's white hands embrace Rüdeger's daughter (1685). The idyllic aspect of this scene remains superficial, and Giselher himself comes to repudiate the note of tenderness which the mention of his white hands helped to convey (cf. 2819). In another instance of the motif – Gotelind's taking the shield off the wall of Bechlaren – the hand has not only a life, but also a culture of its own. As when Kriemhild and Siegfried hold hands, this is a moment "wenn die Hände sprechen." The white hands of Gotelind speak a pithier and more communicative language than language as such. Here, too, however, the hands seem detached from the waking personality. Gotelind acts as though in trance. Her hands are like independent agents, acting without the benefit of reason to give away the shield, the symbol of protection.

And so, whenever hands are said to be doing something, they fail to acquire power by association with their owners. Precisely because of the courtly value suggested by the whiteness of hands, their unexpected *under*-the-surface value – or rather, the very lack of it – becomes more portentous in alluding to the discrepancies between hands and minds than in those instances in which the hand is said to handle the sword, shield, or spear.

4 To quote Schwarze, "Die Frau," 389, note 6: "Diese Formel kehrt in der Poesie jener Zeit häufig wieder; vgl. *Sanct Oskars Leben*, 577; *Tristan*, 484, 36; *Aucassin und Nicolete*, 26, 11: 'ses blances mains'; *Tristan*, 256, 10 findet sich auch 'liehte hende.'"

5 The adjective "wise" in 1069 may be simply to fill out the meter.

The hand imagery in the *Nibelungenlied* tells more about the characters. Together with the motifs of battle anger (chapter II, pp. 31 ff.) and of acquiescence (chapter I, pp. 21 ff.), it suggests a lack of inner substance. The poet does not spell this out, he merely shows us its effects. Though aware of the unconscious – witness Kriemhild's endeavor to keep Siegfried from going to meet the allegedly renewed hostilities of the Saxons (921 ff.) – the poet is not greatly interested in exploiting it. He is interested in some of its manifestations – dreams, for instance, and the way in which hands act independently. But while leaving untouched the dark recesses of his characters' minds, he reveals some of their thoughts nevertheless, by juxtaposition or otherwise, as when he uses the window motif to show that only Kriemhild leaves a window to destroy (chapter I, pp. 20 f.).

It is this lack of inner substance that makes the characters in the *Nibelungenlied* rely on appearances. This fact also accounts for the importance of public opinion. Insults are as bad as they are taken to be, as though whatever they say is thereby made true. Honor thus comes to rely on the opinion of others. At every juncture of the narrative it also inevitably provides impetus to the ever increasing forces of annihilation, precisely because the enhancement and vindication of honor is a central commitment of all the characters. For instance, in the exchanges between Gunther, Hagen, Giselher, and Ortwin after the queens' quarrel, the question of whether Siegfried must die revolves around honor (cf. 866 ff.). The defense of Brunhild's honor as Hagen pretends to understand it (cf. chapter VI, pp. 127 ff.) becomes for Tronje a *Tarnkappe* under whose protection he can strike down Siegfried with impunity. Hagen, for that matter, is a master in the manipulation of honor.

Honor in the *Nibelungenlied*, it should be noted, is exclusively a *diesseits* value, its importance in conjunction with the deity being of little consequence. True, at Siegfried's *Schwertleite* the poet tells how a mass was sung: "got man do ze eren eine messe sanc" (33), but this and other periodic processions to the minster are little more than backdrops adding to the honor and aura of the court. When Siegfried is in church, the poet does not say that he thanks God for Kriemhild, but "er mohte sinen saelden des immer sagen danc"/"*He would always thank his good fortune*" (301). Even Rüdeger's anguished appeals to God are lamentations for the unavoidable loss of honor, not God's but his own (2153). Rüdeger's courtly life as based on honor may be at God's behest, but his bitterness towards God for now despoiling him

of his honor – " 'nu ruoche mich bewisen   der mir ze lebene geriet' "/
" '*Let him who called me to life advise me*' " (2154) – is far from any
Christian acquiescence in the greater glory of God.[6]

The adherence or nonadherence to court etiquette in so far as it
centers around honor may be a two-edged sword, capable of exalting
on the one hand or of insulting on the other (cf. chapter I, p. 14). The
potency of this weapon derives from the deadly seriousness with which
the forms are adhered to. Every departure from the code is fraught
with consequences. Gunther is angry when Etzel's minstrels refuse the
gifts he offers (1490). When he and the other Burgundians arrive in
Gran, Kriemhild departs from the norm by kissing Giselher only.
Hagen reacts immediately, and he immediately draws his conclusions
(1737 f.).

Various forms of honor, then, are often at cross purposes with
each other, and thus one of the main principles of order and cohesion
turns into a principle of division and destruction. Honor sets individuals against each other, and the poet can only stand aghast at the
carnage. The closed, self-referential world of the *Nibelungenlied*, with
no point of reference outside itself, has no answer to its self-generated
destruction. It is "eine selbstmahlende Mühle," an existential plight.[7]

An important feature of the structure of the *Nibelungenlied* is
that of symmetry. Such symmetry – Panzer calls it mere repetition[8] –
is akin to parallelism, but the significant difference lies in the fact that
parallelism participates in the self-referential and self-revealing patterns, whereas symmetry lends regularity and order. With this difference in mind, we can speak of the "Parallelität der Rollen und Schicksale zwischen Sifrit und Rüdiger,"[9] but also of points of symmetry
between them. Whereas Wachinger's reference to parallelism hinges on

6 On Christianity in the epic, see, e.g., A. Schönbach, "Die Nibelungen," in: *Das
Christentum in der altdeutschen Heldendichtung* (Graz, 1897); Nagel, "Heidentum
und Christentum," *Der Horizont*, II (1957), 27–37; *idem*, "Heidnisches und
Christliches im *Nibelungenlied*," *Ruperto-Carola*, X (1958), XXIV, 61–81; Hans
Kuhn, "Heldensage und Christentum," *SP* (1960), 515–24; Weber, *Das
Nibelungenlied*, pp. 125 ff.; Nagel, *Das Nibelungenlied*, pp. 208 ff.
7 On honor in the epic, see, e.g., Jones, "Rüdiger's Dilemma"; Mueller, *The
Nibelungenlied Today*, pp. 9 ff.; H. Naumann, "Die Ritter-Ehre der Stauferzeit,"
Euphorion, XLII (1947).
8 Panzer, *Das Nibelungenlied*, p. 131.
9 Wachinger, *Studien*, p. 95.

the events taking place, the symmetry in the roles of these two figures depends on details that in themselves are not significant. Both Siegfried and Rüdeger are killed with their own weapons; Siegfried is killed from behind by his own spear, and Rüdeger is felled in a face-to-face battle by the sword he has given to Gernot. The difference in this similarity reflects on Hagen's function, or lack of it (cf. chapter VII, pp. 144 f.). Furthermore, Siegfried as well as Rüdeger travels with twelve companions to Worms (64, 2170), and both are separated from their own shields when they receive the mortal spear thrust or sword blow. For that matter, Siegfried sparks gems off his shield when he beats Hagen with it (985); Rüdeger also forces gems off shields in the battle ending in his death (2212). As we have seen, the poet has made good use of this parallelistic motif (cf. chapter I, pp. 10 ff.). Before their deaths, Siegfried and Rüdeger commend (996, 2164) the care of wife and child to the King – who is less responsible for those deaths than is his queen in each instance.

It is not the individual instances of symmetry that are of consequence, but their very abundance. The following enumeration stands by itself. Twice a king decides to woo on hearsay (44 and 329). Twice Siegfried is recognized through a window (84, 411); twice he asks Gunther why he is downcast (153, 883); and twice he is told that the Saxons have announced war (143, 880). Twice Siegfried fights with Alberich (96, 497); twice mention is made of talks between husband and wife in the intimacy of the bedroom (1168, 1400); and twice a queen makes a pretence in order to have relatives invited for a visit (726 ff., 1401 ff.). There are two engagement scenes (614, 1683), and twice we are told that couples to be married are not in a position to consummate their intended union (528, 1358). Twice a queen about to leave her country tries to settle her inheritance (522, 691 ff.); in each instance she is less than completely successful. Twice Gunther is warned not to go abroad (330, 1458 ff.); in each instance he goes anyway. Both Kriemhild (1248) and Rüdeger (2154 ff.) find themselves in a quandary and see no way out of the difficulty besetting them. Both finally choose the world's – that is, their own – rather than God's honor. In the first two *Aventiure* the poet divides his attention between Kriemhild and Siegfried; the portraits reflect each other in alternate descriptions. Symmetry occurs also when two sets of brothers fight each other in the dark of Bavaria (1608 ff.). When Siegfried gets a son, Gunther does also; each child is his uncle's namesake.

Of a rather different order are those cases of symmetry that involve groupings. In strophes 583 and 590 we find companies of ladies and knights going hand in hand. The same happens in strophe 1395, and later in Bechlaren (1667 ff.). In the latter instance there is an explicit indication that protocol is observed: Gotelind goes with the most important guest, Gunther; Rüdeger goes with Gernot; his daughter leads Giselher. Also in Gran we see knights going hand in hand (1804 f.): Dietrich goes with Gunther, Irnfrit with Gernot, Rüdeger with Giselher; Hawart holds Iring's hand; Dankwart goes with Wolfhart. Here, too, rules of protocol and rank are observed, Hagen and Volker being the only two who adhere to their own set of values.

Order of rank also makes for symmetry when large groups are involved. In these, the kings are the focal points towards whom and around whom the entourage is grouped and from which it derives its significance. Instances of such groupings occur during the double wedding ceremony (cf. 617, 626 f.). Official encounters are also full of regulated pomp: when Brunhild arrives in Worms (tenth *Aventiure*) and when Kriemhild arrives in Santen (eleventh *Aventiure*) or meets Etzel (twenty-second *Aventiure*), dignity and circumstance give these encounters the quality of colorful processions meeting each other. These are but a few of the indications that social occasions are formal and never fail to observe strict decorum.[10]

When festivities are threatened or are disrupted by enmity, we have the kings above the groupings. The function of these kings is to be normative; throughout the epic they are, or attempt to be, the centers of authority.[11] If need be, they conciliate, or seek to do so. It is their duty to have order and "fröude" prevail. Elsewhere, kings acquiesce or hide their worries so that harmony and joy may remain unmarred.

Insistence on order and symmetry is also applied in geography: it takes twelve days to travel from Worms to Islant (382), from Bechlaren to the Rhine (1175), from Gran to Worms (1430), and from Worms to the Danube (1515). Time lapses are synchronized also: a decade passes between Kriemhild's departure from and her return to Worms; another ten years pass between her departure for Gran and the visit of the Burgundians.

The order evoked in these symmetrical configurations significantly reflects the principle of order to which the society is committed.

10 Dürrenmatt, *Das Nibelungenlied*, p. 93.

11 Not necessarily in contradiction to this, Weber, *Das Nibelungenlied*, p. 83, speaks of the obvious "Abwertung der Königsgestalten."

Thus seen, the principle of symmetry that lies deeply embedded in the structure of the *Nibelungenlied* cannot be viewed as so many instances of repetitiousness, but constitutes a compelling maturity. The importance of this orderly principle is supported by the considerations that deal with the pace of the *Nibelungenlied*.

The epic is at one moment deliberately slow and majestic, then again fast and turbulent. The references to periods of time support this alternation between slackening and quickening of the pace. The two ten-year periods make the epic as a whole chronologically slow. Elsewhere, important events take place within the space of a few days or even less. Towards the end the pace becomes downright furious, the space narrower. The poet frequently resorts to foreshortening devices to indicate coming events. But in contrast to this is the large amount of direct description which slows the narrative. Descriptions of time-consuming preparations are often detailed, though they do not further the plot, and they are placed so as to give the impression that we are present. They thus appear to consume the full number of days or weeks allotted to the operations themselves. The passages describing the preparations for various festivities or departures, with a richness of detail far in excess of the demands of the story, are typical examples of the poet's method. At first glance, at any rate, many passages seem irrelevant and detachable. To take a well known example, some ten strophes are devoted to Kriemhild's dressing scene in the quarrel episode, but our discussion of it (cf. chapter III, pp. 53 ff.) made it clear that its true significance as a source of insight into Kriemhild's and Brunhild's manner of thinking is not readily apparent.[12] As far as the *action* of the epic is concerned, the passage adds little. Similarly, strophes dealing with festivities and courtly occasions in general seem to add little or nothing to the development of the plot, and provide a slowing effect. On a somewhat different plane, the poet's "I heard" and "I was told" cooperate to the same effect.

Unlike these descriptions and the narrator's comments, the direct discourse contributes to speed. Panzer speaks of "handelnde Reden in den Gipfeln der Fabel."[13] These dialogues are rapid and dynamic because they tend to use verbs of action and because they often allude to the hand as the doer of deeds. In fact, rapidity of dialogue often ob-

---

12 This can also be said of the hunt in the sixteenth *Aventiure*. But see Singer, "The Hunting Contest."

13 Panzer, *Das Nibelungenlied*, p. 132.

scures the course of these interchanges. As a consequence, the characters tend to talk past each other. Misunderstanding is their common failure.[14] Warnings go unheeded and advice is scorned. Only once is this failure to communicate adequately recognized (2333), but the insight comes too late to do any good. What with the tendency of words to go their own stubborn way, it is small wonder that kings seek to impose silence and that the would-be retainers of harmony acquiesce.

Kriemhild and Ute fail to communicate because they fail to define their terms. It is as if each is so introverted in her own thoughts and mold of thinking about love that it does not occur to either of them that the other may be thinking of something else. These misunderstandings are allowed to continue and to warp relationships. Such a failure to clarify lies at the base of the crucial quarrel between the queens.

As Bumke has shown,[15] the participants in the council meeting after the queens' quarrel also talk past each other. They have ears only for their own assumptions and opinions, and it is a bit of an accident that they end with a decision at all. Bumke explains the "vagueness" of the dialogue as due to the various sources with which the poet is working, but viewed from *within* the epic the conversation is but another example of the inability of the characters to explain themselves.

In this connection, Bumke's suggestion that Ortwin's offer to kill Siegfried (869) is perhaps in one of the sources mentioned by Gernot[16] may be true as far as the sources are concerned, but from the present line of reasoning we can only say that Ortwin was also the more belligerent in the encounter scene (cf. chapter VII, p. 121). During that meeting Ortwin had good reason to feel offended by Siegfried, who taunted him in no vague terms. Stopped by Gernot's command to be silent, Ortwin was at the time unable to make Siegfried pay for his insult. Now, in the council meeting, he seizes the opportunity to square the old account.

14 *If* the *Nibelungenlied* were a story centering around the delineation of character, this perpetual misunderstanding and the habitual inadequacy of language as a tool of communication would lead to the Kafkaesque conclusion that each individual stands in isolation. Mowatt and Sacker, *The Nibelungenlied*, p. 7, speak of "a whole series of unperceptive characters in the work."

15 Bumke, "Quellen," pp. 18 ff.

16 *Ibid.*, p. 20. Incidentally, there is little Germanic about Ortwin's – or Kriemhild's – long nurtured thirst for revenge.

These remarks on the pace in the epic show that the poet's art does not fail him when he wants to call upon the reader's capacity to experience things with him. We may think that he works by overt statement rather than by suggestion, yet in the end we find that he has suggested more than the content of his statements. The effect of these statements is cumulative; for instance, as we read from one *Aventiure* to the next, the sense of everything closing and rushing in upon us produces finally a profound claustrophobia. Looking back, we see the beginning of the "maere," colorful and gay with its festivals and *buhurts*. The disappearance of ornament, of clothes and other colorful materials, contributes to this effect by negative suggestion. In the end all that is left of color is the red of blood, and the yellow of gold streaming out of Kriemhild's coffers (cf. 2130).

It could be said that the modification of the poet's sources confirmed this pull in two opposite directions. By selection and addition he has produced a story much more symmetrical than his sources, and he has regularized time and distance to a higher degree than his sources ever warranted. Further instances of symmetry could be cited, but they would not alter our conclusions.

These observations suggest a way of approaching the epic. The symmetry of scene, action, or characterization, the pace of the narrative – now slow and now quickening, the abundance of generalizing details contrasted with pithy concrete descriptions, the predominantly dramatic discourse, all indicate that the *Nibelungenlied* is not the best work in which to look for delicate characterization. For full delineation of character is not called for in the design; nor is it possible, though this does not prevent our appreciating the many subtle hints which give us insight into the various characters.[17]

To suggest, however, that the element of characterization is minor in the epic does not justify turning to the plot and making it the focus of interest. For the epic depends only in part on the virtues that make a good story: swift pace, suspense, variety, intrigue. We encounter all these, but not in all the episodes. The swift pace of one *Aventiure* may slow down to a crawl in the next; suspense as often as not is toned

17 Weber, *Das Nibelungenlied*, p. 195: "Es geht nicht um einzelne konkrete Gestalten, sondern um viel mehr: um Schicksale und Mächte als die in der Tiefe herrschenden Gewalten, und noch mehr: es geht weiterhin um das geistige Objekt dieser Schicksale und dieser Mächte des Untergründigen. Dieses geistige Objekt aber, dessen sich die Finsternis bemächtigt, ist das Rittertum."

down by predictory elements liberally sprinkled throughout the many hundreds of strophes; variety, too, often bows out to the repetitive device of parallelism and symmetry; intrigue appears in the actions of some of the characters but not in the poet's method of presentation; the main events are forecast long before they occur. Thus the structure of the epic works against story interest.

If, then, because of the variance between speed and slowness, brevity and length, dialogues and descriptions, pithiness and elaboration, neither characterization nor plot can supply the basis on which the *Nibelungenlied* is to be read, it seems reasonable to conclude, on the principle that a literary monument should be approached on the basis of its own assumptions, that the epic is centered neither on character nor on plot. We can neither examine nor evaluate it according to canons by which it was not written and which it cannot satisfy. Its very texture, its characters and its action, rather than existing for any great interest in themselves, point to a "representational," a "metaphorical" method. There is in the epic a close correlation among the elements on this level that gives support to such an approach.

I suggest, then, that the *Nibelungenlied* presents a poetic pageant,[18] and that its materials are organized in such a way as to contribute to the complex design expressing the nature of the noble life or, in sharp contrast to it, to show how this life can be threatened and is in fact brought to destruction by counter forces. Hagen and Kriemhild may seem to be the embodiments of these counter forces, but actually they work through all the characters. We thus can speak of the *Nibelungenlied* as the story of a pageant destroyed. It is immediately concerned with noble activities, with pomp, ceremony, dignity, power, love, and chivalry, and with the attempts by the exponents of nobility to invoke perpetually the principle of form and order and *fröude*. The disruption of this order lies at the heart of the epic. The society depicted in it is one in which form is full of significance. Life here is conducted at a dignified, processional pace, and is itself perhaps a reflection – or rather a reproduction – of the order of the universe. What gives this conception of life its perspective, its depth, and its sometimes frenetic seriousness (see 1893 ff.) is its awareness of a formidable, antagonistic

18 Singer, "The Hunting Contest," p. 167, finds that the term "pageant" suggests itself for the hunting scene, and on p. 169 he makes a statement which this chapter suggests to be applicable to the epic as a whole: "The ... pageant is constantly subject to abrupt termination."

element, an ever threatening danger, even in the moments of supreme assuredness. When the arrival of Siegfried in Worms seems to threaten this mode of life, Gunther refutes his claims by referring to orderly inheritance. This counterforce – not to be identified with any specific individual or individuals[19] – falls across the pattern of order, and is exemplified in the sudden turns of plot such as Kriemhild's falcon dream, the bedroom episode, the bear scene,[20] or Volker's killing the Hun at Gran's joust.

The descriptive passages support this interpretation of a pageant destroyed, not only in the parts dealing with knighthood in general, but also in the manner in which the antagonistic destructive forces in this life, no matter how represented or suggested, interrupt the leisure of the narrative. At first the interruptions are only momentary – insignificant clouds on the horizon, as in Siegmund's warning to Siegfried not to go to Worms. Then, presently, they become longer and more momentous with Siegfried's first arrival in Worms and, later, the Saxon war. Ultimately the waves of antagonism follow each other with diminishing intervals, rising higher and higher, until in the end they sweep along all that stands for order and pattern and harmony.

The "hochgeziten" in the epic contribute to the rich texture in the fabric of noble life that the poem presents. That is also the reason why details relating to strength, beauty, and magnificence are in the superlative: they contribute to knightly splendor in all its forms:

286   Do stuont so minnecliche   daz Sigmundes kint,
      sam er entworfen waere   an ein permint
      von guotes meisters listen,   als man im jach,
      daz man helt deheinen   nie so scoenen gesach.

19 Mergell, *Nibelungenlied*, p. 321, for one, thinks that "es dem Dichter darauf ankommt ... den Endkampf nicht als Anstiftung eines einzelnen (sei er Hunne oder Burgunder, Heide oder Christ, König oder Mann), sondern mit der zwingenden Gewalt des Naturereignisses hereinbrechen zu lassen." It would seem, however, in contrast to Mergell that Hagen is also a victim of this "Gewalt des Naturereignisses."

20 This suggestion does not contradict the statements made on this scene by Singer in "The Hunting Contest."

There stood the child of Sieglind, handsome as though drawn on parchment by the cunning hand of a master; indeed, it was said that no handsomer hero was ever seen.

In a strophe like this, for example, the description of Siegfried is more than surface ornamentation. It is linked with a score of other passages as an expression of Siegfried's pre-eminence. Beginning with the second *Aventiure*, all the descriptions of him serve to widen and perpetuate our notion of him as variously the ruler, conqueror, judge, lover, or hunter. Among other details, whether subsequent or not, the splendor of the hoard and the wealth of Santen are directly associated with Siegfried's role.

The establishment of Siegfried's pre-eminence is essential to the meaning of the epic, and it is carried out on the multiple levels characteristic of the poet's whole method of working. There is an obvious correspondence between the quality of these descriptions and Siegfried's position as a central figure. From this vantage point it will not do to suggest that the poet's sympathy lies with the "Germanic" rather than the "courtly" qualities in the epic, or vice versa. The distinction is a false one and works havoc with the endeavor to consider the epic as a homogeneous unit. Attention might be drawn, for instance, to Hildebrand's role in the closing *Aventiure*. It has been said that his killing of Kriemhild issues from his adherence to "ere" and "triuwe" in the Germanic-heroic sense of those terms. But considering the way Kriemhild has debased kingship by laying waste entire realms, in defiance of her royal obligation to preserve and enhance order, peace, and harmony, Hildebrand's action may be regarded as an act of justice. Seen in this manner, the last *Aventiure* is to an important degree to be appreciated for its symbolic value.

Similarly, there is no indication that the poet prefers the courtly life as exemplified in love to the courtly life as exemplified in other knightly activities. Siegfried's position suggests that the worship of Mars is no less an important facet of the orderly noble life than is the worship of Venus. To Siegfried goes the honor in the Saxon war as well as the honor in love, and for a while at any rate he comes out on top in a work in which superlatives are used freely, and *is* the ideal lover, king, judge, warrior, hunter, strong man, and rich man. There is no overt indication that the poet takes a dark view of this hyperbolic Siegfried.

Nor, for that matter, does he draw overt moral conclusions about the force that brings Siegfried to destruction. In a literature where death is one of the most powerful instruments of moral exemplum, the poet goes out of his way to stifle any fixing of blame. Here, too, he tries to retain balance.

Love in this society is taken for granted; it is never in debate. We simply discover how faithfully experience in love exemplifies the partial blindness of all earthly experience. Love, we find, can create dissension between relatives, and can make otherwise active men abject. This kind of balance regarding love, if it precludes satire, does not rule out irony. Indeed, irony is fully consonant with the dignified view. No moral preference is expressed or implied in the many views of love that we encounter: Brunhild's, Kriemhild's, Ute's, Siegfried's, Gunther's, Etzel's,[21] Volker's; Hagen is the only figure who has none. All we can glean from these various types of love is that they create tensions in the very structure of the epic; there is no indication that one type is superior to another. Nor is there indication that a tragic attitude is to be adopted towards any of these loves. The tragedy, if such it may be called, stems from the fact that these loves clash and cause hatreds, and that the

---

21 Nagel, *Das Nibelungenlied*, pp. 84 ff., sees no difference between Gunther's love for Brunhild and Etzel's for Kriemhild. Many critics share this opinion. Mowatt and Sacker, for instance, throughout their *Commentary* see Etzel as a figure whose sexual drive, and little else, determines his relation to Kriemhild. It would seem, however, that Etzel comes to achieve a type of *maze*. The thought whether he " 'sol ... Kriemhild immer geligen bi' "/" '*should ever be loved by Kriemhild*' " (1151) plays a role as well as the question " 'ob si in [sinem] lande krone solde tragen' "/" '*whether she should wear a crown in [his] land*' " (1149). Elsewhere we read that "si was im als sin lip"/"*he loved her as his own life*" (1400) and that "getriuwe was sin muot"/"*his mind was faithful*" (1402) – statements that are not applied to Gunther. And verses like these:

1869 Kriemhilt mit ir vrouwen   in diu venster gesaz
      zuo Etzel dem richen;   vil liep was im daz.

Kriemhild with her ladies sat in the windows beside the mighty Etzel; this pleased him much.

convey Etzel's balanced orientation, in which there is room for warmth as well as satisfaction in Kriemhild's ability to be a consort.

hatreds can work themselves out on a gigantic scale because of the power the haters command.

With these views, it becomes possible to suggest that Siegfried and Hagen, Brunhild and Kriemhild, each in his or her way exemplifies legitimate attitudes of equal "value," and that they balance and supplement each other in providing not moral conflict but variety. To find the real issue in the *Nibelungenlied* we must therefore look not so much at the relationships between them, but at their common position in relation to the world in which they have their being, that is, the would-be orderly and dignified world. And the poet expresses this issue not only through a tension between the ordered structure and the violent ups and downs of the surface narrative – too plainly to be seen to require elaborate analysis – but also through a complication of texture. The impressive patterned edifice of the noble life, its dignity and richness, its regard for law and decorum, its perpetual concern that harmony and "fröude" be retained, all are bulwarks against the ever threatening forces of chaos, and are in constant collision with them. And perhaps the crowning nobility – despite the *diesseits* orientation of the characters – is situated beyond the grasp of social order, and beyond magnificence in any earthly sense. For in the final strophes of the *Nibelungenlied* there may lie hidden a perception of order beyond chaos. When the earthly designs have totally crumbled, types of nobility yet remain: Etzel, still the representative of kingship in so far as he sought to avert chaos, and still capable of seeing the justice of his queen's death; Dietrich von Bern, the representative of nobility in its widest sense;[22] and Hildebrand, the representative of justice.

22 See Nagel, "Dietrichbild," parts I and II.

ABBREVIATIONS

Beiträge Beiträge zur Geschichte
der deutschen Sprache und Literatur
DU Der Deutschunterricht
DVLG Deutsche Vierteljahrsschrift
für Literaturwissenschaft und Geistesgeschichte
EG Etudes Germaniques
GLL German Life and Letters
GR Germanic Review
GRM Germanisch-Romanische Monatsschrift
JEGP Journal of English and Germanic Philology
MLR Modern Language Review
NM Neuphilologische Mitteilungen
PQ Philological Quarterly
SN Studia Neophilologica
SP Studies in Philology
WW Wirkendes Wort
ZfD Zeitschrift für Deutschkunde
ZfdA Zeitschrift für deutsches Altertum
ZfdB Zeitschrift für deutsche Bildung
ZfdP Zeitschrift für deutsche Philologie

BIBLIOGRAPHY

BARTSCH, KARL *Der Nibelunge Nôt, mit den Abweichungen von der Nibelunge liet, den Lesarten sämmtlicher Handschriften und einem Wörterbuche*, I. Bd., Leipzig, 1870

– *Das Nibelungenlied*, 8th ed., Leipzig, 1923

BATTS, M. S. "Die Tragik des *Nibelungenliedes*," Doitsu Bungaku, XVI (1960), 42–48.

– *Die Form der Aventiuren im Nibelungenlied*, in: *Giessener Beiträge*, XXIX (1960)

BETZ, WERNER "Die Gestaltwandlung des Burgundenunterganges von Prosper Aquitanus bis Meister Konrad," in: *Gestaltprobleme der Dichtung: Festschrift für Günther Müller*, Bonn, 1957, pp. 1 ff.

BEYSCHLAG, SIEGFRIED "Das Motiv der Macht bei Siegfrieds Tod," GRM, XXXIII (1951/52), 95–108

–"Das *Nibelungenlied* in gegenwärtiger Sicht," WW, III (1952/53), 193–200

–"Die Funktion der epischen Vorausdeutungen im Aufbau des *Nibelungenliedes*," Beiträge (Halle), LXXVI (1954), 38–55

–"Ueberlieferung und Neuschöpfung: Erörtert an der Nibelungen-Dichtung," WW, VIII (1957/58), 205–13

BOER, R. C. *Untersuchungen über den Ursprung und die Entwicklung der Nibelungensage*, III Bde. (Halle, 1906/07)

BOLLINGER, KATHARINA *Das Tragische im höfischen Epos*, Bonn, 1938

BONJOUR, ADRIEN "Anticipations et prophéties dans le *Nibelungenlied*," *Études Germaniques*, VII (1952), 241–51

BOOR, HELMUT DE *Das Nibelungenlied*, 17th ed., in: *Deutsche Klassiker des Mittelalters*, Wiesbaden, 1963

– *Geschichte der deutschen Literatur*, II. Bd., München, 1964

– *Das Nibelungenlied: Zweisprachige Ausgabe*, Sammlung Dietrich, Bd. 250, o.J.

BOSTOCK, J. K. "The Message of the *Nibelungenlied*," MLR, LV (1960), 200–12

–"Realism and Convention in the *Nibelungenlied*," *MLR*, LVI (1961), 228–34

BUMKE, JOACHIM "Sigfrids Fahrt ins Nibelungenland: Zur achten Aventiure des *Nibelungenliedes*," *Beiträge* (Tübingen), LXXX (1958), 253–68

–"Die Quellen der Brünhildfabel im *Nibelungenlied*," *Euphorion*, LIV (1960), 1–38

–"Die Eberjagd im Daurel und in der Nibelungendichtung," *GRM*, XLI (1960), 105–11

CURTIUS, E. R. *Europäische Literatur und lateinisches Mittelalter*, Bern/München, 1961

DE ROUGEMENT, DENIS *Love in the Western World*, trans. Montgomery Belgion, New York, 1940

DRUBE, HERBERT "Der germanische Schicksalsglaube im *Nibelungenlied*," *ZfdB*, XVII (1941), 161–74

DÜRRENMATT, NELLY *Das Nibelungenlied im Kreis der höfischen Dichtung*, Bern, 1944

EGGERS, HANS *Symmetrie und Proportion epischen Erzählens*, Stuttgart, 1956

–"Vom Formenbau mittelhochdeutscher Epen," *DU*, XL (1959), 81–97

EHRISMANN, GUSTAV *Geschichte der deutschen Literatur bis zum Ausgang des Mittelalters*, II. Bd., München, 1935

EIS, GERHARD "Die Hortforderung," *GRM*, XXXVIII (1957), 209–23

ELLIS, HILDA R. "The Hoard of the Nibelungs," *MLR*, XXXVII (1942), 466–79

FECHTER, WERNER *Siegfrieds Schuld und das Weltbild des Nibelungenliedes*, Hamburg, 1948

–"Ueber die Vergleiche in der fünften Aventiure des Nibelungenliedes," *ZfdA*, LXXXIX (1958/59), 91–99

FLÜGEL, HEINZ "Die Schuld der Nibelungen," in: *idem, Geschichte und Geschicke: Zwölf Essays*, München/Kempten, 1946, pp. 191–219

FOURQUET, JEAN "Zum Aufbau des Nibelungenliedes und des Kudrunlieds," *ZfdA*, LXXXV (1954/55), 137–49

GERZ, ALFRED *Rolle und Funktion der epischen Vorausdeutung im Mittelhochdeutschen Epos*, in: *Germanistische Studien*, XCVII (Berlin, 1930)

HAMMERICH, L. L. "Zu Nibelungenlied 867," *Neophilologus*, XVI (1931), 96–98

HATTO, A. T. *The Nibelungenlied: A New Translation*, Baltimore, 1965

HEMPEL, W. " 'Superbia' als Schuldmotiv im *Nibelungenlied*," *Seminar*, II (1966), 1–12

HEUSLER, ANDREAS, *Nibelungensage und Nibelungenlied: Die Stoffgeschichte des deutschen Epos dargestellt*, Dortmund, 1921

HOLTZMANN, ADOLF *Untersuchungen über das Nibelungenlied*, Stuttgart, 1854

– *Kampf um der Nibelunge Hort gegen Lachmanns Nachtreter*, Stuttgart, 1855

HUISMAN, J. A. "Exkurs über die symmetrische Zahlenkomposition im Mittelalter," in: *Neue Wege zur dichterischen und musikalischen Technik Walthers von der Vogelweide*, Utrecht, 1950

ITTENBACH, MAX *Deutsche Dichtungen der salischen Kaiserzeit*, Frankfurt a.M., 1937

– *Das Nibelungenlied: Dichtung und Schicksalsgestaltung*, Brüssel, 1944

JEISMANN, K. E. "Rüedegers Schildgabe oder der Gehalt der Modi: Ein Unterrichtsversuch," *DU*, XIII (1961), 56–62

JONES, G. F. "Rüdiger's Dilemma," *Studies in Philology*, LVII (1960), 7–21

KETTNER, EMIL "Zur Kritik des *Nibelungenlieds*," VIII Teile, *ZfdP*, XV–XX (1883–88)

KING, K. C. "The Message of the *Nibelungenlied*: A Reply," *MLR*, LVII (1962), 541–50

KIRCHBERGER, LIDA, "The Crown in the *Nibelungenlied*," *Monatshefte*, XLVIII (1956), 261–72

KNORR, FRIEDRICH "Der künstlerische Aufbau des *Nibelungenliedes*," *ZfD*, LII (1938), 73–87

KÖRNER, JOSEF *Das Nibelungenlied*, Leipzig/Berlin, 1921

KRALIK, DIETRICH VON *Die Sigfridstrilogie im Nibelungenlied und in der Thidrekssaga*, I. Bd., Halle, 1941

KROES, H. W. J. "Die Sage vom Nibelungenhort und ihr mythischer Hintergrund," in: *Festgabe für Th. Frings*, Berlin, 1956, pp. 323–37

KUHN, HANS "Kriemhilds Hort und Rache," in: *Festschrift für P. Kluckhohn und H. Schneider*, Tübingen, 1948, pp. 84–100

–"Heldensage und Christentum," *Studium Berolinense*, Berlin, 1960, pp. 515–24

– Review of Gottfried Weber's *Das Nibelungenlied: Problem und Idee*, Stuttgart, 1963, in *ZfdA*, LXXVI (1965), *Anzeiger*, 1–18

–"Der Teufel im *Nibelungenlied*: Zu Gunthers und Kriemhilds Tod," *ZfdA*, XLIV (1965), 280–306

KUHN, HUGO "Ueber nordische und deutsche Szenenregie in der Nibelungendichtung," in: *Edda, Skalden, Saga: Festschrift für Felix Genzmer*, Heidelberg, 1952, pp. 279–306

–"Die Klassik des Rittertums in der Stauferzeit, 1170–1200," in: *Annalen der deutschen Literatur*, hrsg. H. O. Bürger, Stuttgart, 1952, pp. 99–177

LACHMANN, KARL *Ueber die ursprüngliche Gestalt des Gedichts von der Nibelungen Noth*, Berlin, 1816

LEWIS, C. S. *The Allegory of Love*, New York, 1958

LINKE, HANSJÜRGEN "Ueber den Erzähler im *Nibelungenlied* und seine künstlerische Funktion," *GRM*, XLI (1960), 370–85

MAURER, FRIEDRICH *Leid: Studien zur Bedeutungs- und Problemgeschichte besonders in den grossen Epen der staufischen Zeit*, Bern/München, 1951, pp. 13–38

–"Die Einheit des *Nibelungenliedes* nach Idee und Form," *DU*, v (1953), 27–42

–"Ueber den Bau der Aventiuren des *Nibelungenlieds*," in *Festschrift für Dietrich von Kralik*, Wien, 1954, pp. 93–98

MCLINTOCK, D. R. "Les larmes de Brünhilt," *SN*, XXXIII (1961), 307–13

MERGELL, BODO "*Nibelungenlied* und höfischer Roman," *Euphorion*, XLV (1950), 305–36

MORGAN, B. Q. "On the Use of Numbers in the *Nibelungenlied*," JEGP, XXXVI (1937), 10–20

MOWATT, D. G. "Studies towards an Interpretation of the *Nibelungenlied*," *GLL*, XIV (1960/61), 257–70

– *The Nibelungenlied: Translated*, London/New York, 1962

MOWATT, D. G. and SACKER, HUGH *The Nibelungenlied: An Interpretative Commentary*, Toronto, 1967

MUELLER, W. A. *The Nibelungenlied Today: Its Substance, Essence and Significance*, Chapel Hill, 1962

NAGEL, BERT "Probleme der *Nibelungenlied*-Dichtung," *ZfdP*, LXXV (1956), 57–73

–"*Das Nibelungenlied*," *ZfdP*, LXXI (1957), 268–305

–"Heldentum und Christentum," *Der Horizont*, II (1957), 27–37

–"Heidnisches und Christliches im *Nibelungenlied*," *Ruperto-Carola*, 24. Bd. (1958), 61–81

–"Das Dietrichbild im *Nibelungenlied*," I. Teil, *ZfdP*, LXXVIII (1959), 258–68; II. Teil, *ZfdP*, LXXIX (1960), 28–57

– *Das Nibelungenlied: Stoff, Form, Ethos*, Frankfurt, 1965

NAUMANN, HANS "Höfische Symbolik: Rüedegers Tod," *DVLG*, X (1932), 387–403

–"Brünhilds Gürtel," *ZfdA*, LXX (1933), 46–48

–"Die Ritterehre der Stauferzeit," *Euphorion*, XLII (1947)

NEUMANN, FRIEDRICH "Schichten der Ethik im *Nibelungenlied*," in: *Festschrift für Eugen Mogk*, Halle, 1924, pp. 119–45

NORDMEYER, GEORGE "Source Studies on Kriemhild's Falcon Dream," *GR*, XV (1940), 292–99

PANZER, FRIEDRICH *Das Nibelungenlied: Entstehung und Gestalt*, Stuttgart, 1955

PLOSS, EMIL "Byzantinische Traumsymbolik und Kriemhilds Falkentraum,"

GRM, XXXIX (1958), 218–26

RANKE, FRIEDRICH *Gottfried von Strassburg: Tristan und Isold,* Berlin, 1962

–"Die höfisch-ritterliche Dichtung," in: *Deutsche Literaturgeschichte in Grundzügen,* Bern/München, 1961, pp. 58 ff.

RENOIR, ALAIN "Levels of Meaning in the *Nibelungenlied:* Sifrit's Courtship," *NM,* LXI (1960), 353–61

–"*Nibelungenlied* and *Waltharii Poesis:* A Note on Tragic Irony," *PQ,* XLIII (1964), 14–19

RICHTER, WERNER "Beiträge zur Deutung des Mittelteils des *Nibelungen- liedes,*" *ZfdA,* LXXII (1935), 9–47

SACKER, HUGH "On Irony and Symbolism in the *Nibelungenlied:* Two Pre- liminary Notes," *GLL,* XIV (1960/61), 271–81

SALMON, P. B. "Why does Hagen die?" *GLL,* XVII (1963/64), 3–13

SCHLÖSSER, FRIEDRICH *Andreas Capellanus: Seine Minneauffassung und das christliche Weltbild um 1200,* Bonn, 1960

SCHNEIDER, HERMANN *Die deutschen Lieder von Siegfrieds Tod,* Weimar, 1947

SCHÖNBACH, ANTON "Die Nibelungen," in: *Das Christentum in der Altdeut- schen Heldendichtung,* Graz, 1897, pp. 1–56

SCHRÖDER, F. R. "Kriemhilds Falkentraum," Beiträge (Tübingen), LXXVIII (1956), 319–48

SCHRÖDER, W. J. *Das Nibelungenlied: Versuch einer Deutung,* Halle/Saale, 1954

SCHRÖDER, WERNER "Die Tragödie Kriemhilts im *Nibelungenlied,*" *ZfdA,* XC (1960/61), 41 80; 123–60

–"Die epische Konzeption des *Nibelungenlied*-Dichters," *WW,* XI (1961), 193–201

SCHÜTTE, GUDMUND *Siegfried und Brünhild: Ein als Mythos verkannter Roman der Merowingerzeit,* Kopenhagen-Jena, 1935

SCHWARZE, M. "Die Frau in dem *Nibelungenliede* und in der *Kudrun,*" *ZfdP,* XVI (1884), 384–470

SEE, KLAUS VON "Die Werbung um Brünhild," *ZfdA,* LXXXVIII (1957/58), 1–20

–"Freierprobe und königinnezank in der Sifridsaga," *ZfdA,* LXXXIX (1958/59), 163–72

SINGER, C. S. "The Hunting Contest: An Interpretation of the Sixteenth *Aventiure* of the *Nibelungenlied,*" *GR,* XLII (1967)

SPIVACK, BERNARD *Shakespeare and the Allegory of Evil: The History of a Metaphor in Relation to His Major Villains,* New York, 1958

STOUT, JAKOB *Und ouch Hagene*, Groningen, 1963

SZÖVERFFY, JOSEF *"Das Nibelungenlied*: Strukturelle Beobachtungen und Zeitgeschichte," *WW*, XV (1965), 233-38

THORP, MARY "The Unity of the *Nibelungenlied*," *JEGP*, XXXVI (1937), 475–80

TONNELAT, ERNEST *La chanson des Nibelungen: Etude sur la composition et la formation du poème épique*, Paris, 1926

TROJEL, E. (hrsg.) *Andreae Capellani regii Francorum de amore libri tres*, Kopenhagen, 1892

WACHINGER, BURGHART *Studien zum Nibelungenlied: Vorausdeutung, Aufbau, Motivierung*, Tübingen, 1960

WAIS, KURT *Frühe Epik Westeuropas und die Vorgeschichte des Nibelungenliedes*, Tübingen, 1953

WAPNEWSKI, PETER "Rüdigers Schild: Zur 37. Aventiure des *Nibelungenliedes*" *Euphorion*, LIV (1960), 380–410

WEBER, GOTTFRIED *Das Nibelungenlied: Problem und Idee*, Stuttgart, 1963

WEINAND, H. G. *Tränen: Untersuchungen über das Weinen in der deutschen Sprache und Literatur des Mittelalters*, Bonn, 1958

WILLSON, BERNARD " 'Ordo' and 'inordinatio' in the *Nibelungenlied*," *Beiträge* (Tübingen), LXXXV (1963), 83–101; 325–51

INDEX

This book

was designed by

WILLIAM RUETER

under the direction of

ALLAN FLEMING

and was printed by

University of

Toronto

Press